THE MUSLIM LAW OF INHERITANCE

COMPILED FROM
ORIGINAL ARABIC AUTHORITIES
WITH
ARABIC TEXT
OF
SIRAJIYYAH, QUR'ANIC VERSES & HADIS
AND THEIR
ENGLISH TRANSLATION

BY

AL-HAJ MAHOMED ULLAH *ibn* S. JUNG, M.A., LL.D.
OF CHRIST'S COLLEGE, CAMBRIDGE; TRINITY COLLEGE, DUBLIN;
BARRISTER-AT-LAW, LINCOLN'S INN, ADVOCATE, HIGH COURT,
ALLAHABAD AND PROFESSOR, DEAN OF THE FACULTY OF LAW,
UNIVERSITY OF ALLAHABAD

KITAB BHAVAN
New Delhi-110002

The Muslim Law of Inheritance

KITAB BHAVAN
Publishers, Distributors, Exporters & Importers
1784, Kalan Mahal, Darya Ganj,
New Delhi - 1100 02 (India)

Phone : (91-11) 23277392, 23274686,
: (91-11) 23263383
Mob : +91-9953098606

Website : www.kitabbhavan.net
Email : info@kitabbhavan.net
nasri@vsnl.com

First Published in India : 1934
Reprint : 2022

ISBN - 10 : 81-7151-005-1
ISBN - 13 : 978-81-7151-005-4

Book Code No. : M00064

Batch ID : SPRFNS130722

Printed & Published in India by :

Moonis Ali Nasri for Kitab Bhavan
1784, Kalan Mahal, Darya Ganj,
New Delhi - 1100 02 [India]

Dedicated
To the memory of
My Paternal Grandfather
Al-Haj Maulvi M. Samee-Ullah
Khan Bahadur, C.M.G.
and
My Maternal Grandfather
Nawab Server-ul-Mulk, Server-ud-dawlah,
Server Jung Bahadur.

PUBLISHER'S NOTE

This handy book treats of the principles which govern the inheritance of the deceased's property among the Muslims of the Sunni Hanafi Sect. It is based on the original Arabic authorities and quotes them *in extenso* for ready reference. **It contains the text and the translation of the renowned work on Muslim Law named the "Sirajiyyah" with a commentary by the learned author.** The Qur'anic Verses and the Traditions of the Holy Prophet of Islam (peace be upon him) relating to the law of inheritance have also been included.

The book deals exhaustively with the subject of inheritance and leaves nothing to be searched for from elsewhere. The Research Scholars, the Lawyers and the Courts will find in the book a very useful guide and companion. and it can be safely said that the exposition of the law and the manner of its treatment as found in this book is not likely to be found in any other work on Muslim Law of Inheritance, as far as clarity of style and fullness is concerned.

PREFACE

These few pages contain the principles of the Muslim Law of Inheritance. It comprises mainly the Sunni Hanafi Law and is based on the original Arabic authorities. The book contains the text and translation of the Sirajiyyah which was first translated, in 1792, by Sir William Jones and subsequently annotated by Rumsey, and also by S. C. Sircar; but for some reasons I prefer to use my own translation with a commentary and I leave it to my readers to judge it on its own merits. The Quranic verses and the traditions of the Holy Prophet relating to the Law of Inheritance are also included. I am greatly indebted to Dr. Zubaid Ahmad and also to Dr. Mahmud Ullah in assisting me in preparation of this work. I trust the work will meet with the approval of all those interested in the Muslim Law.

M. U.

Law Department,
University of Allahabad.
25th March, 1934.

TABLE OF CONTENTS

THE MUSLIM LAW OF INHERITANCE

The Muslim Law of Inheritance, *Ilm-ul-Faraiz*, is a great achievement of the Muslim jurists. In its minutest details it is a system rendered to perfection, and thus deserves our admiration. Macnaghten in his preliminary remarks, Principles and Precedents of Mohammedan Law, observes:

> In these provisions we find ample attention paid to the interests of all those whom nature places in the first rank of our affections; and indeed it is difficult to conceive any system containing rules more strictly just and equitable[1].

And the tribute paid by Rumsey is no less exalted. He remarks:

> The Mohammedan Law of Inheritance comprises beyond question the most refined and elaborate system of rules for the devolution of property that is known to the civilised world[2].

The dead man's portion

The view that the deceased is entitled to "a dead man's portion" often took the form of placing in the grave things considered as necessaries for the life of the deceased in the next world. Such was the custom particularly in Egypt. Later on in religious surroundings the reservation of the dead man's portion was confined to the property to be spent on charitable objects for the good of the soul of the deceased. This practice exists under the Church as also under the Muslim Law.

Succession to real and personal property

In almost all systems the distinction is made between real and personal property. The natural law of succession refers to personal property. The succession to personal property is governed by one set of rules while succession to immovable property is based on different principles. However the Muslim Law makes no distinction between the succession of real and personal property, nor is there any difference as found under the Hindu Law between ancestral and self-acquired property, nor from mere fact of commensality, the heirs continuing to live together, presumption as to existence of joint family can arise. The well known rule of primogeniture which is the incidence of succession of real property in various systems is not recognised by the Muslim Law at all. Under the Islamic Law all sons inherit equally. The converse case of ulti-

[1] P. V. [2] P. 1 (Preface)

mogeniture, the succession of the youngest son to the estate, is also not recognised.

Intestate succession

Historically intestate succession comes before testamentary succession. The law itself takes into account the fact that the property of the deceased should be applied primarily to the support of persons who were entitled to be first supported by the deceased in his lifetime, and who have greatly suffered by his death. The right of testamentary succession was only to meet exceptional cases for reasons known to the testator himself, and that herein again some restriction was placed on the testamentary power of the person as was the case under the Roman Law that some portion of the property must be left for the descendants of the deceased. Justinian provided by the 18th Novel that a testator should leave at least one-third or one-half of the estate if he has four or more children. The Muslim Law goes further and requires that at least two-thirds shall be left for the near relations of the deceased, by providing that the testator cannot dispose of more than one-third by way of legacies.

Right of ascendants and descendants

Bentham discussing the Law of Succession (Theory of Legislation, Vol. I, Chapter XX) observes:

> On a man's death, the question arises, how ought his property to be disposed of? The legislator should have three objects in view, in framing any laws of succession: (1) To provide for the subsistence of the rising generation; (2) to prevent the pain of disappointment; and (3) to aim at the equalisation of fortunes.

Proceeding thus he discusses some well known propositions, stating in effect that descendants shall be given preference to all. He argues that any other arrangement would be contrary to the accepted view. He says:

> It is quite certain that our children could not exist without us, or some one who should take our place. It is probable that our parents could exist without us, as they existed before we came into being.

Thus briefly the order proposed by Bentham would be thus: namely; (1) Descendants; (2) Ascendants; (3) Collaterals. The Muslim Law takes note of the right of the descendants to inherit from their parents but at the same time places the father and mother of the deceased in the first rank of heirs along with sons and daughters.

The Holy Koran itself contains the sacred text:

> . . . . And the parents of the deceased shall have each of them a sixth part of what he shall leave, if he have a child; but if he have no child, and his parents be his heirs, then his mother shall have the third part . . . . . . Ye know not whether your parents or your children be of greater use unto you . . . .
>
> (Koran IV; II)

Thus under the Muslim Law the parents inherit along with the children of the deceased and are not excluded by them and the argument advanced by Bentham that our parents could exist without us as they existed before we came into being is untenable, from the point of view that usually when grown-up descendants die the parents are old and decrepit and therefore are more in need of assistance, and further the care and services bestowed by the parents on their own children in the past can never be nullified by any consideration of pre-eminence in the matter of affection in favour of the descendants. It is manifest that it is an unhappy contingency for the father or mother to inherit from his own son or daughter, the parents themselves anticipate that their children would inherit from them, but if they should survive contrary to course of nature it is only fit and proper, fair and equitable that they should have the right of immediate succession to their deceased children. Indeed it may be noted that no other system of jurisprudence except the Muslim Law provides for the parents to succeed to the property of their deceased descendants. Under the Hanafi Muslim Law even the grandfather in default of the father excludes full or consanguine brothers and sisters from participating in the right of inheritance, though perhaps in this case the doctrine of the right of ancestors to succeed has been pushed too far The Koran having made no provision for this contingency some of the jurists differ on this point whether the grandfather should exclude full brothers and sisters or should share along with them.

Right of representation

Another distinguishing feature of the Muslim Law of inheritance is that there is no right of representation. The heir is to be ascertained at the time of the death of the deceased, and a person cannot succeed as a representative of some one who had already predeceased the last proprietor. This appears to be a strict rule but it logically follows from the maxim, "*Nemo est hæres viventis*", no one is the heir to a living person. Under the Muslim Law, strictly speaking, a person has not even an incohate right to the property of his ancestor until the death of that ancestor, it is only then the property vests in him absolutely. Therefore it follows that renunciation by a presumptive heir of the right of inheritance during his ancestor's lifetime is invalid and so would be the transfer of *spes successiones*, mere chance of the heir succeeding to the estate of a living person.

Adoption

The Muslim Law does not recognise adoption at all. Hence an adopted son has no legal status and cannot inherit.

The whole estate of a deceased Muslim vests at the moment of his death in his heirs one or more in specific shares though if there are debts of the deceased the property would remain liable for its discharge, and each heir would be liable to pay a sum proportionate to his share of inheritance. Mr. Justice Markby made an attempt to introduce the fiction that the estate itself is owner and stands in the place of the deceased, *'hereditatem dominam esse et defuncti vicem obtinere.'*[1] That the estate does not immediately vest in the lawful heirs and the deceased owner is supposed by a fiction to be represented by the estate itself. Similarly the maxim *"semel heres semper heres"* is not applicable for under the Muslim Law there is no *confusio* of the property of the deceased and that of the heir. The property of the deceased is alone liable for the debts of the deceased. The devolution of the property cannot be made contingent or suspended till payment of debts. The estate devolves immediately upon the legal representatives charged with the debts of the deceased.

Vesting of inheritance

The distribution is effected among the near blood relations of the deceased, and the claimants must establish the cause of inheritance, and there should be no impediment to inheritance. The heirs in general are divided into three distinct groups, the sharers, *zavul-furuz*, the residuaries, *Asabah*, and the distant kindred *zavul-arham*, and some other special classes of heirs follow next in order and finally and lastly in the absence of all classes of heir the inheritance devolves upon the State Treasury *Bait-ul-mal*. The following are the general principles applicable under the Muslim Law of Inheritance.

The rules of distribution

(1) That the person whose property is to be distributed is dead.

(2) The claimant possess the cause of inheritance based upon relationship.

(3) That the claimant is not excluded by existence of any preferable heir and there is no impediment to succession.

(4) The nearer in degree excludes the more remote.

(5) There is no representation.

(6) The strength of consanguinity determines preference.

(7) As a general rule the male sharer takes double the portion of a female sharer of the same degree.

Under the Muslim Law the following may be said to be the primary heirs; they are always entitled to inherit:—

(1) The parents (father and mother); (2) the child (sons and daughters); (3) the heirs by marriage (husband and wife).

[1] Assamathem Nissa Bibee v. Roy Lutchmeeput Singh 4 Cal. 142 [1878]

(The following Chart illustrates the immediate near relations of the deceased.)

The table of near relations, sharers and residuaries

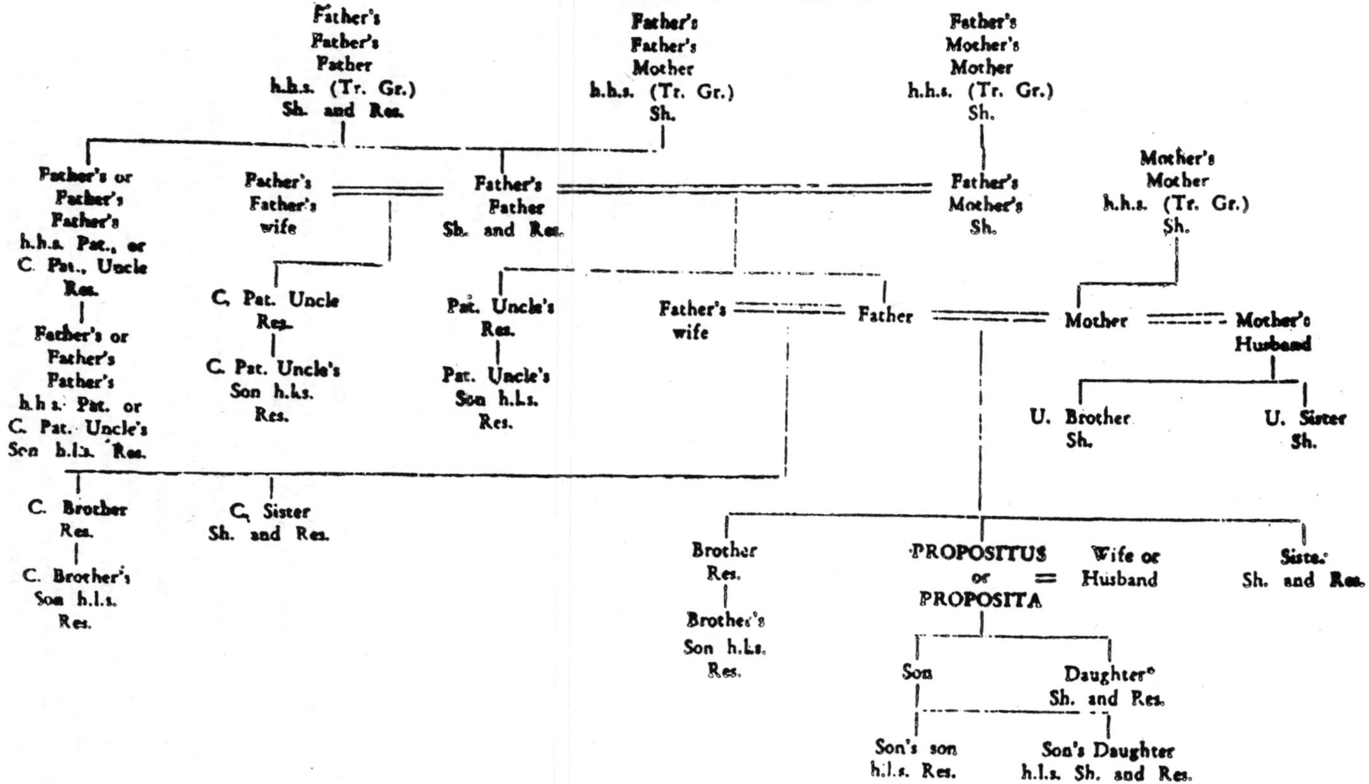

*The daughter's descendants belongs to the distant kindered class

Abbreviations

h.h.s. = How high-soever
h.l.s. = How low-soever
Tr. Gr. = True grandfather or grandmother
C. = Consanguine

Pat. = Paternal
U. = Uterine
Sh. = Sharer
Res. = Residuary

Legislative enactments and law affecting Muslim Law

Upto the middle of the eighteenth century the Muslim Law was the law of the land. In 1757 after the battle of Plassey the supremacy of the East India Company was firmly established. In 1765 the Diwani was conferred upon the Company and it was in 1772 that the Supreme Court of Judicature at Fort William in Bengal was established. The first reference to the preservation and administration of the Muslim Law we find in the Parliamentary enactment 21 George III, Chapter 70, Section 17, which provided:

> That the Supreme Court of Judicature, at Fort William in Bengal shall have full power and authority to hear and determine, in such manner as is provided for that purpose in the said charter or letters patent, all and all manner of actions and suits against all and singular the inhabitants of the said city of Calcutta.
>
> Provided that their inheritance and succession to lands, rents, and goods, and all matters of contract and dealing between party and party, shall be determined in the case of Muhammadans by the laws and usages of Muhammadans, and in the case of Gentus by the laws and usages of Gentus; and where only one of the parties shall be a Muhammadan or Gentu, by the laws and usages of the defendant.

And the same was provided in Bombay and Madras by 37 George III, Chapter 142, Sections 12 and 13. And finally the Government of India Act 1915 (5 and 6 George V, Chapter 61) says:

> The High Courts at Calcutta, Madras and Bombay in the exercise of their original jurisdiction in suits against inhabitants of Calcutta, Madras or Bombay, as the case may be, shall in matters of inheritance and succession to lands, rents and goods, and in matters of contract and dealing between party and party, when both parties are subject to the same personal law or custom having the force of Law, decide according to that personal Law or custom and when the parties are subject to different personal laws or customs having the force of Law to which the defendant is subject. Section 112.

So far as the Company was concerned in 1793 it took the first step to legislate for the Indians and the earliest important legislation was Regulation IV of 1793, Section 15 of which laid down that:

> In suits regarding succession, inheritance, marriage and caste, and all religious usages and institutions, the Muhammadan laws with respect to Muhammadans and the Hindu Laws with regard to Hindus, are to be considered the general rules by which the Judges are to form their decisions.

The Bengal Regulation XI of 1793 also recognises by Section 2 the Hindu and Muslim Law of inheritance. The same is provided in the Bengal Regulation VII of 1832 and in Section 24 of the Bengal Civil Courts Act VI of 1871 and finally Section 37 of the Bengal North Western Provinces and Assam Civil Courts Act

XII of 1887 embodies the same rules.

Section 37 of Act XII of 1877 enacted: That the Civil Courts shall decide questions relating to "succession, inheritance, marriage, or any religious usage or institution" by the Muhammadan Law where the parties are Muslims. Thus the same rules were extended to the North Western Provinces and as a matter of fact there the right to be governed by their own personal laws was previously upheld by the Bengal Regulations III, IV, and V of 1803 *vide* also the Bengal Regulation XLIV of 1795.

Similarly in Oudh, the Oudh Laws Act XVIII of 1876, Sections 3 and 4, in Ajmere Merwara, the Ajmere Merwara Laws Regulation. III of 1877, Sections 4 and 5 provide the same rules. In the Punjab the Punjab Laws Act IV of 1872, Section 5 and in the North-Western Frontier Province the Frontier Regulations VII of 1901 provide as follows:

> In questions regarding inheritance, special property of females, betrothal, marriage, dower, adoption, guardianship, minority, bastardy, family relations, wills, legacies, gifts, partition or any religious usages and institutions, the rule of decisions shall be: (1) Any custom of anybody or class of persons . . . . . (2) The Muhammadan Law in cases where the parties are Muhammadans . . . . . except in so far as such law has been altered or abolished by legislative enactment or is opposed to the provisions of this Act . . . .

As regards Madras the same rules were adopted by the Madras Regulations II, III and IV of 1802 and V of 1803, and finally they were incorporated in the Madras Civil Courts Act III of 1873, Section 16, which says:

> Where in any suit or proceeding, it is necessary for any Court, under this Act, to decide any question regarding succession, inheritance, marriage or caste, or any religious usage or institution (*a*) the Muhammadan Law in cases where the parties are Muhammadans . . . . . shall form the rule of decision unless such law or custom has by legislative enactment been altered or abolished.

The Central Provinces Laws Act XX of 1875, Sections 5 and 6 and similarly the Burma Laws Act XIII of 1898, Section 13 provides the same rules.

In Bombay there are no such definite rules of law, but the law in this respect is laid down by the Bombay Regulation IV of 1827. Section 26 says:

> The law to be observed in the trial of suits shall be Acts of Parliament and Regulations of Government applicable to the case: in the absence of such Acts and Regulations the usage of the country in which the suit arose; if none such appears, the law of the defendant, and in the absence of specifio law and usage, justice, equity and good conscience alone.

So far we have stated what legislative enactments have preserved or guaranteed to administer the Muslim Law in case of the Muslims, but it is clear from some of the concluding remarks, namely, "unless such law or custom has by legislative enactment been altered or abolished" that the then legislatures were apparently of the opinion that they could change, alter or modify the Muslim Law, and in fact by various subsequent enactments they actually altered the Muslim Law. For instance, the rule of Muslim Law that an apostate from Islam cannot inherit from his Muslim relations was abolished by the Caste Disabilities Removal Act XXI of 1850. The right of the master to inherit to the estate of his freed slaves, technically known as the right of residuaries for special causes, became obsolete in consequence of abolition of slavery by the Slavery Act V of 1843. And as regards the right of inheritance of missing persons who cannot be traced, it being uncertain whether they are alive or dead, the rule of seven years provided by Sections 107 and 108 of the Indian Evidence Act would become applicable. And under the Aliens Act of the British Parliament 5 Edw 7 c 13 (1904) and the Aliens Restriction Act 1914, 4 and 5, Geo. 5, c 12 an alien enemy of the British Government cannot inherit the property of any British subject (which term would obviously include Indian Muslims who are British subjects) though they may be so entitled under the Muslim Law. Finally the rule of Muslim Law that in default of heirs the inheritance devolves on the public Treasury *Bait-ul-Mal* is superseded in British India by the law of escheats to the Crown. The rule of primogeniture is not recognised by the Muslim Law according to which all sons inherit equally, but Section 2 of the Oudh Laws Act of 1869 recognises the rule of primogeniture, for the taluqdars of Oudh. The rule that daughters inherit along with the sons has been held judicially to have been superseded by contrary custom found to be in existence among the Muslims, particularly in the Punjab and in Oudh.

And some of the Indian communities who have been converted to the Muslim faith have preferred to follow their old personal laws. Thus the Khojas and Cutchi Memons of Bombay are governed regarding succession and inheritance by the general Hindu Law. The same is provided in the Cutchi Memons Act XLIV of 1920 and Act XXXIV of 1923. Similarly in matters of inheritance the Muslim Borahs of Gujrat and the Girasies of Broach are governed by the Hindu Law. The Khojas and the Memons retain their Hindu Law of Inheritance.

And lastly the Indian Limitation Act, IX 1908 has affected the Muslim Law of inheritance under which system there is no period of limitation at all. All suits based upon inheritance must conform to law of limitation, viz., if they are for recovery of immovable property the period for institution of such suits is 12 years under Article 144. And as regards for recovery of movables the period would appear to be six years under Article 120 of the Limitation Act.

Reprint from Allahabad Law Journal, No. 12 of March 17, 1933

CHAPTER I

§ 1. LAW OF INHERITANCE—'ILM-UL-FARAIZ.

THE RIGHT OF INHERITANCE.—

1. The Muslim Law of inheritance, *'Ilm-ul-Faraiz,* prescribes the mode and manner of succession to a deceased Muslim. After incurring funeral expenses befitting the social status of the deceased, and after payment of his debts in full,[1] all legacies must be paid out of a third of what remains, and finally the whole of the residue is distributed amongst the heirs by right of inheritance. The distribution is effected among the blood relations of the deceased hereinafter mentioned, provided they be in existence at the time of the death of the deceased. The claimants must establish the cause of inheritance which is based upon near relationship, and there should be no impediment to inheritance, *e.g.*, the existence of a preferable heir or otherwise.

CONCEPTION OF PROPERTY.—

2. Under the Muslim Law, there is no distinction between ancestral and self acquired property, nor between real and personal property, and from mere fact of commensality, the heirs continuing to live together, no pre-sumption as to existence of joint family arises.[2]

---

1 The Indian Succession Act XXXIX of 1925 has affected the Muslim Law of inheritance. Under both systems funeral expenses are to be paid first, while the Muslim law speaks about debts in general, the Succession Act (a) gives preference to death-bed charges including fees for medical attendance and board and lodgings for one month previous to the death of the deceased, (b) next the expenses for obtaining probate and letters of administration, (c) next wages due for services rendered to the deceased within three months next preceding his death by any labourer, artizan or domestic servants, (d) debts of every kind must be paid before legacies, and finally the residue is distributed amongst the lawful heirs of the deceased.

2 There is no joint family property vide Mohideen Bee v. Syed Mir Saheb 38 Mad. 1099 (1915), Hakim Khan, v. Gul Khan 8 Cal 826 (1882), As to a partition suit vide Abdur Kader v. Bapubhai 23 Bom. 188 (1898).

Doctrine of Representation.—

3. There is no right of representation under the *Hanafi* Law. The heir is to be ascertained at the time of the death of the deceased, and a person cannot succeed as a representative of some one who had already predeceased the deceased.[1]

Primogeniture Exclusion of sons, daughters.—

4. Under the *Hanafi* Law the rule of primogeniture is not recognised, all sons inherit equally along with the eldest son. But under Anglo-Muslim Law if a custom of strict primogeniture is established then it may be followed.[2] Under the *Shia* Law the eldest son is entitled to his deceased father's signet ring, sword, Koran, and garments provided there are also other assets besides these articles.

The daughters are also entitled to specific share of inheritance hereinafter mentioned, but under Anglo-Muslim Law if there is valid custom excluding daughters from inheritance, it would be followed.[3]

---

1 This appears to be a strict rule but it logically follows, since according to Muslim Law a person has not even an incohate right to the property of his ancestor until the death of that ancestor, if so there could possibly be no claim through such a deceased person who himself had no vested right.

The Holy Prophet himself had suffered from the application of this rule as his own father had predeceased his grandfather. The theory of representation under the Shia Law will be discussed later.

2 The rule of Primogeniture has been applied by the Courts in Mahomed Akul Beg v. M. Kayum Beg 25 W. R. 199 (1876); Ibrahim Ali Khan v. M. Ahsanullah Khan P. C. 39 Cal., 711 (1911) (the Kunjpura estate case).

The Oudh Estate Act I of 1869 Sec., 22 recognises the rule of Primogeniture for the taluqdars and prescribes comprehensive rules.

3 In Jammya v. Diwan 23 All. 20 (1900) evidence was held to be inadmissible to prove any custom inconsistent with the Muslim Law, "regarding succession, inheritance, marriage......or any religious usage or institution" (s. 37 of Bengal Civil Courts Act XII of 1887). The same view was followed in Ismail Khan v. Imtiaz-ul-nissa 4 A.L.J.R. 793 (1907). However on appeal Muhammad Ismail Khan v. Lala Sheokmukh Rai 17 C.W.N. 97 (1912) the Privy Council overruled the view taken by the Allahabad High Court and held that evidence as to family custom should be taken. But my submission is that the view taken by the Allahabad High Court is correct and justifiable, and to hold it otherwise would amount to an interference with the Muslim personal Law. In Ali Asghar v. Collector of Bulandshahr 39 All. 574 (1917) evidence of such family custom was held admissible. And in Muhammad Kamil v. Must. Imtiaz Fatima 36 I.A. 210 (1908), the Privy Council held that where daughters are excluded by custom they should be treated as non-existent for determining shares of heirs.

THE HEIRS IN GENERAL.—

5. A number of blood relations of the deceased are entitled to participate in the inheritance simultaneously. They are divided into three distinct groups the *Zav-ul-Furus*, the *Asabah*, the *Zav-ul-Arham*, and the other kinds of heirs follow next in order.

Zav-ul-Furus, the Sharers.—

(*a*) The sharers are entitled to receive a fixed share allotted to them in a certain order of preference, and mode of succession.

Asabah, the Residuaries.—

(*b*) The Residuaries are those persons who inherit of what remains of the estate after the sharers have been satisfied, and if there should be no sharers, then they take the whole of the inheritance. And in the absence of the residuaries, the residue of the estate, after first distribution amongst the sharers, once more devolves upon them (sharers) in the fixed ratio of their specific shares.

Zav-ul Arham, the Distant Kindred.—

(*c*) The distant kindred are those relations of the deceased who are neither sharers nor residuaries. They are entitled to the residue in all cases where the sharers are not entitled to it.

Successor by contract.—

(*d*) In default of sharers, residuaries or distant kindred, the estate devolves upon the successor by contract if any, that is, a person with whom the deceased had made, a contract of clientship, *mawalat*.[1]

Acknowledged Kinsman.—

(*e*) Next in order of preference comes the fictitiously acknowledged kinsman, that is a person of unknown descent who has been

1 The conditions of the valid contract of clientship are as follows.—

(a) There should be declaration and acceptance.

(b) The declarant should have no heir by 'nasab' consanguinity, he should have attained puberty (majority) and he himself should be a person of "unknown descent."

(c) The acceptor inherits from the declarant provided at the time of the latter's death he has attained puberty (majority).

(d) All children of the declarant born after the contract enter into the 'mawalat.' The Shafii school does not recognise mawalat.

acknowledged by the deceased not through himself but through another.[1]

Such acknowledgment is binding on the acknowledgor and if not withdrawn and he dies leaving no other heirs except such acknowledged kinsman, the estate would devolve upon him. And even as regards bequests exceeding the legal third, the acknowledgee consents is necessary to validate it.

Universal legatee.—

(*f*) The universal legatee is the person to whom the deceased has bequeathed the whole of his property by will, it is a case of universal succession to the ***universitas juris*** of the deceased. There being no heirs such a bequest is valid to the whole extent, and the rule of maximum legal third applicable to bequests is not here applicable.

Bait-ul-mal, Treasury.—Escheats to the Crown.—

(*g*) And finally and lastly in the absence of all above classes of heirs, the inheritance devolves upon the ***Bait-ul-mal***, the public treasury for the benefit of all Muslims.

Under the ***Shia*** Law, there is no escheat to ***Bait-ul-mal***, but the property is to be liquidated among the poor of the city.

In default of all the heirs and persons enumerated above and in British India in preference to the poor or to ***Bait-ul-mal*** there being no such public treasury in India, the whole property of a deceased Muslim escheats to the Crown.[2]

---

1 The kinship may be acknowledged through the father or grandfather e.g., acknowledging a person to be his brother or paternal uncle. If a Muslim dies leaving a wife and no other heir except the acknowledged kinsman, then he will take the residue after deducting the wife's share.

In case of acknowledgment of a person as his brother, if the acknowledgor himself inherits, he would have to share with the acknowledged kinsman, as if with a real brother. Vide also Baillie 1 405.

2 The leading case is the Collector of Masulipatam v. Cavalry 8 Moo. I. A. 498 (1860) (a Hindu case) Where the Privy Council observed when it is made out clearly that by the law applicable to the last owner there is a total failure of heirs, then the claim to the land ceases (we apprehend) to be subject to any such personal law........the law of escheat intervenes and private ownership not existing, the State must be owner as ultimate Lord."

The question came up before the Patna High Court in Khursaidi Begum v. Secretary of State 94 I.C. 433 (Pat. 1926) where it was raised under the

THE CAUSES OF INHERITANCE.—

6. There are three causes of inheritance.—

(*a*) Valid marriage, *sabab*, by reason of marriage, of these there are only two sharers namely the husband and the wife.

(*b*) *Nasab*, consanguinity, sharers by relationship, and of these there are ten sharers.

(*c*) *Wala*, fictitious relationship, special cause of inheritance of these there are several.[1]

THE NUMBER OF SHARERS.—

7. The total number of sharers is twelve only,[2] and four of them are of the male sex and eight are of the female sex.

CAUSE OF INHERITANCE	MALE SHARERS	FEMALE SHARERS
Sabab of Marriage.	1. Husband.	5. Wife.
Nasab, consanguinity.	2. Father. 3. True grandfather. 4. Half-brother by mother (uterine brother).	6. Mother. 7. True grandmother. 8. Daughter. 9. Son's daughter. 10. Full sister. 11. Half-sister by father (consanguine sister). 12. Half-sister by mother (uterine sister).

Shia Law, the Shia community of Gaya represented by their Anjuman had sued the Secretary of State. The Court held that the law of escheat prevailed.

1 i.e., Successor by Contract, Acknowleged kinsman universal legatee, Bait-ul-mal. Wala of Emancipation, is obsolete, in British India.

2 Of the twelve sharers five are always sharers viz., husband, wife, true grandmother, uterine brother, and sister. And the remaining seven sharers are sometimes sharers and sometimes residuaries. The following five heirs are never absolutety excluded by another heir ;—viz., (a) Husband (b) wife or wives (c) father (d) mother (e) child (son, or daughther) ; the remaining seven heirs are liable to be excluded as will be seen later on.

ORINGINAL KORANIC SHARERS.—

8. The following eight sharers are expressly mentioned in the Holy Koran, (1) Husband (2) Wife or wives (3) Daughter (son) (4) Full sister (5) Father (6) Mother (7 & 8) Uterine brother, and uterine sister.

The following four are secondary sharers. (9) Son's daughter (10) Consanguine sister, (11) True grandfather (2) True grandmother.

SHARERS CONVERTED INTO RESIDUARIES.—

9. The following sharers are liable to be converted into residuaries.

1. Father.
2. True grandfather.
3. Mother.
4. Daughter.
5. Son's daughter.
6. Full sister.
7. Consanguine sister.

The following general rules determine the conversion of sharers into residuaries.

(*a*) A female sharer is excluded from inheriting as a sharer and is converted into a residuary by one or more male residuaries of the same degree and consanguine relationship to the deceased.[1]

(*b*) The father and true grandfather are converted into residuaries in default of any descendants of the class of sharers or residuaries *i.e.* they inherit as residuaries in default of children—daughters, sons, son's son, of the deceased.

---

1 The case of the father converting mother, into a residuary is a exception to this rule. The rule of conversion of these females into residuaries is with a view to give to the male member of the same degree and relationship a double share n accordance with the general principle of the law of inheritance.

e.g. The sons convert daughters into residuaries.

The son's son convert son's daughters into residuaries,

Table of Sharers that are under certain circumstances also residuaries.

Sharers.	When Sharers	When Residuaries.
1. Father ...	When there is a child or son's Child.	When there is no child nor son's child.
2. True grand father.	Ditto (in default of father.) ...	Ditto (in default of father.)
3. Mother ...	In all cases except vide next column.	When the father co-exists with mother and spouse only and there is no child, or son's child nor two or more brothers or sisters.
4. Daughter ...	When there is no son ...	When there is a son.
5. Son's daughter.	When there are no two or more daughters and there is no son's son of the same degree and no excluder.	When there is a son's son of the same degree. When there is a son's son of lower degree and she has been excluded.
6. Full sister...	When there is no full brother, nor daughter nor son's daughter and no excluder.	When there is a full brother. When there is a daughter or son's daughter and no excluder.
7. Consanguine sister.	When there is no consanguine brother nor daughter, nor son's daughter and no excluder.	When there is a consanguine brother. When there is any daughter or son's daughter and no excluder.

§ 2. THE TWELVE SHARERS.

Father.—

10. Where there is a son,[1] or son's son, h.l.s. the father, takes one-sixth.

Mother.—

11. Where there are children, or son's children, h.l.s. or two or more brothers and sisters, the mother takes one-sixth.

Where there is no child or son's child h.l.s. the mother takes one-third, unless there be both a wife or husband and a father in which case she takes one-third of what remains after the share of the widow or widower has been satisfied.

Illustrations.

(i)	Widow	1/4	
	Mother	1/4	(1/3 of 3/4)
	Father	1/2	(as residuary)
(ii)	Husband	1/2	
	Mother	1/6	(1/3 of 1/2)
	Father	1/3	(as residuary)
(iii)	Widow	1/4	
	Mother	1/3	
	Father's father	5/12	(as residuary)
(iv)	Husband	1/2	
	Mother	1/3	
	Father's father	1/6	(as residuary)

Husband.—

12. The share of the husband in his deceased wife's estate is one-fourth where there are children or son's children, and if there are no such heirs, he takes one-half.[2]

Wife.—

13. The widow[3] takes one-eighth of the deceased husband's estate where there are children or son's children h.l.s. and if there are no such issue then she takes one-fourth.

---

1 As to its definition vide s 249 true grandmother.

2 The husband is entitled to take his share from the unpaid dower if any still unpaid.

3 The wife's dower if still unpaid would count as an ordinary debt, and must be paid before the assignment of the legal shares, otherwise she would recover the amount from the shares of all the legal heirs and would also contribute from her own share. This share given to the widow is in addition to her claim to the unpaid dower.

The share of two or more wives (not exceeding four) is precisely the same, *viz.* one-eighth or one-fourth to be divided equally between them.

TRUE GRANDFATHER*—

14. Whether there is a father, the true grandfather is excluded from participating in the inheritance.

Where there is a son, or son's son h.l.s. and no father the true grandfather takes one-sixth.

TRUE GRANDMOTHER.*—

15. True grandmothers are excluded from participating in the inheritance by the mother, and paternal grandmothers are excluded where there is a father.

---

*True grandfather means a male ancestor between whom and the deceased no female intervenes.

False grandfather is any male ancestor between whom and the deceased a female intervenes.

A true grandmother is a female ancestor between whom and the deceased no false grandfather intervenes.

A false grandmother is a female ancestor between whom and the deceased a false grandfather intervenes.

False grand parents cannot inherit as sharers nor as residuaries

TABLE OF TRUE AND FALSE GRAND PARENTS.

The true grand parents are indicated by capital letters, the letters F (f) and M (m) stand for father and mother respectively.

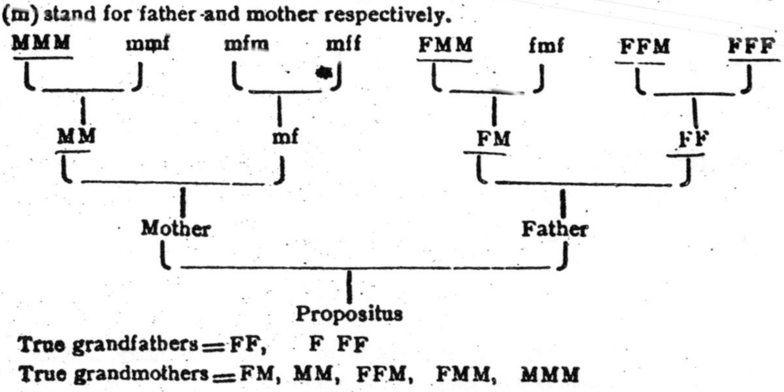

True grandfathers = FF, F FF

True grandmothers = FM, MM, FFM, FMM, MMM

If F is dead then FF and on his default FFF take 1/6 share.

If F and M are dead F M, and MM will divide between them 1/6 but if F is alive he will exclude FM from taking and MM will take the whole one-sixth.

If FM and MM, are dead, then 1/6 will be divided between FFM, FMM, MMM.

However if MM is alive, she will take the whole one-sixth, the nearer in degree excluding the more remote.

Similarly paternal female ancestors h.h.s. except the father's mother are excluded by the grandfather.

The share of the maternal grandmother is one-sixth, and the same is the share of the paternal grandmother where there is no father. Two or more true grandmothers of equal degree divide the sixth equally. The grandmothers nearer in degree exclude the more remote.

DAUGHTER.—

16. The share of a single daughter is one-half where there is no son, and the maximum collective share of two or more daughters is two-thirds.[1]

SON'S DAUGHTER.—

17. Where there is one daughter only, the son's daughter takes one-sixth, but where there are two or more daughters, they take nothing.

Where there is no son, nor daughter, nor son's son, the son's daughters inherit as if in capacity of daughters and take two-thirds if they be two or more, and if there is a single son's daughter she takes one-half of the estate.

SISTER.—

18. Where there is no child or son's child h.l.s. and no father or true grandfather and no full brother, a single full sister takes one-half and if two or more they take two-thirds to be divided equally between them.

---

1 If there is a son the daughter is not a sharer but a residuary, and the rule that the male sharers take double share would apply.

The son would convert the daughter into residuary and the latter would take a share equal to half of that is taken by the son, similarly if there is a son's son h.l.s. the son's daughter takes a share equal to half of that is taken by the former.

2 The brother (f. or c. in sec. 252) converts the sister into a residuary, and the general rule double share to the male members applies.

Consanguine sister.—

19. Where there is no child or son's child h.l.s. and no father or true grandfather, and there being neither full brother nor full sister nor consanguine brother, a single consanguine sister takes one-half, and if two or more they take two-thirds to be divided equally between them.

If there be only one full sister, she will take her half share leaving only the remainder of the maximum collective share (2/3-1/2=1/6) one-sixth for the consanguine sister whether one or more.

Uterine sister—uterine brother.—

20. Where there is no child or son's child or father or true grandfather, the uterine sister takes one-sixth and if two or more they take one-third.

The uterine brother under similar circumstances is entitled to 1/6 of the estate if there are two or more they are entitled to the maximum collective share 1/3 of the estate. In their case the males and females share equally.[1]

Table of Half-blood Relationship.

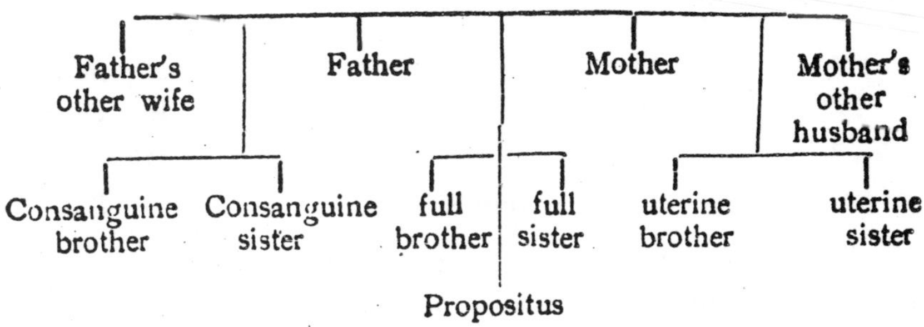

Fixed Portions.—

21. The portion fixed by the Koran are six namely 1/2, 1/4, 1/8, 2/3, 1/3, and 1/6, the object of the Koran was to give

1 The uterine brothers and sisters are cognates and they succeed only as sharer and not as residuaries. Their children are distant kindred.

shares to the females who were excluded under the customary law in ancient Arabia.[1]

Table of Fixed Portion.

Fixed portion.	Of the sharers under certain circumstances.
1/2	Husband, daughter, son's daughter, full sister, consanguine sister.
1/4	Husband, wife.
1/8	Wife or wives.
2/3	Daughters, son's daughters, full or consanguine sisters.
1/3	Mother, uterine brothers or sisters.
1/6	Father, true grandfather, mother, grandmothers, one or more son's daughters, one or more consanguine sisters, uterine brother or sister.

JOINT SHARERS.—

22. In case of several individuals forming one group of sharers, the maximum collective share is to be divided equally among all of them. The following heirs are joint-sharers:—

Joint Sharers.

1. Wives two or more.
2. The grandmothers of the same degree.
3. Daughters two or more.
4. Son's daughters two or more
5. Full sisters ”
6. Consanguine sisters ”
7. Uterine brothers or sisters.

1 The Koran does not specifically mention the true grandfather or true grandmother, they are included under the term "parents" and the expression "female children," includes daughters, son's daughters, and the term "sisters" is deemed to mean full sisters and consanguine sisters.

THE TABLE OF SHARERS

Sharers.	Share.	Conditions under which the share is inherited.	Whether excluded or converted into a residuary.
1. Husband	1/4	When there is a child or son's child (h. l. s.)	Excluded by none.
	1/2	When there is no child or son's child h.l.s	
2. Wife one or more.	1/8	When there is a child or son's chiid (h. l. s.)	Excluded by none
	1/4	When no child or son's child	
3. Daughter	1/2 2/3	if one if two or more } when there is no son	Excluded by none.
	R		Converted into a residuary if there is a son or two or more sons.
Son's daughter.	1/2 2/3	if one if two or more } when no son, or son's son or one or more daughters or higher son's daughter.	Excluded by son, or son's son of higher grade, also excluded by two or more daughters or by two or more sons' daughters of higher grade, or by one daughter together with two or more son's daughters of higher grade.
	1/6	When there is a daughter or higher son's daughter.	
	R		Converted into a residuary by son's son of equal or even lower grade.
5. Father ...	1/6	When there is a son or son's son (h. l. s.)	Excluded by none.
	1/6 plus R.	When there are one or more daughters, son's daughters and there is no son nor son's son.	In this case the father is a sharer and also a residuary.
	R	When no child nor son's child (h. l. s.)	Converted into residuary in the absence of any child.

THE TABLE OF SHARERS—(*Continued.*)

Sharers.	Share.	Conditions under which the share is inherited	Whether excluded or converted into a residuary.
6. Mother	1/6	When there is a child or son's child (h. l. s.) or two or more brothers or sisters whether full blood or half and whether they inherit or are excluded or there is a brother and sister and the father.	Excluded by none.
	1/3	When there is no child nor son's child and not more than one brother and sister.	
	1/3 of R	When there is a wife or husband and the father.	Converted into a residuary by the father.
7. True grand-father.	1/6	When there is a child or son's child (h. l. s.) and no father or nearer true grand-father.	Excluded by the father or nearer true grand-father.
	1/6 ÷ R	When with daughters or only son's daughters.	
	R	When no child nor son's child	Converted into a residuary if there is no descendant sharer or residuary.
8. True grand-mother.	1/6	When no mother and no nearer true grandmother.	Paternal true grand-mother excluded by father or by a true grand-father. Any true grand-mother is excluded by mother or by nearer true grandmother, whether paternal or maternal. Not a residuary.
9. Full sister.	1/2 2/3	If one If two or more } When no child or son's child (h.l.s.) or father or brother.	Excluded by son or son's son (h. l. s.) father or true grandfather. Also excluded as sharer by one or more daughters or son's daughters.

THE TABLE OF SHARERS—(*Concluded.*)

Shares.	Sharer	Condition under which the share is inherited.	Whether excluded or converted into a residuary.
	R		Converted into residuary by full brother, that is when with one or more full brothers subject to not being excluded or when with one or more daughters or son's daughters and no excluder the full sisters one or more become residuaries with daughters i.e. they take the residue after deducting the shares of daughters.
10. Consanguine sister.	1/2 2/3	If one If two or more } When no child or son's child (h. l. s.) or father or brother or full sister.	Excluded by son or son's son, father or true grandfather or by full brother or by full sister when she is a residuary.
	1/6	When with one full sister only, (the sister takes 1/2 and consanguine sister takes (2/3—1/2 = 1/6.)	Also excluded by one or more daughters or son's daughters or by two or more full sisters.
	R		Converted into residuary by a consanguine brother. When there are one or more daughters, or son's daughters and no excluder.
11. 12. { Uterine brother or sister.	1/6 1/3	If one If two or more } When no child or son's child (h. l. s.) or father, (h. h. s.)	Excluded by son or son's son, father or true grandfather, or daughter or son's daughter. Not a residuary.

§ 3. THE RESIDUARIES.

CLASSES OF RESIDUARIES.—

23. There are four classes of residuaries, and each of the preceding class must be exhausted before the next which is excluded, that is the first excludes, the second, the second excludes the third, and the third excludes the fourth.

Class I.

The "offspring" of the deceased *i.e.* his sons and son's sons, *h. l. s.*

Daughters and son's daughters when not sharers.

Class II.

The "root" of the deceased *i.e.* his father and true grandfather *h.h.s.*

Class III.

The "offspring" of the father of the deceased, *i.e.* brothers whether full or consanguine and their sons *h.l.s.*

Sisters whether full or consanguine when not sharers.

Class IV.

The offspring of the true grandfathers *i.e.* paternal uncles and great uncles and their male descendants in the male line.

CLASS I. RESIDUARIES.—

24. According to the Sirayiyah "The offspring of the deceased are his sons first, then their sons in how low a degree soever." Thus in the first instance the residue devolves on the son or sons together and along with daughter or daughters if any. The general rule that the male member takes the double share applies, a daughter thus takes one-half of the share of each son.

If there be no daughter or daughters the risidue is divided equally between the sons, and if alone he takes the whole property.

Similarly the son's daughter takes along with the son's son.

The case of son's daughters with a lower son.

The following problems may usefully be studied.

In this example the female descendant in a nearer degree divided the residue with lower son's son h. l. s. D stands for daughter. S stands for son.

The heirs in the last line have survived the deceased.

(i)

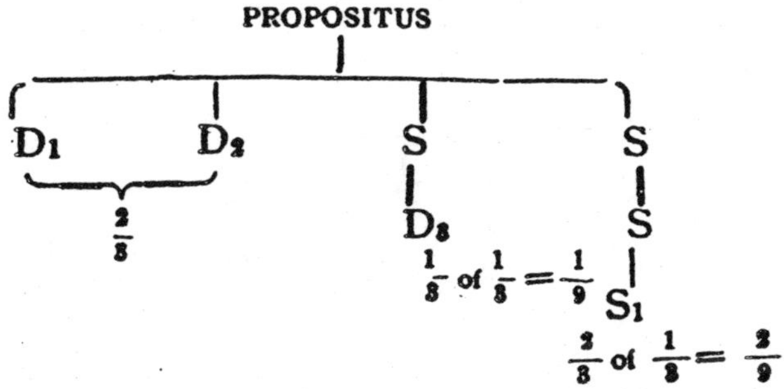

The two daughters D_1 and D_2 exhaust the collective share 2/3, so D_3 if alone would take nothing, but here she shares with S_1 as residuary. D_3 = 1/9 S_1 = 2/9.

(ii)

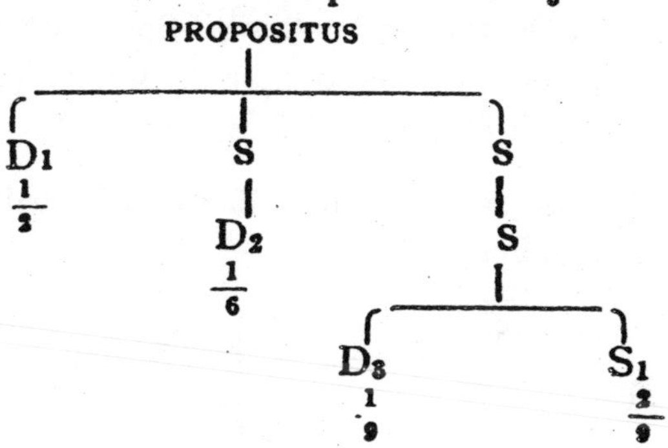

D_1 takes $\frac{1}{2}$

D_2 takes $\frac{1}{6}$ $\left(\frac{2}{3} - \frac{1}{2} = \frac{1}{6}\right)$ the remainder of the collective share.

D_3 and S_1 share the residue D_3 = 1/9 : S_1 = 2/9

(iii)

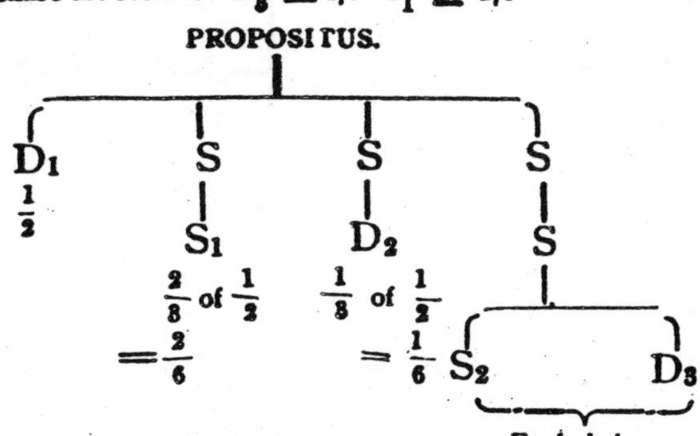

D_1 takes $\frac{1}{2}$

S_1 takes $\frac{2}{3}$ of $\frac{1}{2} = \frac{2}{6}$ D_2 takes $\frac{1}{3}$ of $\frac{1}{2} = \frac{1}{6}$ S_2 and D_3 are excluded.

(iv) PROPOSITUS.

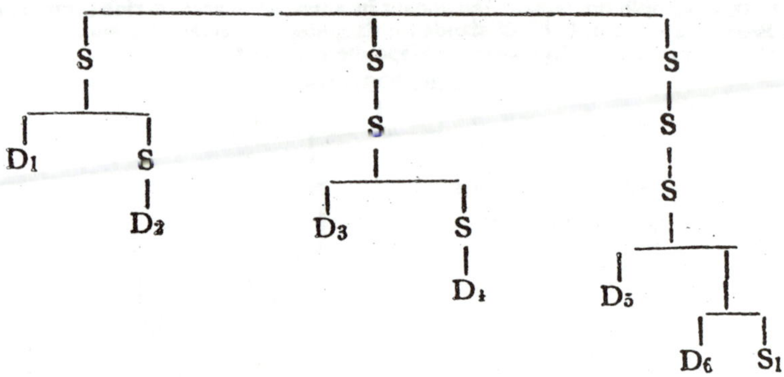

$D_1 = S$ takes 1/2

D_2 and D_3 = take 1/6

D_4 D_5 and D_6 would get nothing if S_1 was not in existence, but now they are made residuaries and take the residue $\left(1-\frac{1}{2}-\frac{1}{6}=\frac{1}{3}\right)$ each taking 1/5 of 1/3 = 1/15, and S_1 takes 2/15.

The following two graphical illustrations will further explain the above proposition.

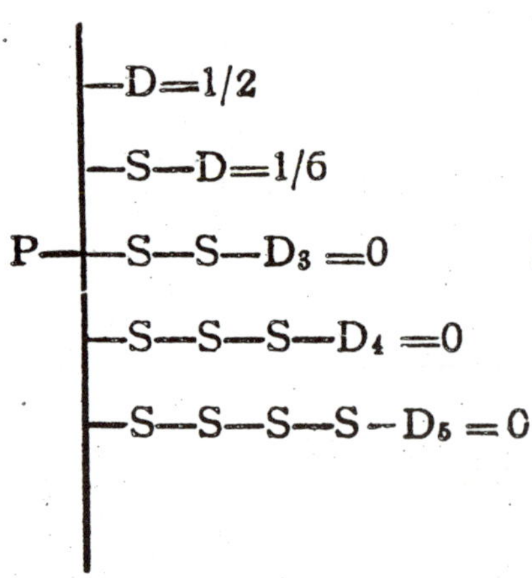

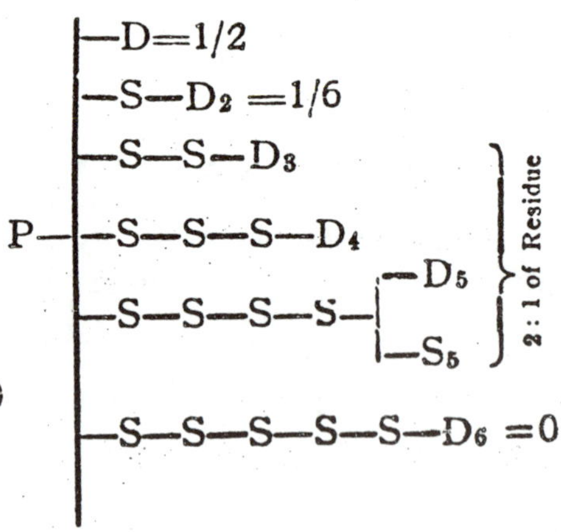

CLASS II OF RESIDUARIES.—

25. In absence of the first class of residuaries, the residue devolves on the second class consisting of the father or the true grandfather.

According to the Sirajiyah "Brothers and sisters whether full or consanguine are all excluded from participating in the inheritance by the father, and even by the true grandfather". This is the view according to Imam Abu Hanifa and *Fatwa* accords with it.

The authorities for and against the right of the true grandfather to exclude full or consanguine brothers and sisters are as follows :—

For—

(1) Hazrat Abu Bakr the first Khalif.

(2) Imam Abu Hanifa, the founder of the Hanafi School.

Against—

(3) Imam Abu Yusuf, } The two famous disciples of Imam
(4) Imam Muhammad } Abu Hanifa

(5) Imam Malik, the founder the Maliki School

(6) Imam Shafi, the founder of the Shafii School.

(7) The eminent jurist Zaid offers some suggestions giving a choice to the grandfather.

(*a*) to take one-sixth as a sharer, or

(*b*) to take as a residuary in capacity of a full brother or

(*c*) take one-third of the Residue.

e.g. ***A Muslim dies leaving a true grandfather, a true grandmother, two brothers and a full sister the grandmother takes 1/6. The residue is 5/6 which according to Imam Abu Hanifa goes to the grandfather. According to Zaid he may elect to take 1/6 as a sharer or as a residuary with brother,*** i.e. ***2/7 of 5/6=5/21. (There being two brothers and one sister), or by the third alternative take 1/3 of 5/6=5/18 which will be better than 5/21 or 1/6.***

Illustration.

		According to Abu Hanifa	According to Zaid
True grandmother	=	1/6	1/6 = 3/18
True grandfather	=	5/6	2/3 of 5/6 = 10/18
Full sister	=	excluded	1/3 of 5/6 = 5/18

The case of the grandfather had caused a considerable difference of opinion among the eminent disciples of the Prophet. Here is a case known as the *Kharqa* which implies an unsettled point. The following are the surviving heirs, mother, grandfather and a sister.

(1) According to

Abu Bakr, First Khalif ...	Mother 1/3	Grandfather 2/3	Sister excluded*
" Zaid	Mother 1/3	Grandfather 4/9	Sister 2/9
" Ali, Fourth Khalif ...	Mother 1/3	Grandfather 1/6	Sister 1/2
" Ibn Abbas ...	Mother 1/3	Grandfather 1/6	Sister 1/2
		or	
	Mother 1/3	Grandfather 1/3	Sister 1/3
" Umar, Second Khalif	Mother 1/3	Grandfather 1/6	Sister 1/2

(ii) Here is a case known as the Hamziyah.

	3 grandmothers	grand-father	full sister	consanguine sister	uterine sister
According to Abu Bakr & Ibn Abbas	1/6 (joint share)	5/6	excluded	excluded	excluded
According to Ali	1/6	1/6	1/2	1/6	excluded

CLASS III OF RESIDUARIES.—

26. In default of Class I and II of residuaries the residue devolves on the full brothers equally, and if there are full sisters then along with them, each sister taking half as much as each brother.

Similarly in default of full brothers and sisters the residue devolves upon the consanguine brothers and sisters in the same manner, the brother taking a double share.

Sister with daughter.—

In default of residuaries of I and II classes and there being no brothers but daughters or son's daughters excluding full or consanguine sisters from inheritance as sharers, such sister or sisters are entitled to take the residue in preference to remote heirs.

This case is the solitary exception to rule that no female is primarily a risiduary but only become so when co-existing with a male residuary.[1]

* This is according to the Hanafi Law.

1 Vide illustration (ii) p 205.

Brother's sons.—

In default of full or consanguine brother, and no sister taking as residuary under the preceding rule, the residue devolves on full brothers, sons to be divided equally between them, and it is immaterial whether they claim their rights through the same or different fathers.

Similary sons of consanguine brothers take the residue if there are no sons of full brothers.

And finally the residue devolves on sons of full or consanguine brothers' sons' sons *h.l.s.* in like order, the nearer degree excluding the more remote, and issue of full brothers excluding the issue of consanguine brothers in the same degree.

Rights of Collaterals

(i) Illustrations

F = Full
S = Sister
Ss = Sisters

B = brother
C = Consanguine

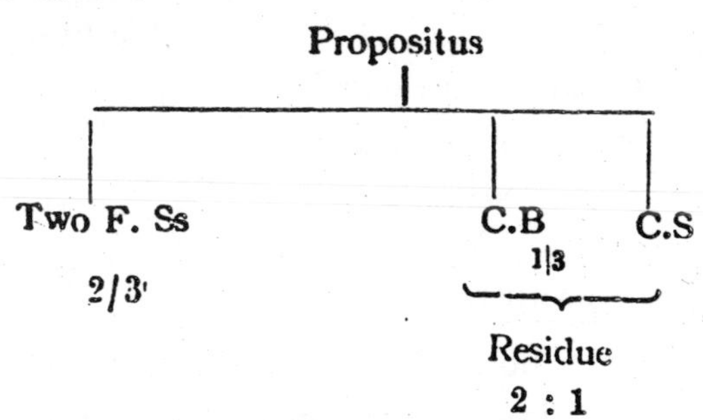

Two F. Ss = 2/3
C. B = 2/3 of 1/3 = 2/9
C. S = 1/3 of 1/3 = 1/9

(ii)

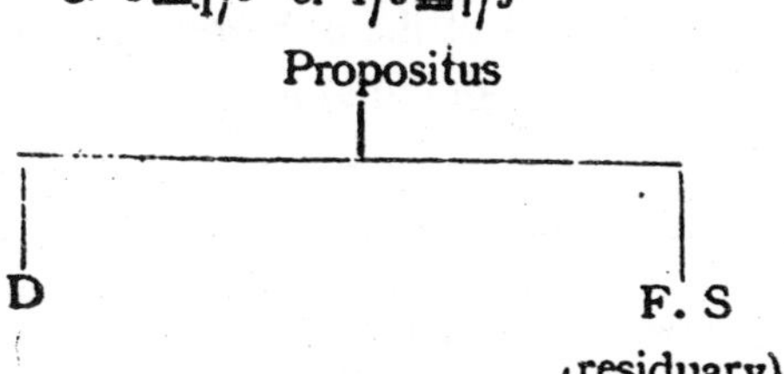

D = daughter = 1/2
F. S = 1/2 as residuary.

(iii)

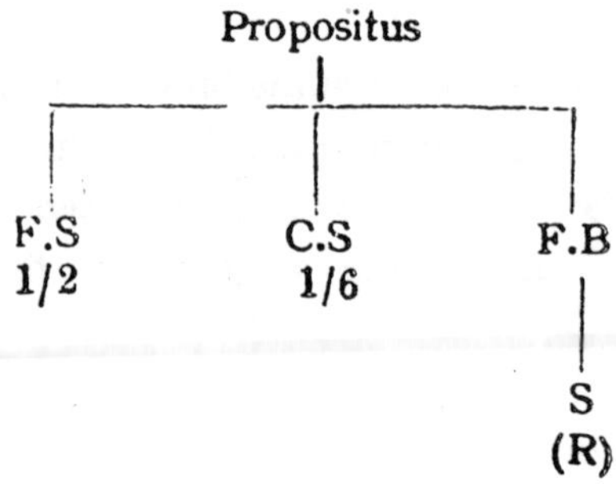

F. S. takes 1/2=3/6

C. S.=(2/3—1/2) =1/6

F. B. S.= the residue=2/6

(iv)

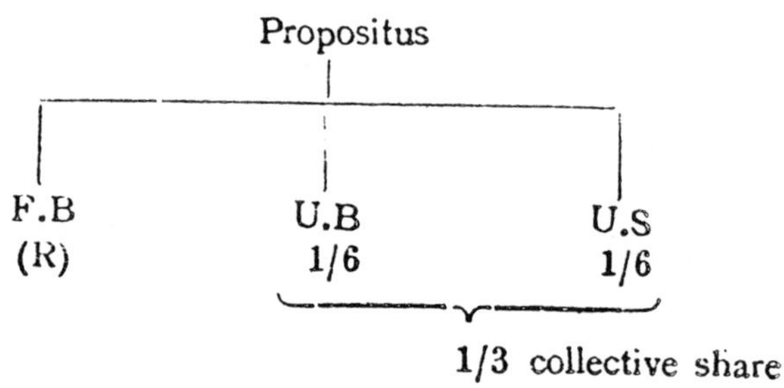

U. B. = uterine brother=1/6

U. S. = " sister 1/6

F. B.= Residue 2/3

CLASS IV OF RESIDUARIES.—

27. If there are no residuaries of class I, II & III the residue devolves on the offspring of the true grandfathers that is, on the paternal uncles, great uncles and their male descendants in the male line.

And finally in default of these the residue devolves on descendants of more remote true grandfathers.[1]

---

1 In Mahomed Haneef v. Mahomed Masoom 21 W. R. 371 (1874) a succession certificate was granted under Act XXVII of 1860 to a person whose paternal ances-or in the fifth degree was related in the sixth degree to the deceased.

In Abdul Samad Sahib v. Chinnathambi Sahib 53 I. C. 873 (Mad. 1918) the true grandfather's descendants succeeded in preference to a daughter's son who belongs o the Distant Kindred class.

CLASS IV OF RESIDUARIES.

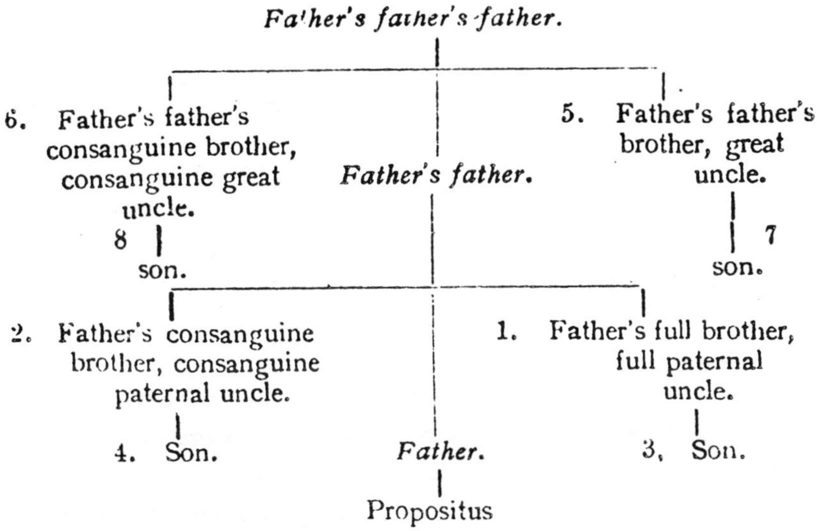

The three lineal ancestors being dead the order of succession is indicated by the figures 1—8.

JURISTIC CLASSIFICATION OF RESIDUARIES.—

28. The residuaries are of two kinds:

1. Residuaries by consanguinity, *nasab*.

2. Residuaries for special causes, this class may be taken to be obsolete in British India as the result of the abolition of the institution of slavery by Act V of 1843.[1]

Residuaries by nasab.—

The Residuaries by *nasab* are further subdivided into three classes (*a*) Residuaries in their own right, (*b*) Residuaries in another's right; (*c*) Residuaries together with another.

1 e.g. Those who succeed to the estate of a manumitted slave etc. The Slavery Act V of 1843 abolished slavery and removed all legal disabilities due to slavery. Vide Sayad Mir .Ujmudinkhan v. Zia-ul-Nissa 6. I. A. 137 (1879), 3 Bom., 422 P.C. In this case a Rajput girl was purchased by the Nawab and she became the mother of a daughter while still a slave. She was later on emancipated and married by the Nawab. Her daughter was married in the Nawab's life time, and the respondents daughters were the issue of that marriage. A male heir of the Nawab claimed the Rajput lady's property to the disherision of her own natural heirs. Held by the Privy Council that by Act v. of 1843 the righ if any of the Nawab's heirs was taken away and that the respondents were entitled to succeed to their grandmother.

(*a*) The first class consists of the male residuaries mentioned in the preceding section *viz.* "The offspring of the deceased or of the father or the true grandfather of the deceased," all in lineal male line, and also the "root" of the deceased, the father or true grandfather *h.h.s.*[1]

(*b*) Residuaries in another's right consists of four females namely daughter, sons's daughter, full sister, and half-sister by father (and in one exceptional case the mother[2] also) who are ***prima facie*** sharers, but are converted into residuaries, when they co-exist with one or more male residuaries of the same relationship to the deceased as the claimant in question.

e.g. ***A daughter co-existing with a son is converted into a residuary by the later. A full sister co-existing with a full brother is converted into a resudiary by the latter.***

(*c*) Residuaries together with another are two female sharers ***viz.*** full sister, and half-sister by father who are converted into residuaries by another female sharer and thereby inherit together.

e.g. ***A full sister co-existing with a son's daughter and not being excluded by any heir becomes residuary together with the son's daughter.***

LIST OF RESIDUARIES.

I. Descendants.—

1. Son or sons.

2. Sons' or sons sharing with daughters, if any, the son taking a double share.

3. Son's sons with son's daughters of equal degree, the former as usual taking a double share, son's son's sons ***h.l.s.*** the nearer in degree excluding the more remote.

---

1 e.g. The sons, son's sons h.l s. The father true grandfather h.h.s. and all male agnates collaterals.

2 When the mother co-exists with the father and there is a spouse of the deceased and there are no other heirs then after the share has been allotted to the spouse the father and the mother take the residue as residuaries.

4. Son's son's sons *h.l.s.* similarly shares with son's daughters of a higher degree or equal degree (son's son's daughter), the male as usual takes a double share, (this case is such that the female sharer in question would get nothing, and all remote son's son's sons and daughters h.l.s. are excluded.)

II. ASCENDANTS—

5. Father.

6. True grandfather, h.h.s. the nearer in degree excluding the more remote.

III. NEAR COLLATERALS—DESCENDANTS OF FATHER.—

7. Full brothers.

8. Full brother with full sister if any, taking a double share.

9. Consanguine brothers;

10. Consanguine brother similarly sharing with consanguine sister if any, in like manner.

11. Full sister where thare is no full brother or any nearer residuary and with one or more daughters or son's daughters, takes the residue if any still not exhausted.

12. Consanguine sister where there is no full or consanguine brother, or any nearer residuary, and with one or more daughters or son's daughters takes the residue if any still not exhausted.

13. Full brother's son's *h.l.s.* the nearer in degree excluding the more remote.

14. Consanguine brother's sons.

15. Full brother's son's sons.

16. Consanguine brother's son's sons.

17. Then follow remoter male descendants of full brother's son's sons, and consanguine brother's son's sons in like manner.

IV. DESCENDANTS OF TRUE GRANDFATHERS *h.h.s.*—

18. Full paternal uncle.

19. Consanguine paternal uncle.

20. Full paternal uncle's son *h.l.s.*

21. Consanguine paternal uncle's son,

22. Full paternal uncle's son's son.

23. Consanguine paternal uncle's son's son.

24. Then follow descendants of full paternal uncle's son's son and consanguine paternal uncle's son's son in like order.

Similarly in like order male descendants of more remote true grandfathers *ad infinitum.*

§ 4. EXCLUSION OF SHARERS

EXCLUSION OF SHARERS.—

29. Of the twelve sharers five are never liable to be excluded from participating in the Inheritance but the other seven sharers are liable to be excluded from the inheritance by presence of some preferable heirs.

Sharers not liable to be excluded.	Sharers liable to be excluded.
1. Husband.	1. True grandfather.
2. Wife, (wives).	2. True grandmother.
3. Father.	3. Son's daughter.
4. Mother.	4. Full sister.
5. Daughter.	5. Consanguine sister.
	6. Uterine brother.
	7. Uterine sister.

The following general principles determine the rules for exclusion of sharers.

(*a*) A sharer is excluded by any person through whom he is related to the deceased, and who may participate as a residuary.

e.g. The father excludes the true grandfather, full sisters, or consanguine sisters.

(*b*) All collateral sharers are excluded by a lineal male decendant or ascendent who can also take as a residuary.

e.g. The son excludes, full sisters, consanguine sisters, uterine brothers and sisters.

(*c*) A remoter sharer is excluded by nearer residuary who is such that would convert such equally nearer sharer into residuaries.

e.g. Son and son's son h.l.s. in nearer degree exclude son's daughters in a lower degree.

(d) A half-blood sharer is excluded by a full-blood residuary who is such that would convert such full-blood sharers into residuaries.

e.g. Consanguine sisters are excluded by full brothers as the latter would convert the full sisters into residuaries

A female full-blood, sharer excludes a half-blood female sharer when the former inherits as a residuary.

e.g. A Muslim dies leaving a daughter, full sister, and a consanguine sister, the latter is excluded by the full sister since she takes as a residuary with the daughter.

EXCLUSION AS SHARERS.—

30. There are three sharers who are excluded without forfeiting their residuary title, and they would inherit if not excluded by other residuaries.

1. Son's daughter.
2. Full sister.
3. Consanguine sister.

The following general principles determine the rules of exclusion as sharers.

Collaterals.—

(a) All descendants of the parents of the deceased are excluded by one or more lineal descendants of the deceased.

e.g. Full sisters, consanguine sisters, are excluded as sharers by one or more daughters or son's daughters [they may inherit as residuaries with the daughters·]

(b) The nearer sharers exclude the more remote sharers, they having taken the maximum collective share fixed for that class.

e.g. Son's daughters are excluded as sharers by two or more daughters or two or more son's daughters of a higher degree or there being one daughter or son's daughter with one or more nearer son's daughters. [Son's daughters may inherit as residuaries with son's sons of the same or a lower degree]

(c) Half-blood sharers are excluded by full-blood sharers of the same degree and who exhaust the maximum collective share fixed for that class[1]

e.g. Consanguine sisters are excluded by two or more full sisters.

1 If the collective share is not exhausted, there being only one such sharer, the half-blood sharer would take the residue.

Table of exclusion as sharers.

The sharers	Exclusion as sharers
1. Son's daughter	Excluded as sharer by two or more daughters or son's daughters of a higher degree, or by one daughter together with one or more son's daughters of a higher degree or by one nearest son's daughter together with one or more nearer son's daughters.
2. Full sister ...	Excluded as sharer by one or more daughters or son's daughters.
3. Consanguine sister	Excluded as sharer by one or more daughters or son's daughters or by two or more full sisters.

There are two sharers who when excluded as sharers are absolutely excluded, for they are not residuaries at all.

1. True grandmother
2. Uterine brother and uterine sister.

The true grandmother (paternal or maternal) is excluded by the mother or nearer true grandmother on that side.

The uterine brothers aud sisters are excluded by one or more child, daughters or son's daughters and as they are not residuaries it means their absolute exclusion.

EXCLUSION BY CONVERSION INTO RESIDUARIES.—

31. In case of three sharers, the father, mother, and daughter exclusion as sharers by conversion into residuaries does not mean absolute exclusion, for they inherit as residuaries, but other sharers, may be absolutely excluded by co-existing residuaries.[1]

---

1 As regards conversion of sharers into residuaries vide sec. 242 ante P. 190.

Table of absolute exclusion of sharers.

Sharers.	When absolutely excluded.
1. True grandfather.	Absolutely excluded by the father or a nearer true grandfather.
2. True grandmother.	A true grandmother excluded by the mother, a nearer true grandmother. Paternal true grandmother excluded by the father or by a true grandfather through whom she is related to the deceased.
3. Son's daughter.	Absolutely exlcuded by son, or son's son of a higher degree.
4. Full sister.	Absolutely excluded by son, or son's son, father, or true grandfather.
5. Consanguine sister.	Ditto and absolutely excluded by full brother or by full sister being a residuary.
6. Uterine brother. }	Absolutely excluded by son or son's son, father, or true grandfather.
7. Uterine sister. }	Also excluded by daughter or son's daughter.

PARTIAL EXCLUSION.—

32. There are five sharers who are sometimes entitled to a maximum share and sometimes to a minimum share owing to co-existence of other heirs.

Table of partial exclusion of sharers.

Sharers.	Share.	Share reduced.	Under what circumstances.
1. Husband.	1/2	1/4	When there is a child or son's child.
2. Wife.	1/4	1/8	Ditto.
3. Mother.	1/3 of the whole.	1/6	When there is a child, or son's child or two or more brothers or sisters.
		1/3 of the Residue.	Ditto and when there is the father and a spouse of the deceased
4. Son's daughter if one if two or more.	1/2 2/3	1/6	When there exists one daughter or son's daughter of a higher degree and is not excluded, nor converted into residuaries.
5. Consanguine sister if one if two or more.	1/2 2/3	1/6	When thre is only one full sister and not excluded, nor converted into residuaries.

§ 5. GENERAL RULES OF INHERITANCE.

THE FUNDAMENTAL RULES.—

33. The right of inheritance of the heirs is generally determined by the following considerations.

(i) The nearer in degree excludes the more remote.

(ii) A person related to the deceased through any person shall not inherit while that person is alive.

(iii) There is no representation.

(iv) The strength of consanguinity determines preference.

(v) If the degree of relationship is equal then as a general rule a male sharer takes double the portion of a female sharer of the same degree.

e.g. a son cannot inherit from his grandfather while the father is alive.
e.g A full-blood relation is preferred to a half-blood.

PRIMARY HEIRS AND THEIR SUBSTITUTES.—

34. The following are the primary heirs; and their substitutes.

Primary heirs :—(1) The child, male or female. (2) The father. (3) The mother. Their substitutes :—(a) Child of a son *h.l.s.* (b) True grandfather. (c) True grandmother.

The primary heirs succeed first and in their default their substitutes inherit the property. The substitutes also exclude all those persons, excluded by the primary heirs. The husband, and the wife are also primary heirs and always inherit.

e. g. If there is a surviving daughter and a son's daughter the former would take 1/2 and the latter 1/6. This may be taken as an exception to the rule.
e. g. the son's child also excludes full brothers or sisters as does the son

PREFERENCE AMONGST HEIRS.—

35. The heirs by *nasab* are subdivided into sharers and residuaries. This classification however does not denote priority of one class over the other so as to exclude that class. No sharer excludes residuaries, in fact all sharers are not entitled to inherit together at one and the same time, some sharers are liable to be excluded by the presence of a sharer or even by a residuary, and again some of the sharers are converted into residuaries and thereby are excluded from receiving their fixed shares.

The primary heirs always inherit.

(a) The heirs by marriage the husband or the wife.

(b) The heirs by consanguinity *viz.* the son or sons, daughter or daughters, father and mother.

Sharers and Residuaries.—

Under the Hanafi system the order is Descendants, Ascendants, and Collaterals. The following general principles determine the order of succession among the sharers and residuaries.

1. As a general rule proximity is determined by the degree of claimants' relationship to the deceased whose property is to be distributed. The strength of consanguinity is another test to determine priority. That is those of the full-blood exclude those of the half-blood. Similarly a nearer residuary excludes the more remote and a residuary of the full-blood excludes a residuary of the half-blood of the same degree.

2. In case of conflict between sharers and residuaries (*a*) a nearer residuary excludes a remoter sharer if the latter is related to the deceased through the former, (*b*) or if the former was either a descendant or an ascendant and the latter was a collateral only, (*c*) or the latter is converted into a residuary.

Illustrations.

(i) A son or son's son excludes a full sister, or a half-sister by father.

(ii) A true grandfather excludes paternal true grandmothers as they are related through him, and under clause (b) he excludes full sisters or half sisters by father.

(iii) A son converts a daughter into a residuary.

3. (*a*) A nearer sharer excludes the more remote, if the latter is related to the deceased through the former who is such that under certain circumstances would take the whole inheritance as a residuary.

(*b*) or the former is a descendant or such an ascendant who under certain circumstances would take the whole inheritance as a residuary, and the latter is a collateral.

(*c*) if the nearer and remoter sharers claim the same Koranic share, and if the former takes the whole share under certain circumstances, the latter would be excluded, but if the former takes the minimum share under certain circumstances, the latter would take the difference between the maximum and the minimum shares allotted.

Illustrations.

(i) A father excludes the true grandfather [this case falls under 3 (a) and also 3 (c)].

(ii) A father excludes the full sister (collateral).

(iii) Two or more daughters exclude the son's daughters, but a single daughter does not exclude the son's daughter (here the two daughters had taken the maximum share viz. 2/3 and there is nothing left for the son's daughters to take, but a single daughter, who is entitled to 1/2 only, enables the son's daughter to take the difference viz. 2/3—1/2 = 1/6.)

4. A nearer sharer does not exclude a remote residuary, here the sharer takes his share first and the residue if any devolves upon the remoter residuary.

Similarly a full-blood sharer never excludes a half-blood residuary.

5. (*a*) Full-blood sharers exclude half-blood sharers if the half-blood sharers are of the same class and claim the same share, and they have taken the maximum share, if not the difference would be given to the half-blood sharer

Illustrations.

Two or more full sisters exclude a half-sister by father and they take the maximum share 2/3, but one full sister does not exclude the half-sister by father, as she takes the share 1/2 leaving 1/6 for the half-sister (2/3—1/2=1/6).

(*b*) A full-blood residuary under the following circumstances excludes a half-blood sharer, namely the former would convert into residuary a full-blood sharer of the same class as the half-blood sharer in question.

e.g. a full brother excludes the half-sister by father as he would convert the full sister into a residuary.

---

§ 6. THE DOCTRINE OF INCREASE AND RETURN.

THE DOCTRINE OF INCREASE.—

36. The doctrine of increase, *'awl*, applies when it is found out that the sum total of the fractions to which several sharers are entitled exceeds unity, then they must all abate rateably. The doctrine of increase operates by increasing the common denominator of the fractions to the total of all the numerators. The numerators are left unchanged, thereby each share is rateably reduced.

Illustrations.

(*a*) A woman dies leaving her husband and two sisters of the whole blood.

Husband	...	1/2=3/6	reduced to ...	3/7
Two full sisters	...	2/3=4/6	" ...	4/7
		7/6		1

(*b*) A woman leaves her husband, her mother and a full sister.

Husband	...	/12=3/6	reduced to ...	3/8
Mother	...	1/3=2/6	" ...	2/8
Full sister	...	1/2=3/6	" ...	3/8
		8/6		1

(*c*) A woman dies ieaving her husband, two full sisters, uterine brother and mother.

Husband	...	1/2=3/6	reduced to	3/9
Two full sisters	...	2/3=4/6	"	4/9
Uterine brother	...	... =1/6	"	1/9
Mother	...	... =1/6	"	1/9
		9		1

(*d*) A woman dies leaving the following heirs.

Husband	...	1/2=3/6	reduced to	3/10
Two full sisters	...	2/3=4/6	"	4/10
Two uterine brothers and two sisters	...	1/3=2/6	"	2/10
Mother ...	...	=1/6	"	1/10
		10/6		1

(*e*) A man dies leaving a widow, mother and a full sister.

Widow	...	1/4=3/12	reduced to ...	3/13
Mother	...	1/3=4/12	" ...	4/13
Full sister	...	1/2=6/12	" ...	6/13
		13/12		1

A person dies leaving a widow, two full sisters, one uterine sister and mother.

Widow	... 1/4=3/12	reduced to	...	1/5
Two full sisters	... 2/3=8/12	...	...	8/15
Uterine sister	... 1/6=2/12	...	...	2/15
Mother	... 1/6=2/12	...	...	2/15
	15/12			1

(g) A person dies leaving the following heirs.

Wife ...	...	1/4=3/12	reduced to	3/17
Two full sisters	...	2/3=8/12	,,	8/17
Two uterine sisters ...		1/3=4/12	,,	4/17
Mother	...	1/6=2/12	,,	2/17
		17/12		1

(h) A person leaves his wife, two daughters, father and mother.[1]

Wife...	... 1/8=3/24	reduced to	3/27
Two daughters	... 2/3=16/24	...	16/27
Father	... 1/6=4/24	...	4/27
Mother	... 1/6=4/24	...	4/27
	27/24		1

Rule of Change of Denominators.—

Thus it will be seen that according to the doctrine of increase, the common denominators that are liable to be increased are as follows:—

Denominators.	Increased up to what limit.
6	7, 8, 9 or 10
12	13, 15 or 17
24	27 only
2, 3, 4, and 8,	not necessary to be increased at all.

1 This case is known as mimberiya, answered by Ali from the pulpit.

Denominator	6	increased to	7	*vide* illustration	(*a*)	page	218
"	"	"	8	"	(*b*)	"	"
"	"	"	9	"	(*c*)	"	"
"	"	"	10	"	(*d*)	"	"
"	12	"	13	"	(*e*)	"	"
"	"	"	15	"	(*f*)	"	219
"	"	"	17	"	(*g*)	"	"
"	"	"	27	"	(*h*)	"	"

THE DOCTRINE OF RETURN.—

37. The doctrine of return, *rad*, applies when after assigning shares to all sharers, there is a surplus, and there being no residuary the residue reverts to the sharers in proportion to their respective shares, this is known as the Return.

The sharers who are entitled to the Return are seven only, one male and seven females. *viz.* uterine brother, or sister, daughter, son's daughter, full sister, consanguine sister, mother and the paternal grandmother. If there be one of such persons only the whole surplus is given to that particular heir.

The Return to sharers.

Sharers not ordinarily entitled to return.[1]	Sharers by *nasab* entitled to return.[2]
1. Husband. 2. Wife (wives).	1. Mother. 2. True grandmother. 3. Daughter. 4. Son's daughter. 5. Full sister. 6. Consanguine sister. 7. } 8. } Uterine brother or sister.

1 If there are no other sharers or residuaries or distant kindred, then the husband or wife take the residue by return.

2 The return may take place to one, two or three of the above mentioned sharers but not to more than three,

Thus the mother (or grandmother), the daughter (or son's daughter) or the sister (full or consanguine together with uterine) take the residue in default of male agnates, and where the daughter or sister are not co-existing. This includes eight sharers, the husband and the wife are excluded from the Return, and the father or the true grandfather are residuaries, so when they co-exist with sharers there is no "Return" at all.

Illustrations.

(*a*) A person dies leaving a wife and a sister.

Wife...	... 1/4
Widow	... 3/4 (1/2 as sharer and 1/4 by Return)

(*b*) A woman dies leaving her husband and a daughter

Husband	... 1/4
Daughter	... 3/4 (1/2 as sharer and 1/4 by Return)

(*c*) A person dies leaving the mother, daughter and son's daughter

Mother	... 1/6=1/6	increased to 1/5
Daughter	... 1/2=3/6	... 3/5
Son's daughters	... 1/6=1/6	... 1/5
	5/6	1

(In this case the share of each shârer is rateably increased. The process is by decreasing the denominators of each sharer so as to make it equal to the sum of the numerators).

(*d*) A person dies leaving the mother, full sister and uterine brother.

Mother	...	=1/6	increased to ... 1/5
Full sister	...	1/2=3/6	" ... 3/5
Uterine brother	...	=1/6	" ... 1/5
		5/6	1

(*e*) A person dies leaving his wife, daughter and mother

Wife	...	1/8	... 4/32
Mother	... 1/6	increased	to 1/4 of 7/8=7/32
Daughter	1/2=3/6	"	3/4 of 7/8=21/32
	4/6		1

Here after assigning the share to the wife the residue is 7/8 which is to be distributed between mother and daughter in the ratio of 1:3 in proportion to their fixed shares, *viz.* 1/4 of 7/8 and 3/4 of 7/8 respectively. This is a simple method. The other process would be as follows :—

Wife ...	...	1/8=3/24
Mother	...	1/6=4/24
Daughter	...	1/2=12/24
	Total ...	19/24, Residue being 5/24

The residue is now to be distributed again between the mother and the daughter in the proportion 1 : 3.

Mother would ultimately receive*	1/6+(1/4 of 5/24)=7/32
daughter	1/2+(3/4 of 5/24)=21/32

A woman dies leaving her husband mother and daughter,

Husband	...	1/4	... 4/16
Mother	...	1/6 increased to	1/4 of 3/4=3/16
Daughter	... 1/2=3/6	,,	3/4 of 3/4=9/16
	4/6		1

(Here after assigning the share to the husband the residue is 3/4, which is distributed between the mother and daughter in the ratio 1:3 in accordance with their original fixed shares.)

Denominator Six.—

In applying the doctrine of Return it will be seen that the denominator 6 is reduced to 2, 3, 4 or 5.

Illustrations.

A person dies leaving the following heirs only.

(*a*) True grandmother	...	1/6	increased to	1/2
Uterine sister ...	...	1/6	,,	1/2
		2/6		1
(*b*) True grandmother	... 1/6 =	1/6	increased to	1/3
2 uterine sisters	... 1/3 =	2/6	,,	4/3
		3/6		1

(*c*) Mother	...	...	1/6 increased to		1/4
Sons's daughter		...	1/2 = 3/6	„	3/4
			46		1

(*d*) Full sister	...	...	1/2 = 3/6 increased to		3/5
Consanguine sister		...	1/6	„	1/5
Uterine sister		...	1/6	„	1/5
			5/6		1

The above rule is followed in initial application even when the heirs co-exist with either the husband or the wife, who are not entitled to the Return.

ILLUSTRATIONS.—

A person dies leaving the following heirs.

(i) Wife	...		... ...	1/4=2/8
Uterine brother		1/6	1/2 of R = 1/2 of 3/4	= 3/8
Uterine sister	...	1/6	1/2 of R = 1/2 of 3/4	= 3/8
		2/6	6 reduced to 2	1
(ii) Wife	...		... ...	1/4
Uterine brother	...	1/6	1/3 of R.= 1/3 of 3/4	= 1/4
Uterine sister	...	1/6	1/3 of R. „	= 1/4
Mother	...	1/6	1/3 of R. „	= 1/4
		3/6	6 reduced to 3.	1
(iii) Husband	...		... ...	1/4 = 4/16
Mother		1/6	1/4 of R. = 1/4 of 3/4	= 3/16
Daughter	1/2 =	3/6	3/4 of R. = 3/4 of 3/4	= 9/16
		4/6	6 reduced to 4.	1
(iv) Wife	...		... ...	1/8 = 5/40
Mother		1/6	1/5 of R. ... 1/5 of 7/8	= 7/40
Two son's daughters	2/3 =	4/6	4/5 of R. ... 4/5 of 7/8	= 28/40
		56	6 reduced to 5.	1

Order of devolution of Return.—

38. The Return devolves in the following order:

(*a*) To the Residuaries

(*b*) In default of (*a*) to the sharers[1]

(*c*) In default of (*a*) and (*b*) to the Distant Kindred

(*d*) In default of (*a*), (*b*) and (*c*) to the heir by marriage[2]

Succession of sharers and residuaries.—

39. The sharers and residuaries succeed briefly in the following manner.

(*a*) The sharers and residuaries may succeed jointly.

or

(*b*) The sharers only may succeed wholly exhausting the estate or there being no residuaries taking the residue by return,

or

(*c*) The residuaries alone may succeed, there being no conversion of sharers into residuaries, or even by excluding remoter sharers.

General Order in British India.—

40. 1. (*a*) The sharers by marriage; (*b*) along with those sharers by consanguinity who are not excluded.

2. The Residuaries taking the residue if any or taking the whole estate in default of (1)

3. In default of No. (2) the residue devolves upon the sharers by consanguinity in proportion to the original fixed shares.

4. In default of sharers by consanguinity and residuaries, the residue devolves upon the Distant kindred.

In default of all these the residue devolves upon the sharers by marriage and next on the successor by contract if any, the acknowledged kinsman, the universal legatee and finally it escheats to the Crown.

---

1 Vide Macnaghten Precedents Inheritance Cases 71 73, 74. Gujjadur Pershad v. Shaikh Abdullah, 11 W. R. 220 (1869).

2 The wife or husband has no claim as against the Distant Kindred, vide Mahomed Noor Bukhsh v. M. Hamedool Haq, 5 W. R. 23 (1866). Koonari v. Dalim 11 Cal. 14 (1884), but as against the State they are entitled to the surplus, vide Mahomed Arshad v. Sajida 3 Cal. 702 (1878), Scobhanee v. Bhetun 1 S. D A. (1811) an old case decided in accordance with the fatawa

LIST OF THE DISTANT KINDRED.

I. DESCENDANTS OF THE DECEASED.[1]

1. Daughter's children and their descendants.
2. Children of son's daughters and their descendants,

II. ASCENDANTS OF THE DECEASED.[2]

3. False grandfathers h.h.s.
4. False grandmothers h.h.s.

III. DESCENDANTS OF PARENTS.[3]

5. Full brothers' daughters and their decendants.
6. Consanguine brothers' daughters and their descendants.
7. Uterine brothers' children and their descendants.
8. Daughters of full brothers' sons h.l.s. and their descendants.
9. Daughters of consanguine brothers' sons h.l.s. and their descendants.
10 Sisters' (whether full consanguine or uterine) children and their descendants.

IV. DESCENDANTS OF IMMEDIATE GRANDPARENTS (TRUE OR FALSE):—

11. Paternal aunts, Father's full sisters and mother's full brothers and sisters i.e., maternal uncles and aunts.
12. Father's consanguine sister's and mother's consanguine brothers and sisters.
13. Paternal aunt's descendants, maternal uncle's and aunt's descendants.
14. Uterine brothers and sisters of father and mother.
15. Full paternal uncles' daughters, and their descendants.
16. Consanguine paternal uncles' daughters and their descendants.
17. Uterine paternal uncles and their children and their descendants.
18. Full paternal uncles' sons' daughters and their descendants.
19. Consanguine paternal uncles' sons' daughters and their descendants.
20. Descendants of remoter ancestors h.h.s. true or false.

---

1 e.g. S D D, S D S = son's daughters' children.
D S S, D S D = grand children of daughters.
D S S S, D S S D = daughters' great grand children.

2 M F. mother's father.
F M F, M M F parents' maternal grandfathers.
M F F, M F M mother's paternal grandparents.

3 The order of succession is as follows.

(a) Full brothers' daughters and full sisters' children or consanguine brothers' daughters and consanguine sisters' children. } with { (b) uterine brothers and sisters' children.
Next in order.
(c) Full brothers' sons' daughters.
Consanguine brothers son's daughters.
(d) Grandchildren of (a) with grand children of (b)
6

THE DISTANT KINDRED.

41. The Distant kindred are those blood relations who are neither sharers nor residuaries.

There are four classes of "Distant kindred"

I. Descendants.

II. Ascendants.

III. Descendants of parents.

IV. Descendants *h.l.s.* of ascendants *h.h.s.*

The Distant kindred may also conveniently be classified into six groups.

1. Descendants of the deceased.
2. Ascendants of the deceased.
3. Descendants *h.l.s.* of the brothers and sisters of the deceased.
4. Uncles and aunts of the deceased.
5. Descendants *h. l. s.* of uncles and aunts of the deceased.
6. Uncles and aunts of the ascendants of the deceased and their issue.

SUCCESSION OF THE DISTANT KINDRED.—

42. The distant kindred are entitled to succeed in two cases (*a*) when there is no sharer or residuary then they are entitled to take the whole estate, or (*b*) when there is the husband or wife only, they take the residue after deducting the share of the spouse.

The rules.—

(1) The general rule that the nearer degree excludes the more remote is applicable to the distant kindred also.

e.g. the daughter's son or daughter's daughter would exclude all other Distant kindred.

(2) Of persons equal in degree, the descendants of sharer's or residuaries are preferred.

e.g. Son's daughter's daughter or son is preferred to daughter's daughter's daughter or son.

Imam Muhammad's system.[1] —

(3) Among the distant kindred equal in respect of propinquity and the condition of their roots, Imam Muhammad proposes a system to examine the sex of the roots and the number of the branches, that is, when tracing the line of descent a difference of sex first appears in the roots, then assign to the male member a portion double that of the female ancestor, by taking account of the claimants descended from that root, for each male root will be considered to be as many males as the claimants descended from that root, and each female root will similarly be considered as many females as are descended from her. Finally what is allotted to the male roots is collected together and is distributed to their descendants. Similarly what is allotted to the female roots is collected together and is distributed to their descendants.

If however in tracing descent there appears a further difference of sex in the pedigree at a lower stage, then what has been allotted to the male or female roots in the higher stage is again assigned and redistributed in the lower stage, and this operation is continued until the actual claimants are finally reached.

In distribution the general rule double portion to the male members is followed. And this method also involves a complicated scheme of succession by representation.

Imam Abu Yusuf's system.—

Imam Abu Yusuf takes no notice of difference of sex in the roots of intermediate ancestors. According to him the sexes of the actual claimants should be taken into consideration in distributing the estate, and very often adopting this method, the result is exactly the opposite to the distribution effected according to Imam Muhammad's system.[1]

---

1 The method of distribution proposed by Imam Abu Yusuf has not been adopted by the Hanafi jurists. The Sirajyah adopts Imam Muhammad's system.

CLASS I—DISTANT KINDRED.—

43. The following is the order of succession among the Distant Kindred of the first class.

(*a*) Daughters' children

(*b*) Sons' daughters' children

(*c*) Daughters' grand children

(*d*) Sons' sons' daughters' children

(*e*) Daughters' descendants h. l. s. and sons' daughters' descendants h. l. s. in like order.

Illustrations.

A person dies leaving heirs as shown in the following tables, and only the heirs in the last line have survived the deceased.

D=Daughter.

S=Son.

(i)

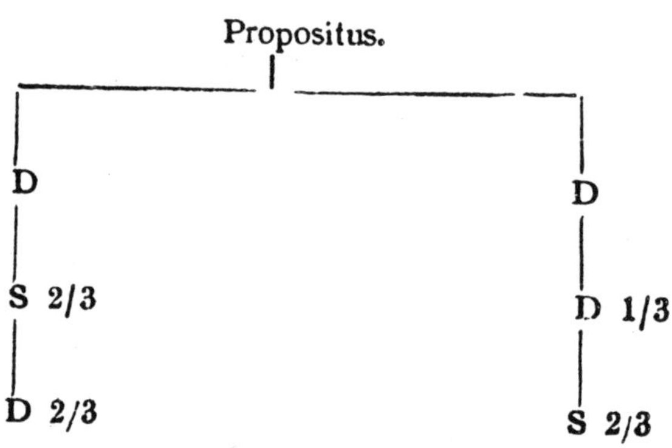

Here the ancestors differ in their sexes in the second line of descent, and there being only one claimant in each line a double share to the male member is assigned at this point and which descends to their claimants respectively.

D S D, daughter's son's daughter 2/3.

D D S, daughter's daughter's son 1/3.

According to Imam Abu Yusuf:—

D S D will take 1/3

D S „ 2/3.

(ii)

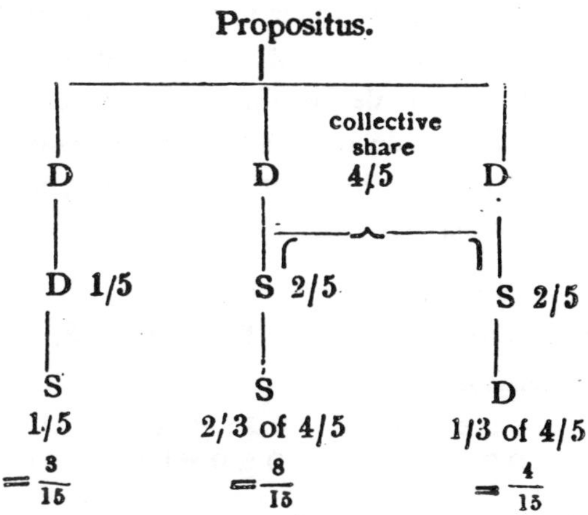

In this case the ancestors differ in their sexes in the second line and there being only one claimant in each line of descent a double share is assigned to the male members at this point and what has been allotted to the male roots (in this case 2/5 each) is collected together (4/5) and is distributed to their descendants, a double share is again assigned to the male members.

D D S=1/5 3/15.
D S S=2/3 of 4/5=8/15.
D S D=1/3 of 4/5=4/15.

According to Imam Abu Yusuf :— D D S=2/5.
D S S=2/5.
D S D=1/5.

(iii)

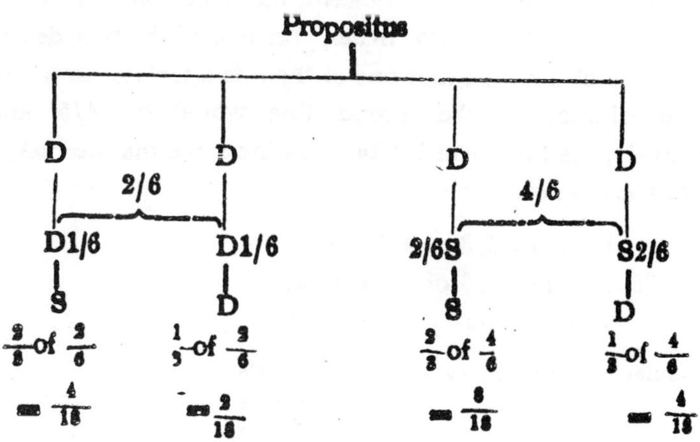

Here also the ancestors differ in their sexes, in the second line and there being only one claimant in each line of descent a double share is assigned to the male members, at this point and what has been allotted to the male roots and female roots *i.e.* 2/6 and 4/6 respectively is distributed to their descendants, a double share is again assigned to their male descendants.

D D S=4/18 D S S=8/18.
D D D=2/18 D S D=4/18.

According to Imam Abu Yusuf :—

D D S=2/6 D S S=2/6.
D D D=1/6 D S D=1/6.

(iv)

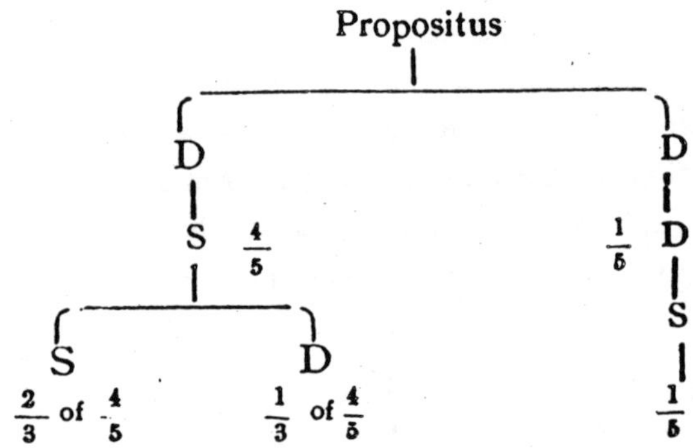

In this case the ancestors differ in their sexes in the second line of descent, and there being two claimants in one line and only one claimant in the other line of descent, the male root in the second line would count as two males, because of the two descendants (irrespective of the fact that one of them is a female member), and thus distribution in the second line would be 4/5 and 1/5 respectively, the final distribution is in the same manner as in the previous examples.

D S S=2/3 of 4/5=8/15.
D S D=1/3 of 4/5=4/15.
D D S=1/5 =3/15.

According to Imam Abu Yusuf :— D S S=2/5.
D S D=1/5.
D D S=2/5.

(v)

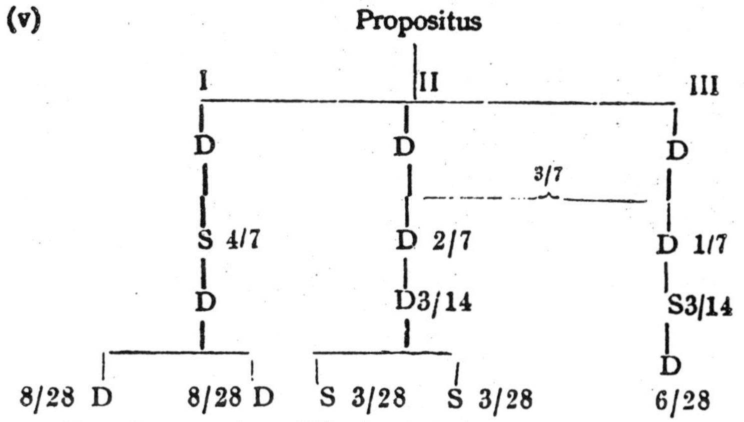

Here the ancestors differ in their sexes in the second line and there being two claimants in the first line of descent they would count as two males and the two claimants in the second line of descent would count as two females, the distribution in the second line would be D S=4/7 ; D D=2 7 ; D D 1/7.

Now 4/7 is inherited by the descendants in the first line equally.

D S D D=2/7 each =8/28

D S D D=2/7 each =8/28

The collective share of D D of the second line II and D D of the third line III is $\left(\frac{2}{7}+\frac{1}{7}=\frac{3}{7}\right)$ and this is to be redistributed to their descendants. There is a further difference of sex between the roots in this collective group in the third descent.[1] The above operation is again to be repeated. There are two male claimants in the second line, but they would be counted as two females, and the only one claimant in the third line would be counted as a male.

Thus D D D=1/2 of 3/7=3/14

D D S=1/2 of 3/7=3/14

And the final distribution to their respective descendants would be

D D D S=1/2 of 3/14=3/28.

D D D S=1/2 of 3/14=3 28.

D D S D=3/14=6/28

According to Imam Abu Yusuf :—

D S D D=1/7.
D S D D=1/7.
D D D S=2/7
D D D S=2/7.
D D D D=1/7

(vi)

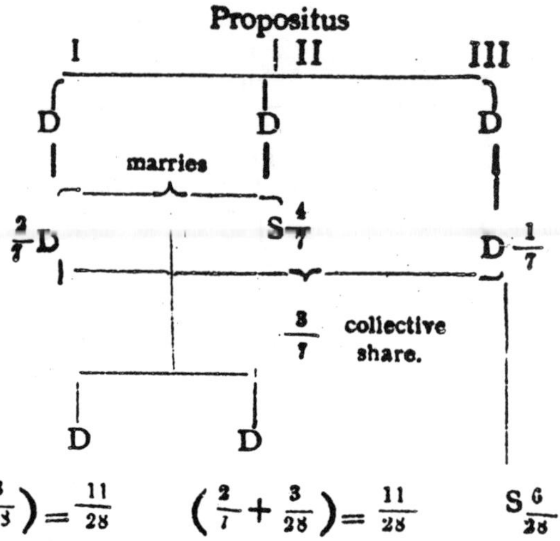

Here the ancestors differ in their sexes in the intermediate line of descent, and there are two claimants in thc first line I of pedigree and two in the second line II of pedigree, but in the former capacity they count as females and in the latter as male members. Hence, the distribution at this stage is as follows :—

I D D=2/7.
II D S=4/7.
III D D=1/7.

Now the share of D S, 4/7 is inherited by his heirs directly 2/7 each, *i.e.* D S D=2 7; D S D=2/7.

The shares of D D (I) and D D (III) is collected together 2/7+2/7=3, 7 and is redistributed to their descendants as follows.

I & II { D D D=1/4 of 3/7=3/28.
D D D=1/4 of 3/7=3/28.

III { D D S=2/4 of 3 7=6/28.

Thus finally because of the marriage of their parents the daughters in the first and second lines inherit in two different capacities, each taking $\frac{2}{7}+\frac{3}{28}=\frac{11}{28}$ each

D=11/28.
D=11/28.
S= 6/28.

(vii)

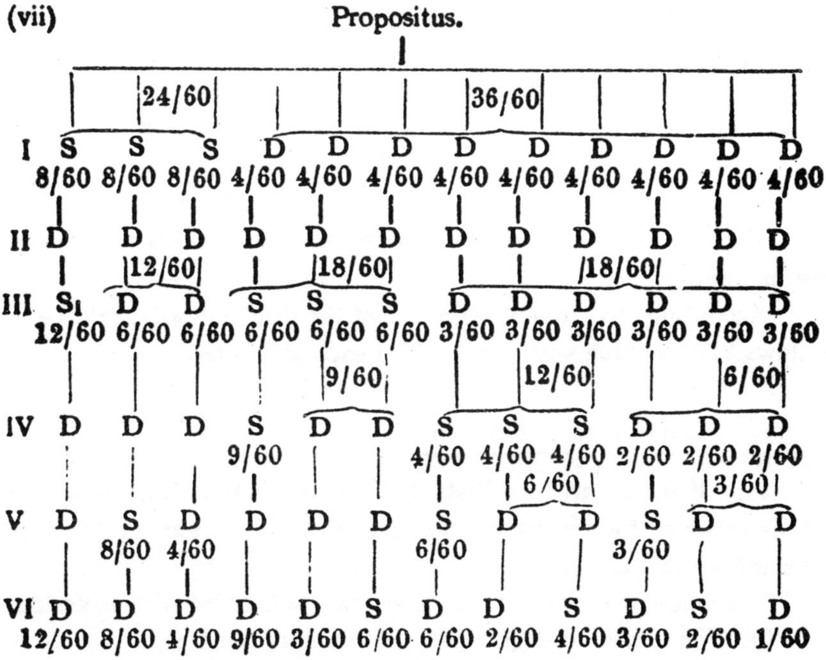

This is a famous illustration given in the Sirajiyah, though not worked out in full, I have made an attempt to arrange it so that at a glance the distribution of shares may be seen.

In Column I the distribution to each son would be 2/15 and to each daughter 1/15 or on the basis of 60 as demominator it would be 8/60 and 4/60 respectively, the three sons taking 24/60 and nine daughters 36/60.

In column II there is no difference of sex at all.

In column III the ancestors differ in their sexes.

S_1 takes 1/2 of 24/60=12/60 which descends to D_1 there being no change of sex in this line of descent.

D and D take 1/4 of 24/60=6/60 each.

And as regards the descendants of daughters, the three sons take 18/60 and six daughters, take 18/60.

---

1 In this case 60 is the L C. D. We could also work it on the basis of 2/15 and 1/15.

In column IV the ancestors differ in their sexes in cases of some of the heirs, and the descendants of sons and daughters are again dealt with separately, the result is as indicated in the chart. In column V the distribution is similarly effected and finally the result is stated in column VI *viz.* 12, 8, 4, 9, 3, 6, 6, 2, 4, 3, 2, 1, respectively.[1]

The general rule of double share to male members applies throughout.

According to Imam Abu Yusuf the distribution would be as follows 2/15 to each son and 1/15 to each daughter.

CLASS II—DISTANT KINDRED.—

44. If there are no Distant Kindred of the first class, the whole estate or the residue would devolve upon the second class of Distant Kindred.

The following general rules determine the order of succession.

(*a*) The nearer in degree exclude the more remote.

e.g. The mother's father excludes the father's mother's father.

(*b*) Among heirs of the same degree those related through sharers or residuaries are preferred, but according to some jurists no such preference is allowed.

(*c*) The heirs on the paternal side take a double share to that of the heirs on the maternal side. That is 2/3 and 1/3 respectively.

(*d*) A male member is entitled to a share double that of a female, and members of the same sex share equally.

e.g. Mother's father's father takes 2/3 and mother's father's mother takes 1/3 of the estate.

(*e*) The special rule of Imam Muhammad as regards the difference of sexes in the ancestors, etc., as stated in the case of first class of Distant Kindred is also applicable.

---

1 A. Rumsey (Inheritance, p. 98) has worked out this chart using letters a b, c...r etc. in a different manner.

CLASS III—DISTANT KINDRED.—

45. If there is no Distant Kindred of the first or second class the estate devolves upon Distant Kindred of the third class. This class consists of the descendants of the brothers and sisters of the deceased.

The following general rules determine the order of succession.

(*a*) The nearer in degree exclude the more remote.

(*b*) Among heirs of the same degree those related through residuaries exclude those related through a Distant Kindred.

e.g The full brother's son's daughter excludes full sister's daughter's son, because full brother's son is a residuary.

(*c*) According to the Sirajiyah among those equal in degree distribution between the heirs is effected by "considering the branches and the roots" that is by assigning to the roots share with reference to number of the claimants in their own line of descent respectively in accordance with Imam Muhammad's system.

(*d*) In the case of issue of uterine brothers or sisters, difference of sex is not taken into consideration in the intermediate roots nor in the claimants, they all share equally.

Illustrations.

F = Full B = Brother.
C = Consanguine U = Uterine.

(i)

C. B.	F. B.	U. B.
|	|	|
S	S	S
|	|	|
D	D	D

In this example the full-brother's son's daughter F. B. S. D. excludes uterine brother's son's daughter U. B. S. D. according to the rule "among claimants of equal degree those related through a residuary exclude those related through a Distant Kindred." And further as the heirs of full-blood exclude those of half-blood on the father's side, consanguine brother's son's daughter C.B. S. D. is also excluded. Hence F. B. S. D. is alone entitled to the whole property.

(ii)

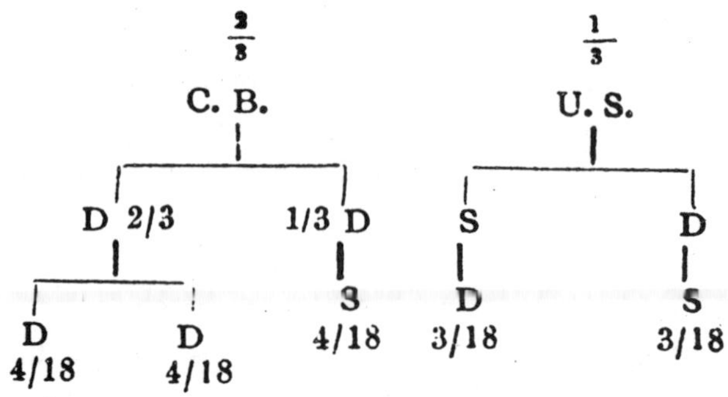

The uterine sister has two branches, and 1/3 is the legal share which is taken equally by them 1/2 of 1/3=1/6 each. The residue 2/3 devolves upon the consanguine brother, and one of the two intermediate daughters has two branches, while the other has only one branch, hence the distribution is 2/3 and 1/3 respectively which devolves upon their descendants.

C.B. D.S.=1/3 of 2/3=2/9 =4/18
C.B. D.D.=1/2 of 2/3 of 2/3=2/9 =4/18
C.B. D.D.= " " =2/9=4/18
U.S. S.D.=1/6 ... =3/18
U.S. D.S.=1/6 ... =3/18

(iii)

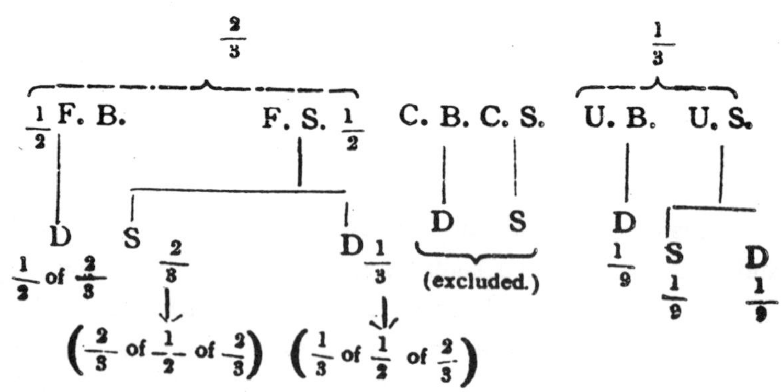

In this example all claimants are equally near to the deceased and are related through residuaries or sharers. The legal share of two are more uterine brothers and sisters is 1/3 and is equally allotted to their branch, the residue 2/3 goes to the full-brothers and sisters.

The full-blood heirs exclude the half-blood heirs, therefore, descendants of consanguine brother and sister take nothing.

The full-sister F.S. having two branches takes equally with F.B. who has only one branch, and their shares go to their branches respectively and the rule of double portion to male applies.

F. B. D. = 1/2 of 2/3=1/3=3/9.
F. S. S.=2/3 of 1/2 of 2/3=2/9.
F. S. D.=1/3 of 1/2 of 2/3=1/9.
U. B. D. 1/3 of 1/3 =1/9.
U. S. S. " =1/9.
U. S. D. " =1/9.

(iv)

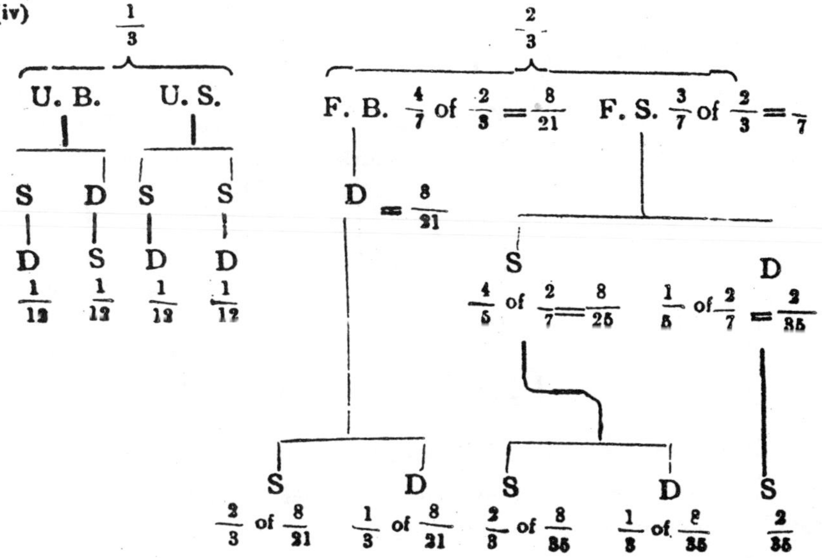

The legal share of uterine brother and sister = 1/3 and the grand children of the uterine brother and sister will divide 1/3 equally between them each taking 1/4 of 1/3 = 1/12 = 105/1260

U.B.S.D.=1/12 U.S.S.D.=1/12.
U.B.D.S.=1/12 U.S.S.D.=1/12.

The residue 2/3 devolves upon full brother and sister.

The full brother F.B. has two branches and the full sister F.S. has three branches therefore, the distribution would be F.B. (two males) 4/7, and F.S. (three females) 3/7 which would devolve on their descendants respectively, the rule double portion to the male members would also apply.

F.B. D.S. = 2/3 of 4/7 of 2/3 = 16/63 = 320/1260.
F.B. D.D. = 1/3 of 4/7 of 2/3 = 8/63 = 160/1260.

As regards the full sister's descendants the roots in the second line also differ and F. S. S. has two branches F. S. D. has only one branch, hence the distribution is F. S. S. (two males) 4/5 and F. S. D. (one female) 1/5 which devolves on their own descendants respectively, the male taking a double portion.

F. S. S. S. = 2/3 of 4/5 of 3/7 of 2/3 = 16/105 = 192/1260.
F. S. S. D. = 1/3 of 4/5 of 3/7 of 2/3 = 8/105 = 96/1260.
F. S. D. S. = 1/5 of 37 of 2/3 = 2/35 = 6/105 = 72/1260.*

Illustrations

(v)

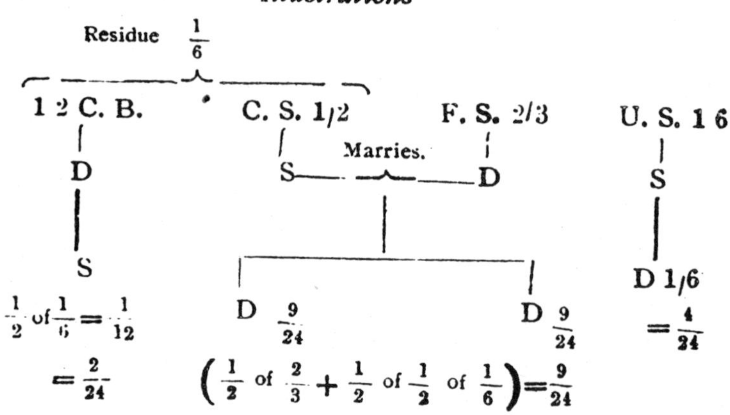

In this example F.S. full sister has two branches and she would therefore take 2/3 (two females' legal shares) which would devolve upon her descendants equally.

The uterine sister would take 1/6 which would devolve upon her only branch D.

The residue 1/6 would devolve upon the residuaries consanguine brother and sister. Here the consanguine brother has only one

*The least common denominator is 1260.

branch and the consanguine sister has two branches, therefore they take equally, and this would descend to their descendants respectively. Because of the marriage of C. S. S. and F. S. D. their descendants inherit in two different capacities, from C. S. and F. S. respectively.

From F. S. and C. S. :—

C. B. D. S. =	1/2 of 1/6 = 1/12	= 2/24.
F. S. D. D. + C. S. S. D. =	1/2 of 2/3 + 1/2 of 1/2 of 1/6	= 9/24.
F. S. D. D. + C. S. S. D. =	" + "	= 9/24.
U. S. S. D. =	1/6	= 4/24.

CLASS IV—DISTANT KINDRED.—

46. If there be no Distant Kindred of class I, II, or III the estate would devolve upon the Distant Kindred of the fourth class.

The following general rules determine the order of succession,

(*a*) The paternal relations together take a double share to that taken by the maternal relations. That is 2/3 is taken by the paternal side and 1/3 by the maternal side.

(*b*) Those of the full-blood exclude those of the half-blood by the father or mother and those of the half-blood on the father's side exclude those of the half-blood by the mother.

(*c*) If the claimants are equal in some respects, *i.e.* in degree, and relationship, then the issue of residuaries are preferred.

(*d*) Among equal claimants distribution is effected by considering the sex of the roots and the number of the branches in accordance with Imam Muhammad's scheme of distribution.

(*e*) As regards ascendants of uncles and aunts of the deceased and their descendants those related through a nearer ancestor exclude those related through a remote ancestor. And among those related through the same ancestor the nearer exclude the more remote.

(*f*) If the claimants are equal in degree and relationship the issue of a residuary is preferred.

(*g*) The general rule that a male member takes a share double to that of a female is also applicable.

TABLE OF UNCLES AND AUNTS.

Paternal Side 2/3.		Maternal Side 1/3.	
	Share.		Share.
1. Father's full sister (Paternal aunt).	2/3	Mother's full brother	2/3 of 1/3
		,, ,, sister.	1/3 of 1/3
		(maternal uncle and aunt).	
2. Father's consanguine sister.	2/3	Mother's consanguine brother.	2/3 of 1/3
		Mother's consanguine sister.	1/3 of 1/3
3. Father's uterine brother.	2/3 of 2/3	Mother's uterine brother.	2/3 of 1/3
Father's uterine sister.	1/3 of 2/3	Mother's uterine sister.	1/3 of 1/3
4. Father's full brother's daughter ...		Mother's full brother's children.	
5 Father's full sister's children ...		,, ,, sister's children.	
6. Father's consanguine brother's daughter		Mother's consanguine brother's and sister's children.	
7. Father's consanguine sister's children ..			
8. Father's uterine brother's children ...		Mother's uterine brother's. and sister's children.	
,, ,, sister's childre n ...			

The claimants are stated in order of priority 1—8. The bracket { denotes that these heirs have inter se no priority. It should be noted that no heir on the paternal side excludes any claimant on the maternal side who is within the same generation.

Father's full sister = Paternal aunt.
Father's half-sister by mother = Father's uterine sister.
Father's half-brother by mother = Father's uterine brother.
Father's half-brother by father = Father's consanguine brother.
Father's half-sister by father = Father's consanguine sister.
Mother's full brother = Maternal uncle.
Mother's full sister = Maternal aunt.

Mother's half-sister-by mother = Mother's uterine sister.
Mother's half-brother-by mother = Mother's uterine brother.
Mother's half-brother-by father = Mother's consanguine brother.
Mother's half-sister-by-father = Mother's consanguine sister.

As regards the descendants of the brothers and sisters of the grandparents, the allotment of paternal side 2/3 and maternal side 1/3 is further subdivided, and in case of each higher generation it would again be subdivided. The descendants take what is allotted to their own ancestors.

Paternal Side 2/3.		Maternal Side 1/3.	
Father's father's side 2/3 of 2/3.	Father's Mother's side 1/3 of 2/3.	Mother's Father's side 2/3 of 1/3	Mother's mother's side 1/3 of 1/3.

Illustrations.

Uncles and aunts.—

The heirs in the left hand column are the only surviving claimants.

1. Father's full-sister = 2/3
   Mother's half-sister-by-mother = 1/3

2. Father's full sister = 2/3
   Father's uterine sister (excluded by father's full sister).
   Mother's full brother = 2/9
   Mother's full sister = 1/9

3. Father's half-sister-by father = 2/3
   Mother's full sister = 1/3

4. 2/3 { Father's half-brother by mother = 2/3 of 2/3 = 4/9
   Father's half-sister by mother = 1/3 of 2/3 = 2/9
   1/3 { Mother's full brother = 2/3 of 1/3 = 2/9
   Mother's full sister = 1/3 of 1/3 = 1/9

5. 2/3 { Father's half-sister-by-mother = 2/3
   1/3 { Mother's half-brother-by father = 2/3 of 1/3 = 2/9
   Mother's half-sister-by father = 1/3 of 1/3 = 1/9

6. Father's full sister's son = 2/3

Mother's half-sister's daughter = 1/3

7. Father's full brother's daughter = 2/3

Mother's half-sister's daughter = 1/3

Issue of a residuary.—

8. F. C. S. = Father's consanguine sister

F. C. B. = Father's consanguine brother

D = Daughter S = Son.

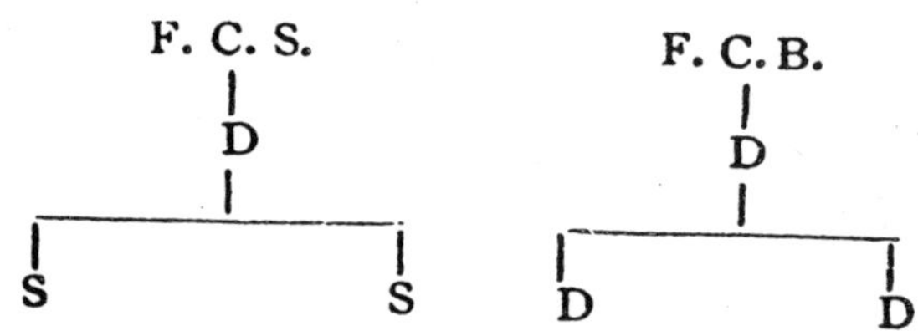

In this example F. C. B. is a residuary but F. C. S. is not a residuary, since the descendants of a residuary are preferred they alone take the whole estate.

9. F. B. = Father's full brother.

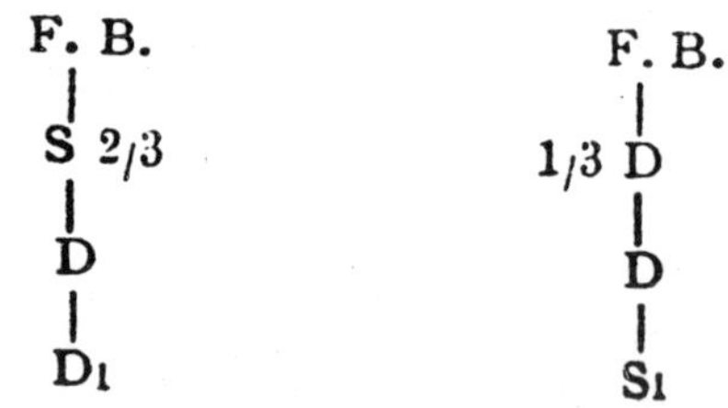

Here in the first line the ancestors differ in their sexes and S takes 2/3, D takes 1/3 which devolves upon their descendants respectively.

D1 = 2/3.

S1 = 1/3.

SIMPLE ILLUSTRATIONS.

Distribution according to Imam Muhammad.—

1.		Daughter's son ...	... 2/3
		Daughter's daughter	... 1/3
2.		Two sons of daughter	... 4/5 each 2/5
		Daughter's daughter	... 1/5
3.		Daughter's son's daughter	... 1/2=3/6
		Daughter's daughter's son	... 1/3=2/6
		Daughter's daughter's daughter	... 1/6=1/6
4.		Daughter's daughter's son	... 3/15
		Daughter's son's son	... 8/15
		Daughter's son's daughter	... 4/15
5.	2/3	Uterine brother's daughter	... 1/9 each
		Uterine sister's son	... 1/9 "
		Uterine sister's daughter	... 1/9 "
	2/3	Full brother's daughter	... 1/2 of 2/3 = 1/3=3/9
		Full sister's son	... 2/3 of 1/2 of 2/3=2/9
		Full sister's daughters	... 1/3 of 1/2 of 2/3=1/9
6.		Uterine brother's daughter	... 1/6
		Uterine sister's son	... 1/6
		Full sister's son ...	... 1/2=3/6
		Consanguine brother's daughter	1/6
7.	2/3	Full paternal aunt	... 2/3=6/9.
		Cansanguine paternal aunt	... excluded.
	1/3	Full maternal uncle	... 2/3 of 1/3=2/9
		Full maternal aunt	... 1/3 of 1/3=1/9
8.		Consanguine paternal aunt	... 2/3
		Full maternal aunt...	... 1/3
9.	2/3	Uterine paternal uncle	... 2/3 of 2/3=4/9
		Uterine paternal aunt	... 1/3 of 2/3=2/9
	1/3	Full maternal uncle	... 2/3 of 1/3=2/9
		Full maternal aunt	... 1/3 of 1/3=1/9
10.	1/3	Uterine brother's sister's daughter	each 1/12=3/36
		Uterine brother's daughter's son ...	" 1/12=3/36
		Uterine sister's sister's daughter ...	" 1/12=3/36
		Uterine sister's sister's daughter ...	" 1/12=3/36
	2/3	Full brother's daughter's son...	2/3 of 2/3=4/9=16/36
		Full brother's daughter's daughter	... 1/3 of 2/3=2/9=8/36

§ 8. THE SHIA LAW OF INHERITANCE

THE HEIRS IN GENERAL.—

47. There are three classes of heirs under the Shia Law.

(1) The heirs by marriage.

(2) The heirs by nasab, consanguinity

(3) Heirs by *wala* special cause.

The first class excludes the second, and the second excludes the third.

(1) The heirs by marriage.—

The husband and the wife.

(2) The heirs by nasab.—

The heirs be *nasab* are subdivided into three classes.

I. (i) Parents.

(ii) Children, issue, h. l. s.

II. (i) Grandparents h.h.s. (true and false).

(ii) Brothers and sisters or their descendants h.l.s.

III. Brothers and sisters of ancestors, that is, paternal and maternal uncles and aunts of the deceased and of his parents and grandparents h. h. s. and their descendants h. l. s.

(3) Heirs by wala.—

Under the Shia Law there are three kinds of heirs by *wala*.

(i) Heirs by *wala* of emancipation.

(ii) Heirs by *wala* of patronage

(iii) Heirs by *wala* of *Imamat.*

The first two are obsolete in British India since the passing of the Slavery Act V of 1843.

In default of heirs by marriage and *nasab* the estate is vested in the *Imam,* the spiritual head of the community and according to some it is to be utilised for the benefit of the poor, which can now be done by Imam's representatives the *mujtahids,* or by the community itself. In British India it seems that the law of escheat would prevail as against the claims of the community.[1]

1. Vide Sec. 288 page 188.

Khursaide Begum v. Secretrary of State 94. I. C. 488 (Pat. 1926)

THE SHARERS.—

48. Under the Shia Law there are nine original sharers *zufars* of these the following three are always sharers, husband, wife, and mother and the other six are sometimes heirs by relation, *"Zu qarabat."*

The descendants of sharers are also sharers.

Cause of inheritance	Male sharers	Female sharers
Sabab of marriage	1 Husband	4 Wife
Nasab, consanguinity...	2 Father 3 Half-brother by mother (uterine brother)	5 Mother 6 Daughter 7 Full sister 8 Half-sister by father (consanguine sister) 9 Half-sister by mother (uterine sister)

Of the nine sharers the husband and wife are heirs by affinity, and the mother, father, daughter are the heirs of the first class, and full sister, consanguine sister, uterine brother or sister belong to the second class. There are no sharers in the third class of heirs at all.

THE TABLE OF SHARERS.

Sharers.	Share.	Conditions under which the share is inherited.	Whether excluded or converted into Residuaries.
1. Husband ...	1/4	When there is a descendant male or female h.l.s.	Not excluded.
	1/2	When there is no issue.	
2. Wife ...	1/8	When there is a descendant male or female h.l.s.	Not excluded.
	1/4	When there is no issue.	
3. Father ...	1/6	When there is a descendant male or female h.l.s.	Not excluded.
	R.		When there is no issue

TABLE OF SHARERS.—*concluded.*

Sharers.	Share.	Conditions under which the share is inherited.	Whether exlcuded or converted into Residuaries.
4. Mother ...	1/6	When there is a descendant male or female h.l.s.	Not excluded.
		When there are two brothers, or one brother and two sisters, or four sisters (full or consanguine) co-exisiing with the father.	
	1/3	When there is no issue nor two or more brethren.	
5. Daughter...	1/2 2/3	If one. If two or more. } When there is no son.	Not excluded.
	R.		When there is a son (one or more).
6. Full sister...	1/2 2/3	If one. If two or more. } When there is no parent or descendant or full brother or father's father.	Excluded by parent or descendant or father's father.
	R.		When there is a full brother.
7. Consanguine sister.	1/2 2/3	If one. If two or more. } When there is no parent, or descendant, or full brother, or sister or consanguine brother or father's father.	Excluded by parent, or descendant etc.
	R.		When there is a consanguine brother.
8 & 9 Uterine brother or sister.	1/6 1/3	If one. If two or more. } When there is no parent or descendant and no maternal grandparent.	Excluded by parent or descendant.
	R.		When there are maternal grandparents 1/3 is divided between them and the grand-parents.

EXCLUSION OF SHARERS.—

49. The general principle of exclusion is based on well-known general rules :—

(i) Proximity of the ancestor.

(ii) Proximity of the claimants,

(iii) The strength of consanguinity.

TABLE OF EXCLUSION.

Sharers	Whether excluded
1 Husband ...	Nos. 1—5 not excluded at all.
2 Wife ...	
3 Father ...	
4 Mother ...	
5 Daughter ...	
6 Full sister ...	Excluded by parents or issue.
7 Consanguine sister	Ditto and also by full sister or full brother.
8 Uterine brother or 9 Uterine sister ...	Excluded by parents or issue.

THE HEIRS BY RELATION.—

50. The heirs by relation, *Zu-qarabat*, are of two classes :—

(*a*) The following sharers are under certain circumstances also heirs by relation (1) Father, (2) Daughter, (3) Full sisters, (4) consanguine sisters, (5 & 6) and uterine brothers and sisters.

(*b*) The real heirs by relation, *zu-qarabat*, consist of the following consanguine relations.

(*a*) The sons and the children of sons h. l. s. and of daughters.

(*b*) The grand-parents h. h. s.

(*c*) Full brothers.

(*d*) Consanguine brothers.

(*e*) Full or consanguine brother's issue h. l. s.

(*f*) Brothers and sisters of the ancestors h. h. s. and their issue h. l. s.

The descendants h. l. s. of residuaries are also residuaries.

JURISTIC CLASSIFICATION OF RESIDUARIES.—

51. The relations *zu-qarabat* may be classified into two groups.

I. Directly related to the deceased.

(*a*) Original residuaries.

II. Representatively related to the deceased.

(*b*) Representative sharers.

(*c*) Representative residuaries.

(A) The following are original residuaries directly related to the deceased.

(1) The father when there is no descendant,

(2) The daughter when there is no son.

(3) The sons in their own rights.

(B) The following are representative sharers, that is, those related through a sharer, and thereby inheriting the fixed allotted share in a representative character under certain circumstances.

(*a*) Maternal grand-parents.

(*b*) Uterine brothers and sisters.

(*c*) Maternal Uncles and aunts and their descendants.

(*d*) The daughter's children.

(*e*) The decendants of full or consanguine sisters.

(*f*) The descendants of uterine brother's and sisters.

(C) The following are representative residuaries, that is, relations related through an original residuary, and thereby inheriting the portion of the residue of the original residuary.

(*a*) Descendants of sons.

(*b*) Descendants of daughters co-existing with son's son of the same grade.

(*c*) Paternal grand-parents and their descendants.

(*d*) Full brothers or consanguine brothers and their descendants.

(*e*) Full sisters or consanguine sisters and their descendants.

(*f*) Brothers and sisters of the father and of paternal ancestors and their descendants.

THE TABLE OF RESIDUARIES.

Heirs.	Kind of Residuaries.	Under what circumstances.
1. Father ...	Original residuary ...	When there is no issue.
2. Daughter ...	" " ...	When there are sons.
3. Sons ...	" " ...	In their own right.
4. Maternal grandparents.	Relations of the mother. Representative sharers.	In default of issue take 1/3 of the estate.
5. Uterine brothers and sisters.		When they co-exist with maternal grandparents, they take 1/3 with the grandparents.
6. Brothers and sisters of the Mother and their descendants.		They are consanguine heirs of the third class, and take 1/3 as representing mother.
7. The descendants of daughters.	Representative sharers ...	In default of the son's descendants of the same degree the issue of a single daughter takes 1/2 and those of two or more take 2/3.
8. & 9. The descendants of full sisters or Consanguine sisters.	"	In default of dercendants of brothers of the same degree and in default of paternal grandparents the issue of one sister takes 1/2 and if two or more 2/3.
10 & 11. The descendants of uterine brothers and sisters.	" ...	In default of maternal grandparents the issue of an uterine brother or sister take 1/6 and those of two or more take 1/3 and with maternal grandparents they divide the mother's share 1/3.
12. Descendants of sons h.l.s.	Representative residuaries ...	They are always residuaries.
13. Descendants of daughters h.l.s.	" " ...	When with son's descendants of the same degree.

THE TABLE OF RESIDUARIES.—*concluded.*

Heirs.	Kind of Residuaries.	Under what circumstances.
14. Paternal grandparents.	Relations through the father. Representative residuaries.	When there is no father and they divide the residue with full brothers or consanguine brothers.
15. Full brothers or consanguine brothers their descendants.		When there is no father they divide the residue with paternal grandparents.
16. Full sisters or consanguine sister or their descendants.		When co-existing with paternal grandparents or with brother (f or c) or their descendants of the same degree.
17. Brothers and sisters of the father or of paternal ancestors and their descendants.		These are residuaries in the right of the father.

Distribution between Sharers and Residuaries.—

52. The sharers at first take their respective shares and if are also residuaries then the residue goes to them, but if the residuaries are alone then they are entitled to the whole property.

The representative sharers and representative residuaries take the portion of original sharers or residuaries through whom they are related to the declared. Similarly their descendants the remoter representatives take *per stirpes* in like order.

The descendants of sharers succeed as sharers, and of residuaries succeed as residuaries.

Illustrations.

(i) Children h. l. s. of a son take the portion of their father.

(ii) Children of the daughter take the share of that daughter.

(iii) The grandchildren of a son or daughter take the portion of the son or daughter 'per stirpes'

Distribution per stirpes.—

(i)

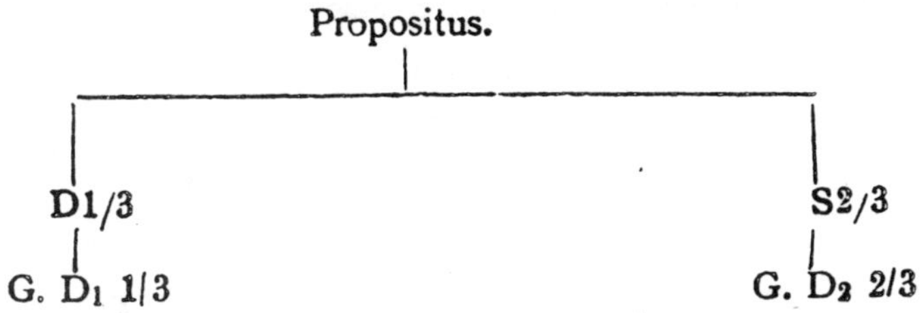

D = Daughter G. D. = Granddaughter.

S = Son

A Shia Muslim dies leaving two granddaughters G D_1 and GD_2 from a pre-deceased daughter and a son.

G. D_1 inherits her mother's share = 1/3

G. D_2 „ „ father's share = 2/3

Under the Hanafi Law G. D_2 is a sharer and would take the whole property.

(ii)

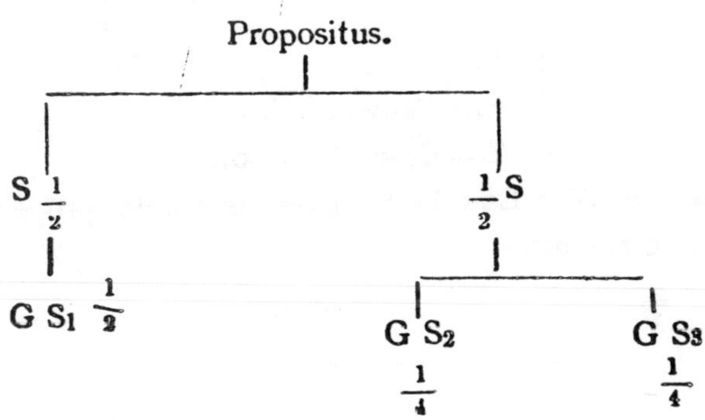

S = son

G. S. = Grandson

A Shia Muslim dies leaving G. S_1 a grandson from one son and G. S_2, G. S_3 grandsons from another son. Their respective fathers inherit one-half each which descends to their issue.

that is G. S_1 lakes 1/2

G. S_2 „ 1/4 } 1/2

G. S_3 „ 1/4

---

1 Under the Hanafi Law the division is 'per capita' i.e. per claimants } G. S_1 = 1/3, G. S_2 = 1/3, G. S_3 = 1/3

The descendants of brethern paternal or maternal take the portion of the brother's or sister's *per stirpes.*

(iii)

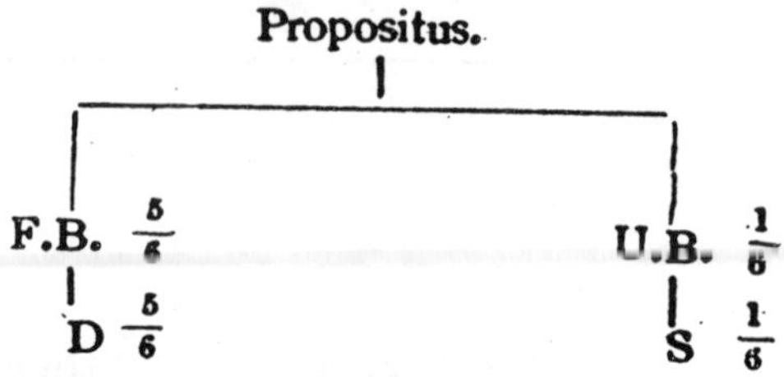

D = Daughter S = Son

F. B. = Full brother, a residuary[1]

U. B. = Uterine brother, a sharer

F. B. D. = 5/6 as a residuary

U. B. S. = 1/6 as a sharer

(iv)

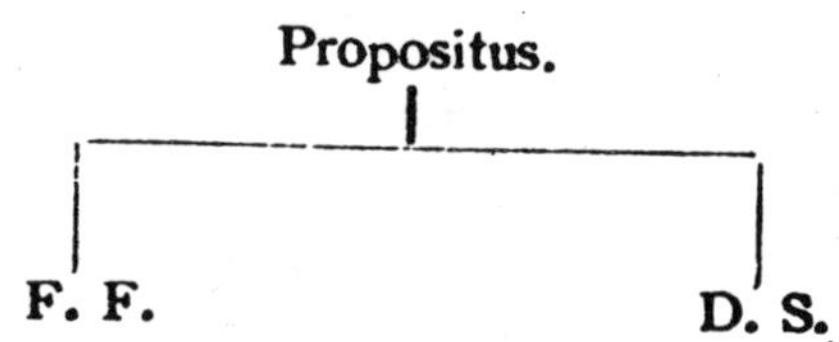

F. F. = Father's father

D. S. = Daughter's son

Under the Shia Law D. S. takes the whole property being an heir of the first class.[2]

(v)

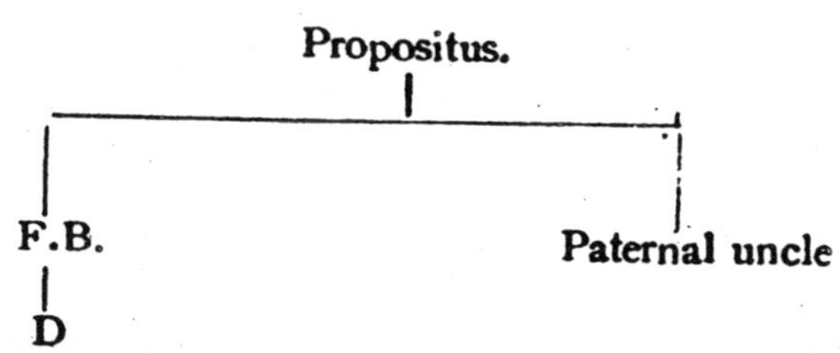

F. B. = Full brother

Under the Shia Law F.B.D. being an heir of the second class takes the whole property[3]

---

1 Under the Hanafi Law, F.B.D. and U.B.S. are distant kindred of the third class and F. B. D. will take 5/6 U. B. S. " 1/6

2 Under the Hanafi Law, F. F. would take the whole property D. S, being a distant kindred.

3 Under the Hanafi Law, the full paternal uncle would take the whole property excluding F. B. D. a distant kindred.

§ 9. DISTRIBUTION AMONG HEIRS UNDER SHIA LAW.

HEIRS BY MARRIAGE.—

53. The husband or the wife is never excluded[1] but inherits along with other heirs. Their fixed shares are not liable to be reduced.[1]

CHILDLESS WIFE.—

54. If the widow has no child or the child was born and died in the life-time of her husband, she is entitled to take one-fourth share in the personal estate including the value of household effects, buildings and trees, but she cannot inherit out of the land, immoveable property, belonging to her deceased husband.[2]

MUTA WIFE.—

55. A temporary marriage in *muta* form does not entitle either party to inherit *inter se*, unless they had expressly agreed to this effect, at the time of *muta* marriage.[3]

1 In the first instance it is not liable to be increased by application of the doctrine of return, but if there are no heirs to take the residue the husband can take the surplus. but the wife is in no case entitled to the surplus under the Shia Law. The Imam now the State is preferred to her. Ameer Ali however thinks that in default of heirs she should get the surplus.

2 Ballie II. 295.

Sahibzadee Begum v. Himmnt 14 W. R. 125 (1870). Umdutoonissa v. Aslo 20 W. R. 297 (1873). Umardaz Ali v. Wilayat Ali 19 All. 169 (1896). Mir Ali Hussain v. Sajuda Begam 21 Mad 27 (1897). Aga Mahomed v. Koulsom Beebee 25 Cal. 9 (1897). Parbati v. Muzaffar Ali 34. All. 289 (1921). Shaukat Ali v. Anwar-ul-Haq 55 I.C. 745 (Lah. 1920) Durga Das v. M. Nawab Ali 48 All. 557 (1926). (The widow takes a fourth share in the proceeds of the sale of the buildings).

3 Under the Shia Law there are two kinds of marriages (1) permanent (2) temporary. The "muta" marriage is for a fixed definite period of time, it is dissolved on the eflux of the term but may be re-newed by mutual consent. There is a dower also. The number of muta wives is unlimited. In case of muta marriage contracted for a long period say 99 years, it can be dissolved according to some jurists by making a gift of the unexpired portion of the term to the wife. The consent of the wife is not essential for acceptance of the gift of the term, the dower however would become due immediately. According to some jurists there is no divorce except by the Zihar mode in case of muta form of marriage. As to

CLASS I—HEIRS.—

56. The first class of heirs as stated consists of :—

(*a*) Parents (father and mother)

(*b*) Descendants h.l.s.

These heirs are entitled to inherit along with the husband or wife. The following rules govern the order of distribution

(i) The nearer excludes the more remote.

(ii) Sons if alone are residuaries and are entitled to take the whole estate.

The daughters if alone are sharers, and when co-existing with son's, they become residuaries, and the rule of double share to male members would apply.

(iii) In default of sons and daughters their descendants of equally near degree take *per stirpes* that is the portion of the person through whom they are descended. In this sense the doctrine of representation is recognised by the Shia Law.[1]

Illustrations.

S=son D=daughter

(i)

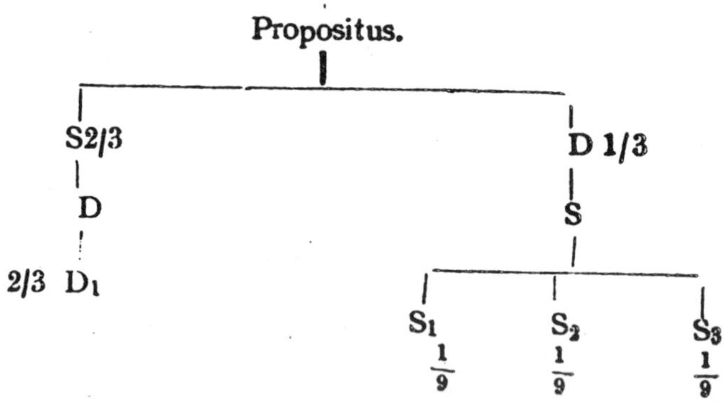

muta marriage vide Luddan Sahiba v. Miza Kamar Kadr. 8 Cal. 736 (1882); Mohomed Abid Ali Kumar Kadar v. Luddim Sahibe 14 Cal. 276, (1886) where the husband gave away the unexpired term and then sued in a Civil Court for a declaration that the relation of husband and wife had terminated and that she was not entitled to maintenance.

1 It is equally applicable in the ascending line. Vide Sec. 290.

In the first line S and D take 2/3 and 1/3 respectively which devolves upon their own descendants.

D_1 takes 2/3

S_1 , S_2 , S_3 ,= 1/9 each (all together 1/3)

(ii)

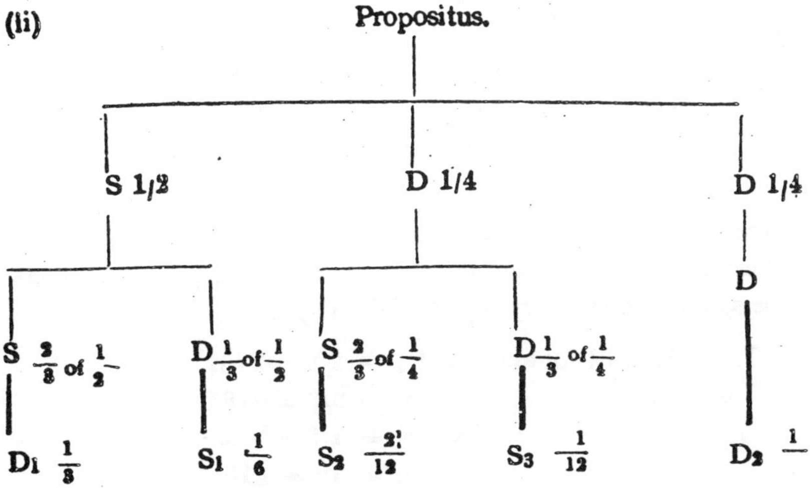

In the first line the distribution is 1/2 and 1/4 each to one son and two daughters respectively, which devolves upon their respective descendants subject to the rule of double share to male members. The distribution is thus effected by applying the rule of double share to male members with that of succession by representation.

D_1 takes 1/3,=4/12 S_2 takes 2/12 D_2 takes 1/4=3/12

S_1 „ 1/6,=2/12 S_3 „ 1/12

(iii)

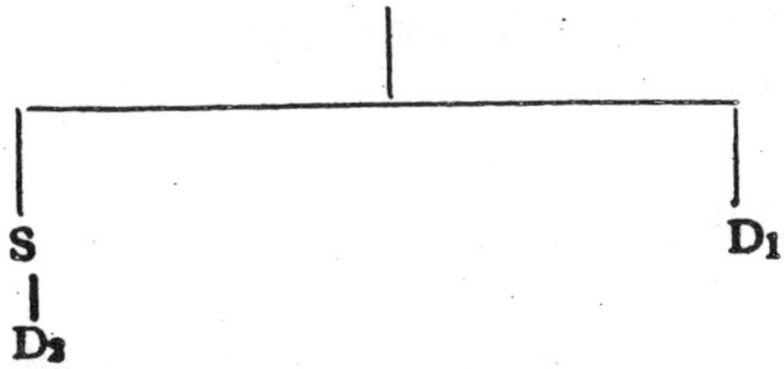

In this example the daughter D_1 is the nearest living descendant and therefore under the Shia Law takes the entire property.

(iv)

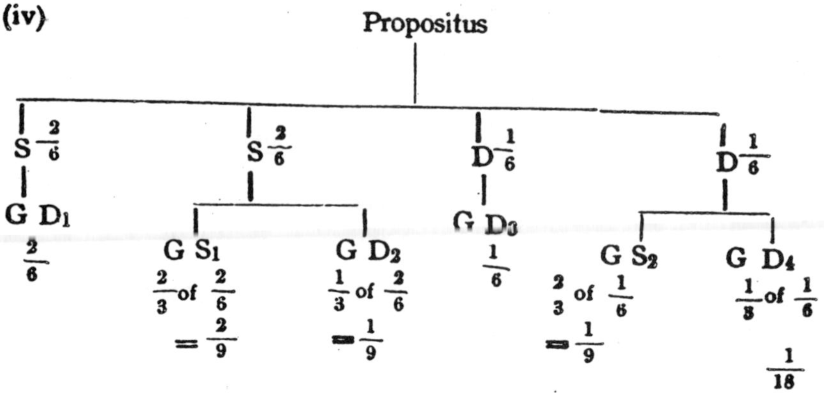

The respective issue of sons and daughters inherit their shares as indicated in the chart, and the rule of double share to the male members and succession by representation applies.

Thus the distribution is as follows:—

G D1 = 2/6 = 6/18
{ G S1 = 2/9 = 4/18
{ G D2 = 1/9 = 2/18
G D3 = 1/6 = 3/18
{ G S2 = 1/9 = 2/18
{ G D4 = 1/18 = 1/18

Parents.—

(i) If the father and mother co exist, the mother's share is 1/6 or 1/3 as the case may be (*vide* the Table of Sharers), and the father takes the residue. But if there is the mother only and no father, she takes 1/3 and if there is the father only and no mother, he takes the residue.

(ii) In case of parents co-existing with the male descendants of the deceased the father takes 1/6 and the mother takes 1/6 as her share, but if co-existing with the daughters or their issue, they all inherit as sharers.[1]

CLASS II—HEIRS.—

57. The second class of heirs consists of :—

(*a*) Grandparents h.h.s. related through the father or mother.

(*b*) Brothers and sisters full or half and their descendants h.l.s.

1 This is subject to general rule about increase or return of surplus.

Thus there will be three alternative modes of succession.

(*a*) Grandparents alone.

(*b*) Grandparents with brothers and sisters or their descendants,

(*c*). Brothers and sisters or their descendants alone.

General Rules of Succession of Grandparents.—

(i) The "nearer in degree excludes the more remote."
e.g. ***Mother's mother excludes father's father's father.***

(ii) The grandparents on the mother's side are representative sharers on behalf of the mother, and take 1/3, and the grandparents on the father's side are representative residuaries and take the residue, and the general rule of double share to the male members applies. The residue may comprise the whole estate.

(iii) The remote grandparents succeed in default of near grandparents and take by representation analogous to that of ***per stirpes*** as applicable in the case of descendants. That is they take the portion of the immediately related grandparent, and in case of several claimants through the same grandparent, they divide the portion of the immediate grandparents.

(iv) The rule of double share to a male applies to remote grandparents, if no female intervenes between them and the deceased, and if a female intervenes, they divide equally without distinction of sex.

(v) In case of grandparents of the same sex the division is made equally ***per capita.***

Illustrations.

Grandparents alone :—

(i) Father's father =2/3.
Mother's mother =1/3.

(ii) Maternal grandmother = 1/3.
Paternal grandmother = 2/3.

(iii)

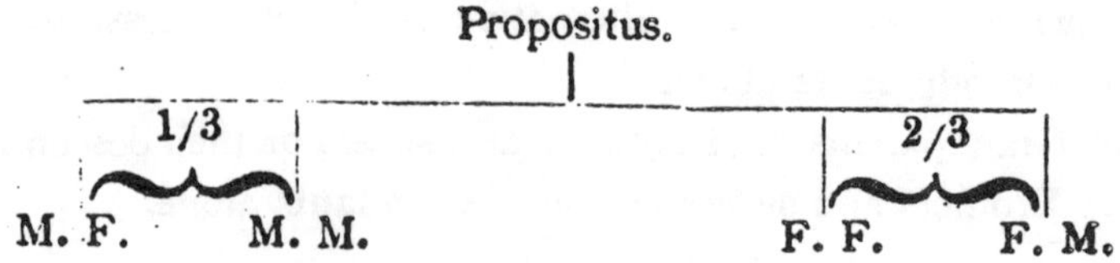

2/3.	F. F. Father's father	... 2/3 of 2/3 = 4/9 = 8/18.
	F. M. Father's mother	... 1/3 of 2/3 = 2/9 = 4/18.
2/3.	M. F. Mother's father	... 1/2 of 1/3 = 1/6 = 3 18.
	M. M. Mother's mother	... 1/2 of 1/3 = 1/6 = 3/18.

(iv)

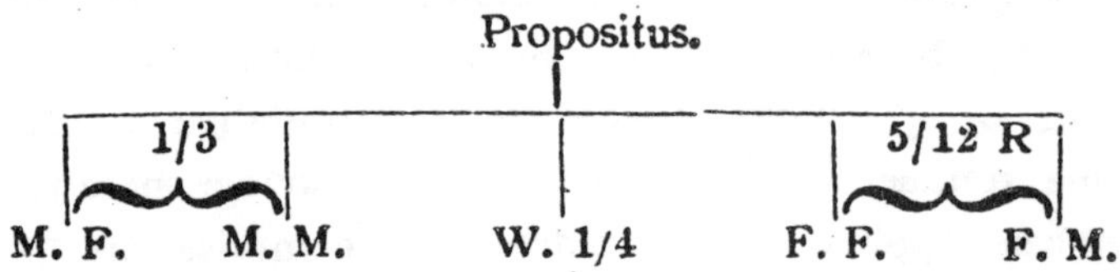

After assigning to the wife 1/4 and to mother's relations 1/3, the residue 5/12 goes to the father's relations. The distribution is thus as follows :—

	W. takes	...	1/4 ...	= 9/36
1/3	M. F. Mother's father	...	1/2 of 1/3 = 1/6	= 6/36
	M. M. Mother's mother	...	1/2 of 1/3 = 1/6	= 6/36
Residue 5/12	F. F. Father's father	...	2/3 of 5/12 = 10/36	= 10/36
	F. M. Father's mother	...	1/3 of 5/12 = 5/36	= 5/36

(v)

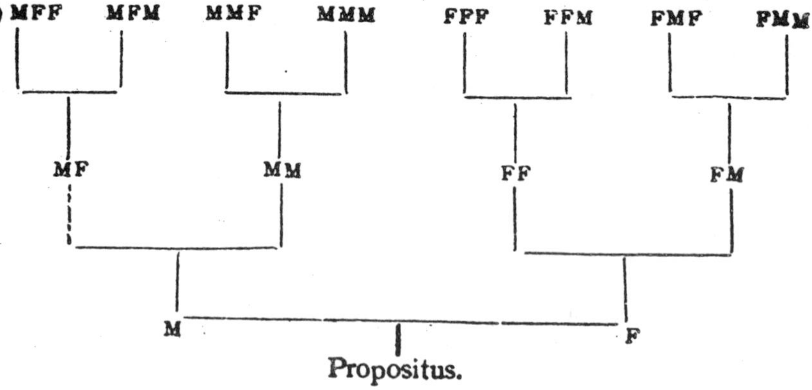

M = Mother F = Father.

M F F, F M F, M M F, and M M M are sharers related through the mother, and therefore take 1/3, and divide it equally

1/4 of 1/3 = 1/12 each. The residue 2/3 is taken by F F F, F F M, F M F and F M M which is divided in the first instance in the proportion of 2 : 1, between father's father's relations and father's mother's relations, *i.e.* 2/3 of 2/3 = 4/9 and 1/3 of 2/3 = 2/9 respectively. the collective share 4/9 is again assigned subject to the general rule of double share to the male members. The collective share of 2/9 would be equally divided as a grandmother intervenes in that line.

Thus the distribution is as follows :—

2/3	4/9	F F F ...	2/3 of 4/9	= 8/27	=	32/108.
		F F M ...	1/3 of 4/9	= 4/27	=	16/108.
	2/9	F M F ...	1/2 of 2/9	= 1/9	=	12/108.
		F M M ...	1/2 of 2/9	= 1/9	=	12/108.
1/3		M F F ...	1/4 of 1/3	= 1/12	=	9/108.
		F M F ...	" "	= "	=	9/108.
		M M F ...	" "	= "	=	9/108.
		M M M ...	" "	= "	=	9/108.

Grandparents with brothers and sisters.—

When grandparents co-exist with brothers and sisters the paternal grandmother and grandfather take as would a full-brother and sister, and the maternal grandparents as uterine brother or sister.

The mother's parents and half brethren by mother, if any divide their collective share of 1/3 equally *per capita.*

The father's parents and full or half-brothers by father divide the residue, the father's portion *per capita*, subject to the rule of double share to the male members. All general fundamental rules are also applicable.

Illustrations.

(i)		Paternal-grandfather	... 2/3 (as full-brother)
		Full-sister	... 1/3
(ii)	1/3	Uterine brother	... 1/6
		Maternal grandmother	... 1/6 (as uterine sister)
		Two full-sisters	... 2/3
(iii)	1/3	Maternal grand-mother	... 1/9 (as uterine sister)
		Uterine brother	... 1/9
		Uterine sister	... 1/9

	2/3 {	Paternal grandfather	... 1/3 (as consanguine brother
		Paternal grandmother	... 1/6 „ „ sister
		Consanguine sister	... 1/6
(iv)	1/3 {	Mother's father	... 1/2 of 1/3 = 1/6 = 3/18
		Mother's mother	... 1/2 of 1/3 = 1/6 = 3/18
	2/3 {	Father's father	... 2/6 of 2/3 = 4/18 (as full brother)
		Father's mother	... 1/6 of 2/3 = 2/18 (as full sister)
		Full brother	... 2/6 of 2/3 = 4/18
		Full sister	... 1/6 of 2/3 = 2/18
(v)		Paternal grandfather	... 1/2 (as full-brother)
		Full-brother's son	... 1/2 by representation his father's share.

Brothers and sisters alone.—

The succession of full or half-brothers and sisters is also effected under the general fundamental rules, as regards propinquity, nearness of relationship, and strength of consanguinity etc., *e.g.* the full-blood excludes half-blood by the father, but half-relations by the mother are not excluded.

Illustrations.

(1)	Husband	...	1/2.
	Full-sister	...	1/2.
(2)	Wife	...	2/4.
	Full-brother	...	3/4 (as residuary).
(3)	Husband	...	1/2 = 3/6.
	Full-brother	...	2/3 of R = 2/3 of 1/2 = 2/6.
	Full-sister	...	1/3 of R = 1/3 of 1/2 = 1/6.
(4)	Daughter of half-sister by mother		= 1/6 (her mother's share).
	Daughter of full sister		= 1/2 + 2/6 Residue = 5/6.*
	Son of half-brother by father		= excluded by full sister's daughter.
(5)	Son of half-brother by mother		= 1/6 (her mother's share).
	Son of full sister		= 1/2 + 2/6 Residue = 5/6.*

* The daughter in (4) and son in (5) first take their mother's share 1/2 and also the residue.

As regards the descendants of brothers and sisters they would take according to the principle of representation.

(6)

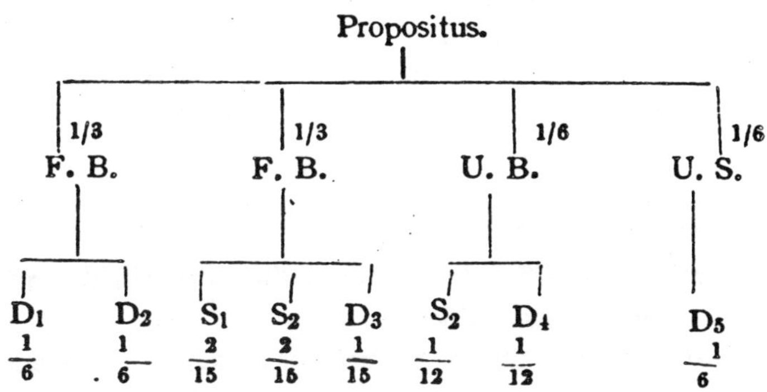

F. B. Full-brother U. B. Uterine brother U. S. Uterine sister.

We first assign the shares to brothers and sisters, which descends to their descendants and the rule of double share to the male members applies, and the uterine relatives inherit equally.

D_1	= 1/6	= 30/180	D_3	= 1/15	= 12/180
D_2	= 1/6	= 30/180	S_2	= 1/12	= 15/180
S_1	= 2/15	= 24/180	D_4	= 1/12	= 15 180
S_2	= 2/15	= 24/180	D_5	= 1/6	= 30/180

CLASS III—HEIRS.—

58. In default of the first and second class of heirs the estate devolves on the third class of heirs which consist of the brothers and sisters of the ancestors of the deceased and their descendants.

The following is the order of priority among the heirs.

(1) Paternal and maternal uncles and aunts of the deceased and next their descendants h.l.s.

(2) Paternal and maternal uncles and aunts of the parents of the deceased and next their descendants h.l.s.

(3) Remoter uncles and aunts of the remote ancestors and next their descendants h.l.s.

All those related through a nearer ancestor are preferred, and again among the claimants the nearer exclude the more remote the exception being the case of full paternal uncle's son co-existing with a consanguine uncle.[1]

(a) Those of the full-blood exclude those of the half-blood related through the same ancestor.

(b) The brothers or sisters of the mother are the representative sharers and those of the father are representative residuaries.

Rules of Distribution.—

(a) Assign 2/3 of the estate to the paternal side and 1/3 to the maternal side.

(b) Assign to uterine paternal or maternal uncles and aunts if any 1/3 and if only one then 1/6.

(c) The rule of double share to the male members is applicable to the relations on the paternal side.

(d) In default of the maternal side the paternal side is entitled to the whole and *vice versa.*

(e) The distribution among the descendants of uncles and aunts is *per stirpes,* in accordance with the doctrine of representation, the heirs take their parents' shares.

Illustrations.

A person dies leaving the following heirs :—

1. Husband = 1/2
   Maternal aunt = 1/3
   Paternal uncle = residue 1/6
2. Full paternal uncle = 2/3
   Maternal aunt = 1/3
3. Full paternal uncle = 2/3
   Full „ aunt = 1/3

---

1 The preference given by the Shia jurists to father's full brother's son over the consanguine uncle is perhaps due to their respect for Ali the fourth Khalif. Hazrat Ali was son of Abu Talib, full paternal uncle of the Prophet and Hazrat Abbas was his consanguine uncle. Hazrat Ali is regarded as the first rightful successor to the Holy Prophet. Hence this case of preference of the paternal uncle's son to the consanguine uncle.

4\. 2/3 {
Full paternal uncle 5/6 of 2/3 = 5/9 = 10/18
Consanguine paternal uncle excluded
Uterine paternal uncle 1/6 of 2/3 = 1/9 = 2/18

1/3 {
Full maternal uncle 5/6 of 1/3 = 5/18
Consanguine maternal uncle excluded
Uterine maternal uncle 1/6 of 1/3 = 1/18

Here the first distribution on the paternal and maternal side was 2/3 and 1/3 respectively, half-blood relations are excluded by full-blood relations and by applying ordinary rules of distribution and computation the estate is distributed as above.

5\. *Full maternal uncle 1/2
,, ,, aunt 1/2

6\. 2/3 {
Full paternal uncle 2/3 } 2/3 of 2/3 of 2/3 = 8/27 = 16/54
,, ,, aunt 1/3 } 2/3 of 2/3 of 1/3 = 4/27 = 8/54
Uterine ,, uncle 1/2 } 1/3 of 2/3 of 1/2 = 1/9 = 6/54
,, ,, aunt 1/2 } ,, ,, = 1/9 = 6/54

1/3 {
Uterine maternal uncle 1/2 of 1/3 = 1/6 = 9/54
Uterine maternal aunt 1/2 of 1/3 = 1/6 = 9/54

7\. 2/3 {
Full paternal uncle 2/3 } 2/3 of 2/3 of 2/3 = 8/27 = 32/108
Full paternal aunt 1/3 } 2/3 of 2/3 of 1/3 = 4/27 = 16/108
Consanguine ,, uncle excluded
Uterine ,, ,, 1/2 } 1/3 of 2/3 of 1/2 = 1/9 = 12/108
Uterine ,, aunt 1/2 } ,, ,, = 1/9 = 12/108

1/3 {
Full maternal uncle 1/2 } 5/6 of 1/3 of 1/2 = 5/36 = 15/108
Full ,, aunt 1/2 } ,, ,, = 5/36 = 15/108
Consanguine ,, ,, excluded
Uterine ,, uncle 1/6 of 1/3 = 1/18 = 6/108

---

* According to the rule of distribution (d) the maternal side takes the whole in default of paternal side and the uterine relations inherit equally.

Case of double Inheritan ce.

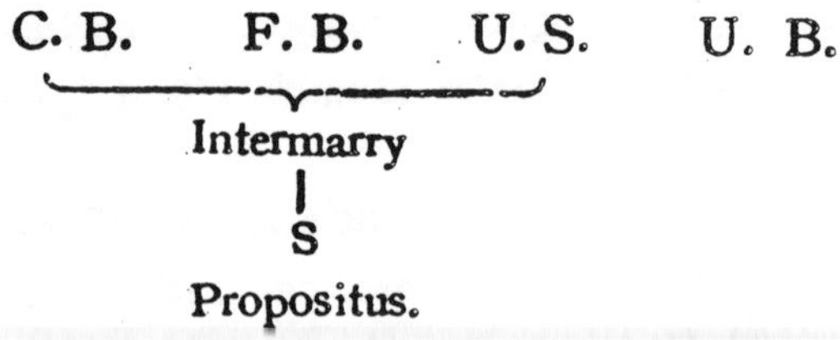

C=Consanguine F=Full U=Uterine.
B=Brother S=Sister.

C. B. and U. S. intermarry and leaving a son who also dies leaving F. B. and U. B.

F. B. is doubly related to S as his consanguine paternal uncle and also as his uterine maternal uncle.

2/3 { F. B. as consanguine paternal uncle 2/3=12/18

1/3 { F. B. as uterine maternal uncle 1/6 of 1/3 =1/18
U. B. as full „ aunt 5/6 of 1/3=5/18

Thus F. B. takes in all 2/3+1/18=13/18

Descendants of uncle and aunts :—

(*a*)

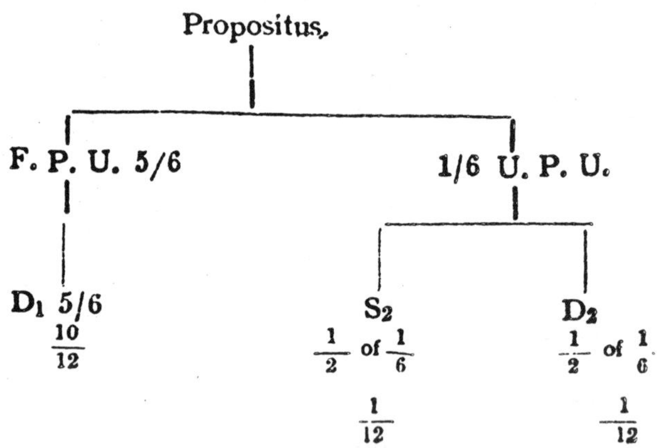

F. P. U.=Full paternal uncle...5/6 Residue
U. P. U.=Uterine „ „ ...1/6 Legal share

$D_1 = 5/6 \qquad = \frac{10}{12}$

$S_2 = \frac{1}{2} \text{ of } \frac{1}{6} \qquad = \frac{1}{12}$

$D_2 = \frac{1}{2} \text{ of } \frac{1}{6} \qquad = \frac{1}{12}$

(b)

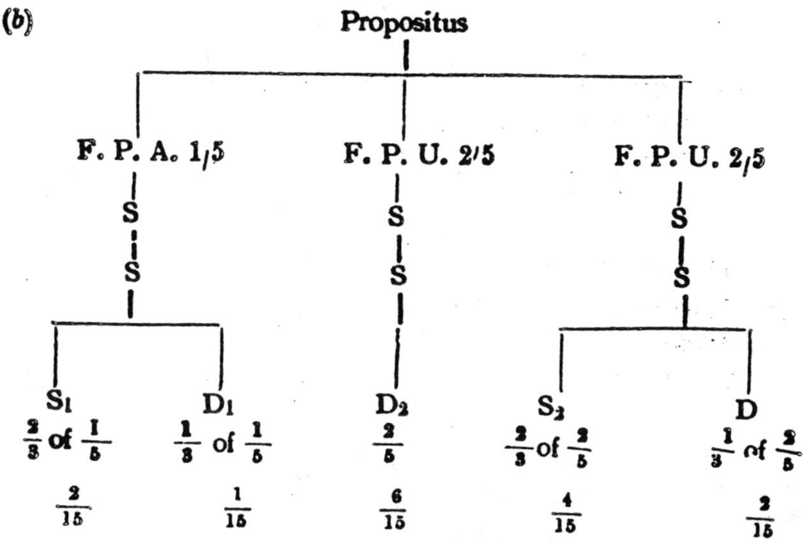

F. P. A.—Full paternal aunt = 1/5 } which descends
F. P. U.— „ „ uncle = 2/5 } to their
F. P. U.— „ „ „ = 2/5 } descendants

$$S_1 = \frac{2}{3} \text{ of } \frac{1}{5} = \frac{2}{15}$$

$$D_1 = \frac{1}{3} \text{ of } \frac{1}{5} = \frac{1}{15}$$

$$D_2 = \frac{2}{5} = \frac{6}{15}$$

$$S_2 = \frac{2}{3} \text{ of } \frac{2}{5} = \frac{4}{15}$$

$$D_3 = \frac{1}{3} \text{ of } \frac{2}{5} = \frac{2}{15}$$

§ 10. DOCTRINE OF INCREASE AND RETURN UNDER SHIA LAW.

DOCTRINE OF INCREASE.—

59. Under the Shia Law if the sum total of the shares exceed unity, then the shares of the spouse, father, mother (and maternal representative sharers), and uterine brother and sisters remain unaffected, but the fraction in excess of unity is deducted from the share of the daughters, full or consanguine sisters.

Illustrations.

(i) Husband ... 1/4 = 3/12
Father ... 1/6 = 2/12
Mother ... 1/6 = 2/12
Daughter* ... 1/2 = 6/12 reduced to 6/12 – 1/12 = 5/12

(Excess = 1/12) 13/12

(ii) Husband ... ... 1/4 = 3/12
Mother ... ... 1/6 = 2/12
Two daughters ... 2/3 = 8/12 reduced to 8/12 – 1/12 = 7/12

(Excess = 1/13) 13/12

(iii) Widow ... ... 1/8 = 3/24
Father ... ... 1/6 = 4/24
Mother ... ... 1/6 = 4/24
Two daughters 2/3 = 16/24 reduced to 16/24 – 3/24 = 13/24

(Excess = 3/24) 27/24

(iv) Husband ... ... 1/2 = 3/6
Two full sisters ... 2/3 = 4/6 reduced to 4/6 – 1/6 = 3/6

(Excess = 1/6) 7/6

(v) Husband ... ... 1/2 = 6/12
Two uterine brothers 1/3 = 4/12
Two full sisters ... 2/3 = 8/12 reduced to 8/12 – 6/12 = 2/12

(Excess = 6/12) 18/12

The result would be the same if there were instead of two full sisters two consanguine sisters.

(vi) Husband ... ... 1/2 = 6/12
Uterine sister ... 1/6 = 2/12
Consanguine sister 1/2 = 6/12 reduced to 6/12 – 2/12 = 4/12

(Excess = 2/12) 14/12

* If there were two daughters they would take 2/3 = 8/12 and the excess in this case would be 3/12 which would be reduced from 8/12 – 3/12 = 5/12, or 5/24 each

DOCTRINE OF RETURN—

60. After assigning shares to the sharers if there is a surplus, residue, still in hand, and there are no residuaries entitled to inherit (*i.e.* of the class of the sharers) the residue reverts to the sharers in proportion to their respective shares.

Exception.—

(*a*) The husband or widow is not entitled to the return if there is a consanguine heir, but if there is no other heir the husband is entitled to the residue in preference to the Crown. The surplus would escheat to the Crown if there is a wife only, for she is never entitled to the return.

(*b*) The mother is not entitled to the return if there co-exist the father, two brothers, or one brother and two sisters, or four sisters whether of full or half-blood by the father.

(*c*) Uterine brothers and sisters are not entitled to the return if there co-exist a full sister, but they share in the residue along with a consanguine sister.

SIMPLE CASES

(i)	Father ...	... 1/6 = 1/6	increased to	1/4
	Daughter	... 1/2 = 3/6	...	3/4
		4/6		1

(ii)	Mother ...	... 1/6	increased to	1/4
	Daughter	... 1/2 = 3/6	...	3/4
		4/6		1

(iii)	Father ...	... 1/6	increased to	1/5
	Mother ...	... 1/6	...	1/5
	Daughter ...	... 1/2 = 3/6	...	3/5
		5/6		1

EXCEPTION (a)

(iv) Wife	...	... ...	1/8=5/40
Father	1/6	increased to (1/5 of R.) 1/5 of 7/8	=7/40
Mother	1/6	... (1/5 of R.) 1/5 of 7/8	= 7/4
Daughter	1/2=3/6	... (3/5 of R.) 3/5 of 7/8	=21/40
	5/6		1

(v) Husband	...	... ...	1/4=4/16
Father	1/6	increased to (1/4 of R.) 1/4 of 3/4	=3/16
Daughter	1/2=3/6	... (3/4 of R.) 3/4 of 3/4	=9/16
	4/6		1

EXCEPTION (b)

(vi) Mother	1/6	... (not entitled to return)	=4/24
Father	1/6	increased to (1/4 of R.) 1/4 of 5/6	=5/24
Daughter	1/2=3/6	... (3/4 of R.) 3/4 of 5/6	=15/24

Two full brothers (excluded heirs of the second class).

EXCEPTION (c)

(vii) Uterine brother ...	1/6	... ...	1/6
Uterine sister ...	1/6	... ...	1/6
Full sister*	1/2=3/6+1/6	by return	=4/6
	5/6		1

(viii) Uterine sister ...	1/6	... ...	1/6
Full sister	1/2=3/6+2/6	by return	5/6
	4/6		1

* If there were only an uterine sister and a consanguine sister the latter would participate in the residue along with the uterine sister as follows :—

Uterine sister ...	... 1/6	increased to	1/4
Cons : sister ...	...1/2=3/6	" "	3/4
	4/6		1

§ 11. IMPEDIMENTS TO SUCCESSION

61. According to the Sirajiyah there are four impediments to succession.

(i) Slavery.
(ii) Homicide.
(iii) Difference of religion.
(iv) Difference of country.

SLAVERY.—

62. That the fact of slavery of the claimant is an impediment to succession has now become obsolete in British India by the Slavery Act V of 1843.[1]

HOMICIDE.—

63. Under the *Hanafi* Law intentional or unintentional homicide of the proprietor by claimant is a valid impediment to inheritance, and under the Shia Law, it is an impediment only if it be intentional, if it is unintentional or justifiable it is not a bar to succession.

Under the *Hanafi* Law homicide by an infant or a person of unsound mind or in the course of war or when inflicting punishment under the law is not a valid impediment.

DIFFERENCE OF RELIGION.—

64. A non-Muslim is not entitled to inherit from a Muslim, and a Muslim also cannot inherit from a non-Muslim by birth.

Apostate.—

Under the Muslim Law if an apostate from Islam has died, then his estate devolves on his Muslim heirs,[2] but he himself cannot inherit from his Muslim relations, however under Anglo-Muslim Law he is entitled to inherit and *vice versa*. The caste Disabilities Removal Act XXI of 1850 has removed the disabilities of an apostate heir to inherit whether from a Muslim or from a non-Muslim by birth or by apostasy. The Act says, "So much

1 Vide Ujmuddin v. Zialulnissa 3 Bom. 422 (1879).

2 According to some jurists and also the Shafii jurists the acquisition of an apostate after his apostacy, goes to the Bait-ul-mal.

of any law or usage now in force within the territories subject to the Government of the East India Company as inflicts on any person forfeiture of rights or property, or may be held in any way to impair or affect any right of inheritance, by reason of his or her renouncing or having been excluded from the communion of any religion, or being deprived of estate, shall cease to be enforced as law in the Courts of the East India Company and in the courts established by Royal Chapter within the said territories."[1]

DIFFERENCE OF COUNTRY.—

65. It still appears that a non-Muslim by birth would beexcluded from inheriting from a Muslim as provided by the Muslim Law.

Under the Shia Law want of Islam on the part of the claimant is an only bar to inheritance, that is, the property of any deceased person whether a Muslim or non-Muslim can be inherited by a Muslim heir.

Under the Muslim Law, Muslims though owing different allegiance are entitled to succeed to each other, but non-Muslim residents domiciled in a Muslim State are not so entitled. In the modern International Law, this involves the question of allegiance, nationality, and domicile and under Anglo-Muslim Law an alien enemy of the British Government cannot inherit the property of any British subject including Indian Muslims.[2]

---

1 Vide Khunni Lal v. Gobind Krishna Narain 33 All. 356 (1911), and S. 9 of the Bengal Regulation Act of 1832.

In Vaithilinga Odayar v. Ayyathorai Odayar 40 Mad. 118 (1917), the court held that the Act XXI of 1850. does not benefit the descendants of converts, thus dissenting from Bhagwant Singh v. Kallu 11 All. 100.

If a person apostatises and dies, then curiously according to Abdul Gaffar v. Ma Piva Shin (Rang. 1926) 98 I.C-155. his Muslim father cannot inherit, but under the Muslim Law he is entitled to inherit.

2 Vide the Aliens Act 1905 5 Edw 7. C. 13 and the Aliens Restriction Act 1914. 4 and 5 Geo. 5-C-12.

§ 12. MISCELLANEOUS CASES.

66. The following special cases may be considered.

1. Rights of heirs in the womb.
2. Transfer of vested inheritance owing to the death of an heir.
3. Missing heirs.
4. Hermaphrodite heirs.
5. Persons dying together.
6. Succession with reference to death-illness, *Marzul-Maut*,
7. Rights of insane, blind or deformed persons.
8. Rights of illegitimate children.

RIGHTS OF HEIRS IN THE WOMB.—

67. (*a*) A child in the womb of its mother, will be entitled to inherit, if born alive,[1] in case its father is living, within the minimum period of gestation,[2] and in case of divorce of its mother or death of the father, if born within the maximum period[3] of gestation allowed by the Sunni Law, or the Shia Law.

(*b*) A child born dead does not inherit both under the Sunni and the Shia Law, but under the Hanafi Law, if intentional violence has been done to the mother, then the child will be presumed to have been born alive.

If the child is born alive and dies subsequently, then its own heirs inherit from it.

The effect of the birth of a child.—

A child on birth may affect the existing heirs in several ways:—

(*a*) It may absolutely exclude all the existing heirs or some of the heirs.

(*b*) it may reduce the shares of existing heirs by application of the doctrine of increase or it may deprive the heirs of the return.

---

1 If born alive, that is, if the greater part of the body came out, it shall inherit, and it is considered sufficient if it came with its head and the whole of its breast, or with its feet upto its navel. The existence of life is made out by a voice, weeping, or any little movement of the body.

2 Vide Ch. IV Secs. 55 & 56, p. 49.

(*c*) The sex of the child born would determine its own heritable right as sharer or as residuary, and would accordingly affect other existing heirs.

(*d*) It may merely be an addition to an existing class of heirs and may take along with them.

Child as Excluder.—

If the child in womb may possibly be an absolute excluder of all existing heirs, then the estate is not to be distributed, until its birth, but if it cannot be an absolute excluder, then a preliminary distribution may be effected, considering the possibility of the child being a male or a female, and the smallest shares may be given to the existing heirs reserving the remainder for final distribution after the birth of the child on ascertaining its sex.

Illustrations.

(i) A person dies leaving a full brother's pregnant widow and a brother's son's son.

In this example if a male child is born within the lawful period of gestation it would absolutely exclude brother's son's son and would take the entire property, and if a female child is born, she would be a distant kindred, and would take nothing as against the brothers' son's son. Therefore the estate cannot be distributed, until the birth of the child.

(ii) A person dies leaving a pregnant wife and a full brother.

In this example if a male child is born, it would exclude the brother and partially exclude its own mother, and if a female is born it would reduce the residue of the brother. Hence it is not a case of absolute exclusion, therefore the heirs, the wife and the brother may be given the smallest possible shares respectively on basis of their own right of inheritance.

The following are the possibilities:—

	Wife.	Child.	Full brother.
I. If a son is born ...	1/8	7/8	0
II. If a daughter is born ...	1/8	1/2	Residue 3/8
III. If a child is born dead or is under the law held to be illegitimate	1/4=2/8	0	3/4=6/8

Thus on examining these shares, we find that the wife's smallest share is 1/8, and that of the brother is zero. Consequently the wife may take 1/8, and the residue 7/8 will not be distributed, till the birth of the child. And if a son is born he will take 7/8, but if a daughter is born, she will take 1/2 leaving 3/8 for the brother, and if a dead child is born or is declared illegitimate, and thus is not entitled to inherit, the wife will get 1/8 more to make up her legal share 1/4 and the residue 6/8 (3/4) will go to the brother as a residuary.

(iii) A person dies leaving a pregnant wife, his father and mother. This is also a case of birth of a partial excluder :—

The following are the possibilities :—

	Wife	Child.	Father.	Mother.
I. If a son born ...	1/8	Residue	1/6	1/6
	3/24	13/24	4/24	4/24
II. If a daughter is born ...	1/8	1/2	1/6+R. (1/24)	1/6
	3/24	12/24	5/24	4/24
III. If a dead child is born ...	1/4	0	=2/3 of R.	1/3 of R.
			2/3 of 3/4	1/3 of 3/4
			6/12	3/12
	6/24	0	12/24	6/24

Thus the wife may take ... 3/24 }
Father " ... 4/24 } The smallest shares.
Mother " ... 4/24 }

And the residue 13/24 will not be distributed, till the birth of the child, thereafter the final distribution will take place, and according to the sex of the child the shares will be affected.

DEVOLUTION OF VESTED INHERITANCE.—

68. According to the Muslim Law on the death of a person his eatate vests immediately in the lawful heirs in terms of their legal portions. Thus every case of inheritance under the Muslim Law is a case of vested inheritance, though actual distribution might

not have taken place at all. . Such an heir may die before the actual distribution of the estate, and the share, though undivided, which had vested in him, would be inheritable by his own heirs. This devolution of vested inheritance, owing to the death of the heir is known as *munaskhat*. The other heirs may also be heirs to the deceased heir, if so, they would inherit in both capacities, it would be a case of " repeated inheritance" sometime a case of double or threefold devolution of inheritance.

The general rules of distribution would be applicable, that is, first assign shares to the original claimants including the dead heir, and thereafter distribute the estate vested in the dead heir to his own heirs.

(1) A person X dies leaving a son, a daughter, and a consanguine brother.

Before the distribution of the estate the son dies leaving the above heirs namely the sister and the consanguine uncle.

	Son.	Daughter.	Consanguine uncle.
I. Distribution on X's death ...	2/3	1/3	0 excluded
II. Distribution on the Son's death ...		1/2	1/2 as residuary.
Distribution in terms of son's estate (2/3) ...		1/2 of 2/3	1/2 of 2/3
		1/3	1/3
It is a case of double inheritance, I and II		1/3+1/3	0+1/3
		2/3	1/3

Thus the daughter takes 2/3 and the consanguine uncle 1/3

MISSING PERSONS, AND HEIRS.—

69. A "missing person" is a person who cannot be traced at all, his whereabouts being unknown, it being uncertain whether he is living or dead.

No one can succeed to the estate of a missing person, until his death is established or a certain period has elapsed. Under the old Muslim Law, the period was ninety years from the date of the birth of the missing person, and according to some jurists it is four years from the date of missing. This is also the Maliki Law and the period under the Shafii Law is seven years, and under the Shia Law it is ten years. Under Anglo-Muslim Law it would be governed by the Indian Evidence Act. (Sections 2, 107 and 108), which provides thus:—"When the question is whether a man is alive or dead, and it is proved that he has not been heard of for seven years by those who would naturally have heard of him if he has been alive, the burden of proving that he is alive is shifted to the person who affirms it."[1]

Missing heir.—

A missing heir cannot inherit, unless he reappears within the period of presumption of life as stated above. Under the Muslim Law his share of Inheritance is reserved, in case he should present himself, and after the expiry of the period, the reserved portion would be distributed again.

Illustration.

A person leaves two daughters, a missing son and a son's son.

	Two daughters.	Missing son.	son's. son.
I. If the missing son is alive	1/2	1/2	0
	3/6	3/6	0
II. „ „ is dead	2/3	0	1/3
	4/6	0	2/6

The two daughters may take 3/6, but nothing can be given to son's son, and residue 3/6 will be reserved, if the son presents himself within the period he takes 3/6, if not the daughters will again take 1/6 and the residue 2/6 will go to the son's son.

---

1 As to missing persons and heirs.

Vide. Mazhar Ali v. Budh Singh 7 All. 297.

Jafri Begum v. Amir Muhammad 7 All. 822.

Moolla Cassim v. Moolla Abdur Rahim 32 I. A. 177, 33 Cal. 173.

Hermaphrodite heirs.—

70. A person whose sex is doubtful is known as hermaphrodite. A hermaphrodite is entitled to the smallest share that he would get as a male or a female.[1] Hence it is to be seen on two different computations what share could be assigned to such a person.

(i) A person dies leaving a husband, father, mother and a herma-phrodite.

	Husband.	Father.	Mother.	Hermaphrodite.
If the hermaphrodite is taken as a female person	1/4	1/6	1/6	1/2
Reduced to unity by the doctrine of increase ...	3/13	2/13	2/13	6/13
If the hermaphrodite is taken as a male person	1/4	1/6	1/6	5/12 R.

Now 5/12 is smaller than 6/13, therefore here the hermaphrodite inherits as a male person.

(ii) According to the Sirajiyah if a man leaves a son a daughter and an hermaphrodite, the hermaphrodite will take the share of a daughter, it being the smallest allotment.

Persons dying together.—

71. If two persons die together and it cannot be established who died first, then under the Hanafi Law the death is presumed to be simultaneous, and the one cannot inherit from the other, their estate would be inheritable by their own descendants.

Shia Law.—

Under the Shia Law in case of mutual succession of persons dying together in some accident, two or more series of computations should be made, with regard to their respective heirs, as claimants to one of such persons and finally the said computations are to be added up to make the final allotment.

---

1 According to Ibn Abbas a hermaphrodite is entitled to a moiety of the two shares that is half of the shares of a male and a female member.

Illustration

A Muslim dies together with his son in some accident, leaving his wife and mother. The father and the son have left Rs. 2400 each.

	Wife	Mother	Son
I First computation assuming that the father died before the son	1/8	1/6	17/24 residue
	3/24	4/24	17/24
	Rs. 300	Rs. 400	Rs. 1700

	Son's Mother	Grandmother	Father
II Second computation assuming that the the father died after the son.	1/3	0	2/3
	Rs. 800	0	Rs. 1600

Now from the first computation 17/24 or Rs. 1700 devolves exclusively on the son's mother, and from the second computation 2/3 or Rs. 1600/- father's share would devolve on the wife and the grandmother in the ratio of 1 : 3

Wife		Mother
1/4	:	3/4
Rs. 400		Rs. 1200

Thus the final result is adding up shares assigned to the wife *i.e.* son's mother Rs 300 + Rs. 1700 + Rs. 800 + Rs. 400 = 3200 and to the mother *i.e.* son's grandmother Rs. 400 + 0 + 0 + Rs. 1200 = Rs. 1600

SUCCESSION—DEATH ILLNESS.—

72. If a person pronounces divorce, in death illness *marz-ul-maut* and dies during his wife's *iddat,* then under Hanafi Law, the wife is entitled to inherit from him, but she will not be entitled to inherit if she herself had asked her husband to repudiate her irrevocably or she obtains a *khula* divorce, or exercises the option of puberty or obtains divorce by reason of her husband's impotency.

The wife is also entitled to inherit if the husband makes *ila,* or *lian* while in *marz-ul-maut.* However if the wife were to die before her husband, the latter would not be entitled to inherit from her, as he has forfeited his right, by his own voluntary act of repudiation.

If the wife abandons Islam during her death illness, and dies during *iddat*, her husband would be entitled to inherit from her.

Under Shia Law, if a woman is divorced by her husband in his death-illness, her right of inheritance continues for one year, and she will inherit from him, if her husband dies within one year from date of divorce, provided also that the woman remains unmarried during this period of time, and if the woman were to die first, her husband cannot inherit from her, as is the case under the Hanafi Law.

Under the Shia Law, if a man in death illness marries and dies, without consummating the marriage, his wife shall not Inherit from him, but if the wife were to die in his life-time he would inherit from her. And if a woman in death-illness marries and her husband were to die in her life-time, she shall inherit from him, though the marriage was not consummated, and if the woman dies first and before consummation, the husband would inherit from her.[2]

INSANE, BLIND, DEFORMED PERSONS.—

73. Under the Muslim Law insanity, blindness or any form of bodily disability is not a bar to inheritance.[3]

ILLEGITIMATE CHILD.—

74. Under the *Sunni Hanafi Law* an illegitimate child does not inherit from the father, it inherits from the mother and her relations and they inherit from him,[4] but under the *Shia* Law such a child is not entitled to inherit from the mother or her relations nor do they inherit from him.[5]

---

1 As to what is marz-ul-maut vide Sec. 51. Pp. 45 and 46.

2 Under the Hanafi Law marriage in death-illness is allowed but the husband cannot fix more than the proper dower.

Ballie Digest 11, 340, 341.

3 Vide Mahar Ali v. Amani 2 B.L.R.A.C. 306. (1869).

4 Bafatum v. Bilaiti Khanum 30 Cal. 683 (1903). A Muslim woman dies leaving her husband and an illegitimate son of her full sister, the husband takes 1/2 and the illegitimate son 1/2 as a distant kinsman.

5 Sahebzadee Begum v. Himmut Bahadoor 12 W. R. 512 on review 41. W. R. 125 (1870).

The Seven rules of the Muslim Law of Inheritance.

In addition to the fundamental principles of distribution of inheritance the Muslim jurists have formulated seven rules for the actual working out of the shares of the heirs. They may be called the rules of computation or the arithmetical processes or formulas for working out the actual allotment of shares. The unique feature of this Arabian system is that it avoids the use of fractions altogether, though the fixed Koranic shares are in terms of fractions viz., 1|2, 1|4, 1|8, 2|3, 1|3 and 1|6. An attempt is here made to explain the Arabian method of computation and also to note side by side the modern arithmetical process in solving out the same problems.

There is no doubt that we can distribute the shares without taking into account these seven rules by adopting ordinary arithmetical process, and perhaps for this reason several writers of Anglo-Muhammadan Law have not devoted much attention to these rules. However if these rules are not actually necessary for working out of the shares, they are nevertheless useful in assisting speedy solution of problems; at least they should be studied for the sake of knowledge alone. We may substitute all these rules into one simple rule, viz., first assign shares to the heirs and if the shares are equally divisible *inter se* and thus exhaust the property leaving no remainder it is a case of perfect distribution if not in each case reduce the fractions assigned to each class of heirs to the lowest common denominator in order to obtain a perfect solution[1]. We finally obtain fractions of such numerators with the common denominator that the number of numerators are equally divisible among each class of heirs.

I have taken the seven rules and the examples from the Sirajiyah the famous work on the law of inheritance. Three of these

---

[1] If the sum total of the assigned shares i.e., of the fractions exceeds unity we apply the doctrine of increase and reduce all the shares proportionately, and if there is some surplus left over after assigning the shares we apply the doctrine of return to increase the shares proportionately. However the doctrines of increase *awl* and return *rad* are part of the fundamental principles of distribution, so they are not included in the seven rules of computation, but while working out the seven rules we have to apply the doctrine of increase and return as a matter of course.

rules are by reason of the difference in the respective shares and in the numbers of the heirs and the four rules are based upon a comparison of the numbers of the different classes of the heirs.

The following technical terms have been used.

Technical Terms

1. *Tamasul-Adaddain,* equal numbers. The numbers are said to be equal *tamasul* when they agree and leave no fraction when one is divided by the other, e.g., 3 and 3; 4 and 4.

2. *Tadakhul-adaddain,* concordant, they are such two numbers that the smaller exactly divides the other leaving no fraction, e. g., 2 and 4; 3 and 6; 3 and 9.

3. *Tawafaq-adaddain,* composite, they are such two numbers that have a common factor, e.g., 8 and 20; 4×2=8 and 4×5 =20, hence 4 is the common factor; in 12 and 18; 6×2=12; 6×3=18, 6 is the common factor, and 7 is the common factor of 14 and 21.

4. *Tabayun-adaddain,* that is numbers which have no common factor nor can one divide the other, e.g. 3 and 5; 9 and 10; 7 and 10; etc.

(*i*) *Wafq* is the factor other than the common factor in respect to any two numbers, e.g., take the numbers 8 and 20; 2×4=8; and 5×4=20; here 4 is the common factor and the *wafq* factor is 2 and 5 respectively of 8 and 20.

(*ii*) The term *Musla* means the shares into which the property is actually divisible initially by reason of the claimants. The fixed Koranic shares are 1|2, 1|4, 1|8,

1. e.g., A woman leaves her husband, her mother and a full sister.

Husband	1/2	3/6 ....reduced to	3/8.
Mother	1/3	2/6	2/8.
Full sister	1/2	3/6	3/8.
		8/6	1.

Here there was an excess of 2|6 hence the shares are reduced proportionately.

2. e.g., A person leaves his mother and a son's daughter.

Mother		1/6 increased to	1/4
Son's daughter	1/2	3/6	3/4
		4/6	1

Here there was surplus of 2|6 hence the shares are increased proportionately.

2|3, 1|3 and 1|6, and they may be assigned alone or jointly to certain heirs. In the first case the *musla* is their denominator and when they come jointly the *musla* will be the least common multiple of the denominators. Therefore the possible cases of *musla* are 2, 3, 4, 6, 8, 12 or 24.

To sum up. The numbers are of four kinds. When they are identical they are called *mutamasil,* if not identical they may be *mutadakhil,* one measuring the other, or they may be *mutawafiq,* having a common factor or they may be *mutabayin,* that is not divisible *inter se* or if divisible at all by the number one only.

First Rule

The First Rule is that the heirs have their shares assigned without leaving any fraction, that is the property is divisible among the heirs leaving no remainder, e.g., a Muslim leaves, his father, mother and two daughters. The distribution will be as follows and it leaves no remainder.

Father		1|6
Mother		1|6
Two daughters	2|3	4|6 (each 2|6)

The *musla* in this case is 6, the father receiving one share, and mother one share and the daughters two each.

The above example is given in the *Sirajiyah,* several others may be suggested. In the following cases a person dies leaving these heirs:—

Two daughters	2|4, each 1|4, one share as residuaries.	
One son	2|4, as a residuary.	
Husband	1|4	one share.
Son	2|4	two shares as residuary
Daughter	1|4	one share as residuary
Widow	1|4	one share.
Brother	3|4	three shares as residuary.
Mother	1|6	one share.
Son	5|6	five shares as residuary.
Widow	1|8	one share.
Son	7|8	seven shares as residuary.

Second Rule

The Second Rule is when the shares assigned to one particular class of heirs is not divisible between them without leaving a fraction on account of their numbers, but the assigned share and the number of the heirs are *twafuq* have a common factor. The rule here is to multiply the *musla* (or *awl* increase if any) by the *wafq* of the number of heirs, e.g., a person leaves his father, mother and ten sisters.

Father		1|6
Mother		1|6
Ten sisters	2|3	4|6

Here the *musla* is 6, father receives 1, mother 1, and ten sisters 4 shares. But the number of heirs 10 is not divisible by 4, the assigned share but 10 and 4 are *twafuq*, i.e., 2×2=4; and 2×5=10, hence the common factor *twafuq*, is 2. Hence the *wafq* factor of the heirs 10 is 5. Our rule is to multiply the *musla* with the *wafq* that is 6 by 5 and we get 30.

In other words the father receives 5 shares, mother 5 shares, 10 daughters in all 20 shares 2 shares each.

The following example is with the incident of the doctrine of *awl*, increase. A woman dies leaving her husband both parents and six daughters.

Husband	1|4	3|12
Father	1|6	2|12
Mother	1|6	2|12
Six daughters	2|3	8|12
		15|12

The *musla* being 12 the distribution is as follows, husband 3, father 2, mother 2, and the daughters 8. But the assigned shares 8 are not divisible equally among the 6 daughters without leaving a fraction. However 8 and 6 are *twafuq* 2×4=8, 2×3=6 and the *wafq* factor of 6 is 3.

Our rule is to multiply the *musla* by the *wafq* factor, of the number of heirs that is 12×3=36.

Therefore the husband is entitled to 9, father 6, mother 6, and 4 to each daughter. In all 24 for six daughters. Adding up the numerators we find that its sum is 45 while the denominator is 36. So the doctrine of increase becomes applicable, thus we increase the shares to 45.

Another simple process would be first to apply the doctrine of increase and then the rule stated above, that is, multiply the *awl* with the *wafq* factor of the number of heirs.

Husband	1|4	3|12	reduced to unity	3|15
Father	1|6	2|12	,,	2|15
Mother	1|6	2|12	,,	2|15
Six daughters	2|3	8|12	,,	8|15
		15|12		1

Here the *awl* is 15 and since 8 is not divisible equally among 6 daughters, the *wafq* factor of 6 is 3, i.e., 2×3=6; 2×4=8, the common factor being 2. Hence we multiply *awl* by *wafq*, that is, 15×3=45 and get 45 shares thus distributing the property as above, to the husband 9 shares, to the father 6, mother 6, and 6 daughters 24, each 4 shares.

The above two examples may also be worked out by our modern arithmetical process bearing in mind that all shares must be ultimately reduced to a common denominator. First we must reduce the shares to a common denominator in accordance with the assigned shares, and again the denominator will have to be altered by reason of number of shares in the other classes.

Father......1|6 reduced to apparent common denominator 1|6
again reduced to common denominator........5|30
Mother ....1|6..............................1|6
..................................5|30
Ten daughters..2|3..............................4|6
each 2|30 in all......................20|30

Husband..........1|4 reduced to apparent C. D. 3|12 applying
increase reduce the shares..........................3|15
Father ....1|6......................2|12.......
....2|15
Mother ....1|6......................2|12.......
....2|15
Six daughters......2|3......................8|12......
....8|15

15|12

the share of each daughter is 8|15×1|6=4|45 each in all 24|45 and again reducing all shares to the denominator 45 we get.

Husband ....9|45
Father ....6|45
Mother ....6|45
Six daughters..................24|45 each 4|45.

The Third Rule is when the shares assigned to one particular class of heirs are not divisible between them without leaving a fraction on account of their numbers, and the assigned share and the number of the heirs are not *tawafuq*, have no common factor, but they are *mutabayin*, in this case the rule is to multiply the *musla* or *awl* by the number of the heirs.

Third Rule

e.g., a man leaves his father and mother and five daughters.

Father ....1|6..................1|6.
Mother ....1|6..................1|6.
Five daughters ....2|3..................4|6.

The *musla* is 6, the father receives 1, mother 1, and five daughters 4. And 5 and 4 are not *tawafuq* but are *mutabayin*, have no common factor. Applying the rule we multiply the *musla* by the number of heirs, viz., 6×5=30. Therefore the father receives 5, mother 5, and daughters 20 shares each daughter 4 shares.

We may also work it out as follows:—

Father..........1|6..........1|6 again reducing it to common denominator ....5|30
Mother ....1|6..........1|6...5|30
Five daughters ...2|3..........4|6 each daughter 4|30 in all ....20|30

In the following illustration the doctrine of increase becomes applicable. A woman leaves her husband and five full blood sisters.

Husband............1|2.....3|6 applying increase reducing to unity 3|7 reducing to common denominator......15|35
Five full sisters......2|3......4|6..........................4|7 each 4|35 ....in all 20|35

Here the *musla* is 6, applying increase reducing it to unity *awl* is 7 and to get the shares we multiply *awl* by the number of heirs, viz., 7×5=35 the estate is divisible as above to the husband 15 shares, to the 5 full sisters 20 shares each 4 shares.

A woman leaves her husband true grand-mother and three uterine sisters.

Husband..........1|2........3|6 again reducing it to common denominator ....9|18
Tr. Gr.-mother.....1|6........1|6..3|18
Three uterine sisters.1|3........2|6.......... each 2|18.................... in all 6|18

The *musla* here is 6, but 2 is not divisible among 3 uterine sisters. Hence we multiply *musla* by the number of the heirs viz., three sisters, that is, 6 by 3 we get 18 shares, which is distributed as follows:—To the husband 9 shares, to the true grandmother 3 shares and to 3 uterine sisters 6 shares to each 2 shares.

Special case of 2nd and 3rd Rules

The above Second and Third Rules are based on the assigned shares and the number of heirs being *mutawafuq* or *mutabayin* but they may also be *mutadakhil*, one measuring the other. This will have two forms, the assigned shares, may be more or less than the number of heirs. e.g., a person leaves his mother, 2 daughters and uncle.

Mother		1|6
Two daughters	2|3	4|6
Uncle		1|6 residue.

Here there is *tadakhul* between 4 and 2, the assigned shares and the number of the heirs and the former are more than the latter, but if the number of heirs are more than the assigned shares, the case would be governed as in the case of *tawafuq* as discussed in the second rule. The rule is to multiply the *musla* with the *wafq* of the number of heirs, e.g., a person leaves 2 true grand-mothers 8 daughters and 2 uncles.

Two Tr. gr. mother		1|6		2|12
Eight daughters	2|3	4|6	each 1|12 in all	8|12
Two uncles residue		1|6		2|12

The *musla* is 6, and 8 and 4 are *tadakhul* and the number of heirs are greater than the assigned shares. The *wafq* factor of 8 is 2, the common factor of 4 and 8 being 4 by reason of *tadakhul*. Hence we multiply *musla* by *wafq* that is 6×2 and get 12 and the 2 True grand-mothers receive 2 shares, 8 daughters 8 shares and 2 uncles 2 shares.

Fourth Rule

The Fourth Rule is when the shares assigned to two or more classes of heirs are not divisible by their respective numbers without leaving fraction but the numbers of heirs are *tamasul*, equal. The rule is to multiply the *musla* (or *awl*) by the *tamasul* number of any of these classes.

A person leaves 6 daughters, 3 true grand-mothers, and 3 uncles.

Six daughters	2|3	4|6
Three Tr. gr.-mother		1|6
Three uncles		1|6 residue

Here the *musla* is 6; and 6 daughters receive 4 shares, 3 true grand-mothers 1 share and three uncles 1 share. It will be noticed that 2 is the common factor of 6 and 4. The *wafq* factor of 6 is 3. (2×3=6; 2×2=4). Thus all three numbers are *tamasul* they being in threes in each class. Hence multiply 6 by 3 and we get 18 shares, consequently 6 daughters receive 12 shares, 3 true grand-mothers, 3 shares, i.e., one each, and three uncles 3 shares that is one each

We may also work out the above example as follows:—

Six daughters .... 2|3 .... 4|6 each 2|18 in all
12|18 thus reducing to common denominator .... 12|18.
Three Tr. Gr.-mother .... 1|6 each 1|18 in all
.... 3|18
Three uncles the residue .... 1|6 each 1|18 in all
.... 3|18

The Fifth Rule is that first assign shares and if the numbers of some classes of heirs are found to be divisible by the number of the other classes, that is there is *tadakhul*, the rule is to multiply the *musla* by the largest number in the classes.

Fifth Rule

A person leaves 4 wives, 3 true grand-mothers and 12 uncles.

Four wives	1|4	3|12
Three gr.-mother	1|6	2|12
Twelve paternal uncles	residue	7|12

There is *tadakhul* between the numbers, 4, 3 and 12.

The *musla* here is 12, and the largest number of one class of heirs is 12 uncles, hence applying the rule we multiply *musla* 12 by 12 and get 144. The distribution will be as follows:—

Four wives receive 36 shares each 9 shares.

Three true grand-mothers 24 shares each 8 shares.

Twelve uncles 84 shares each 7 shares.

The above illustration may also be worked out thus:—

Four wives .... 1|4 .... 3|12 reducing to common denominator .... 36|144

Three Tr. gr.-mother .... 1|6 .... 2|12 .... 24|144

Twelve uncles the residue ...... 7|12 .. each .... 7|144 in all .... 84|144

Some easy cases under these Rules.

A person dies leaving his wife, mother, brother and three sisters.

Widow gets her share 1|4 .... 3|12

Mother .... 1|6 .... 2|12

Residue .... 7|12 to be divided between the brother and 3 sisters.

The *musla* is 12 and applying the rule that is multiply *musla* by the number of sharers in this case 5 (namely, three sisters and one brother equivalent to two more sisters), we get $12 \times 5 = 60$. Thus the widow is entitled to 15 shares, mother to 10, and the residue 35 is to be divided between one brother and three sisters, the brother receiving double share, namely, 14 to brother and 7 to each sister that is 21 shares to 3 sisters.

We may also work it out thus:—

Widow .... 1|4 .... 3|12 reducing it again to common denominator .... 15|60

Mother .... 1|6 .... 2|12 .... 10|60

Brother as residuary .... 2|5×7|12 .... 14|60

Three sisters .... 3|5×7|12 .... 21|60

Similarly in the following cases both the Arabian method and the modern arithmetical process is used:—

A person leaves a widow, a brother and three sisters.

Widow ....1|4 reducing to common denominator..5|20
Brother ....2|5×3|4..........................6|20
Three sisters ....3|5×3|4..........................9|20

The *musla* is 4 and we multiply it with 5 the number of heirs, one brother is equivalent to two sisters and also there are three sisters and get 20 shares, which is distributed as above.

A person dies leaving two daughters, a son's son and a son's daughter.

Two daughters ....2|3....................6|9
Son's son ....2|3×1|3=2|9 ....2|9
Son's daughter ....1|3×1|3=1|9 ....1|9

Here the *musla* is 3 and applying the rule we multiply it by the number of heirs, viz., three (one son is equivalent to two daughters and also there is one daughter) that is 3×3=9 shares which is divided as above.

A person leaves, the widow, a sister and four brother's sons.

Widow ....1|4...........1|4...........4|16.
Sister ....1|2...........2|4...........8|16.
Four brother's sons the residue 1|4, i.e., 1|16 each in all 4|16.

The *musla* here is 4 and applying the rule we multiply it by the number of heirs viz., 4×4=16 we get 16 shares which is distributed 4 to the widow, 8 to the sister and 1 to each brother's son, in all four shares to four of them.

A person leaves his wife and two sons.

Widow ....1|8......................2|16
Two sons...the residue...7|8 equally, 7|16 each in all 14|16

The *musla* here is 8, and applying the rule we multiply *musla* by the number of heirs, viz., 8×2=16 shares which is distributed as above.

A person leaves his wife, two daughters and a son.

Widow ....1|8..... reducing to common denominator 4|32
Son ....1|2 of 7|8 residue 7|16...................14|32
Two daughters ..1|2 of 7|8 ......7|16 each 7|32...........14|32

The *musla* here is 8 and applying the rule we multiply *musla* by the number of the heirs four (two daughters and one son equivalent to two daughters) 8×4=32 shares distributed as above, widow 4, son 14, and each daughter 7 (to both 14).

A person leaves his wife, two sons and a daughter.

Widow ....1|8...............5|40
Two sons ....4|5 of 7|8 residue 28|40 each 14|40
Daughter ....1|5 of 7|8 residue ..7|40

The *musla* here is 8 and applying the rule we multiply *musla* by the number of the heirs 5 (one daughter and 2 sons equivalent to 4 daughters) 8×5=40 and distribute as above, widow 5, son 14 each and to daughter 7.

A person leaves two wives, six daughters and five sons.

Two widows....	1|8 reducing to common denominator		16|128
Five sons.....	10|16 of 7|8 residue	....	.70|128
Six daughters ..	6|16 of 7|8 residue	....	.42|128

The *musla* here is 8; and we multiply it with the highest number of heirs of one class, viz., 16 daughters (6 daughters and 5 sons equivalent to 10 more daughters in all 16) that is 8 by 16 gives 128 and the distribution is as above to the widows 18, that is 8 each, to the sons 70 that is 14 each and to daughters 42 that is 7 to each daughter.

A person leaves his father, two widows, five sons and two daughters.

Two widows ....1|8.... 3|24 reducing to common denominator .... 36|288.....each 18|288
Father .... 1|6.... 4|24 .... 42|288
Five sons......10|12 of 17|24 residue..170|288 in all each 34|288
Two daughters..2|12 of 17|24 residue...34|288.....each 34|288

The *musla* here is 24 and applying the rule we multiply by the largest number in the class, namely, 12 (2 daughters and 5 sons equivalent to ten daughters). That is 24 by 12 which gives 288.

A person leaves three widows, six sons and six daughters.

Three widows...........1|8 reducing to common denominator 18|144 each 8|144
Six sons................12|18 of 7|8 residue................ 84|144 each 14|144
Six daughters...........6|18 of 7|8 residue................ 42|144 each 7|144

The *musla* here is 8; and we multiply it by the largest number in the class namely 18 (6 daughters and 6 sons equivalent to 12 daughters) that is 8 by 18 and we get 144 which is distributed as above; 3 widows 18 shares that is 6 each, and 6 sons 84 shares that is 14 shares each, and 6 daughters 42 shares that is 7 each.

Sixth Rule

The Sixth Rule is when after assigning shares we see that some of the numbers of the heirs are *mutawafiq* that is have a common factor then the rule is to multiply the *wafq* of the first number by the second number and multiply the product by the *wafq* of the third number, and if the resulting product be *mutawafiq* multiply it, and so on until finally you multiply the last product itself by the *musla*.

e.g., A man leaves 4 wives, 18 daughters, 15 true grand-mothers and 6 uncles.

Four wives	1|8	3|24.
Eighteen daughters	2|3	16|24.
Fifteen Tr. gr.-mothers	1|6	4|24.
Six uncles		residue 1|24.

The *musla* here is 24.

As regards the first and second numbers viz., 4 and 18, the common factor is 2 (2×2=4 and 2×9=18) and so the *wafq* of 4 is 2. The rule is to multiply the *wafq* of first by the second number i.e. 2 by 18=36.

Now the product 36 and the third number 15 have 3 as the common factor (3×12=36 and 3×5=15) so the *wafq* of 15 is 5. And the rule is to multiply the product by *wafq* of the third number, 36×5=180.

Now we see that there is *tadakhul* between 180 and 6 the last number so it needs no further multiplication.

Finally we multiply the *musla* by the ultimate product viz., 24 by 180 and we get 4320 shares which are distributed as follows.

Four wives receive	540 shares	each 135 shares.
Eighteen daughters	2880 shares	each 160 shares.
Fifteen Tr. gr.-mothers	720 shares	each 48 shares.
Six uncles	180 shares	each 30 shares.

The above problem has been worked out in an admirable manner as suggested by the author of the Sirajiyah. Some Muslim jurists have worked it out in a different manner, a mode suggested by the author of Sharifa.

The author of the Sharifa solves it thus:—

A man leaves 4 wives, 18 daughters, 15 true grand-mothers, and 6 uncles.

Four wives	1|8	3|24.
Eighteen daughters	2|3	16|24.
Fifteen Tr. gr.-mothers	1|6	4|24.
Six uncles		1|24. residue.

The *musla* here is 24.

Four wives cannot have the three shares divided between them without leaving fraction; and 4 and 3 are *mutabayin* so we retain 4 as it is. Similarly as regards the number of daughters 18 and the shares 16, they are *tawafuq* i.e., 2×9=18 and 2×8=16 so we retain 9. Again the numbers 15 and 4 are *mutabayin* so we retain 15, and similarly we retain 6. Hence the numbers that we retain are 4, 9, 15 and 6. Again the numbers 4 and 6 are *tawafuq* i.e., 2×2=4, 2×3=6 and multiplying we obtain 12 (i.e. by multiplying half of any of these numbers by the other, i.e. 4×3 or 2×6

=12 which is really the L. C. M.). Similarly 12 and 9 are *tawafuq* by 3 so we obtain 36 so are 36 and 15 *tawafuq* by 3 so we multiply 36 by 5 and obtain 180, (the same result is obtained if we find out the L. C.M. of 4, 9, 15, 6; or the L. C. M. of 4, 18, 15, 6= 180) and finally multiplying it by the *musla* 24 we get 4320 which is distributed as follows:—

Four wives 540 shares—each 135, 18 daughters 2880 shares, each 160, 15 true grand-mothers 720 shares, each 48, and 6 uncles 180 shares, each 30.

The same example may be worked out in a different manner by our modern methods of arithmetic, we should simply bear in mind that the fractions should be reduced to one common denominator.

Four wives . . . . 1|8 . . . . 3|24 each 3|96
in all 12|96 . . . . 540|4320.
Eighteen daughters . . . . 2|3 . . . . 16|24 each 16|432
in all 288|432 . . . . 2880|4320.
Fifteen Tr. gr.-mothers . . . . . . 1|6 . . . . 4|24 each 4|360
in all 60|360 . . . . 720|4320.
Six uncles . . . . residue 1|24 each 1|144
in all 6|144 . . . . 180|4320.

The L. C. M. of 96, 432, 360, 144=4320.

2 | 96, 432, 360, 144
2 | 48, 216, 180, 72
2 | 24, 108, 90, 36
2 | 12, 54, 45, 18
3 | 6, 27, 45, 9
3 | 2, 9, 15, 3
2, 3, 5, 1

$2 \times 2 \times 2 \times 2 \times 2 \times 3 \times 3 \times 3 \times 5 = 4320.$

There is some difficulty in understanding the Seventh Rule as stated in the Sirajiyah and possibly for this reason the author of the Sharifa has adopted a different process in working the sixth as well as the seventh rule. The rule is thus stated in the Sirajiyah. When after assigning shares we see that the numbers of classes of heirs are *mutabayin* the rule is to multiply the first number by the second, and the product by the third, and so on until the resulting product is multiplied by the *musla*. A person leaves 2 wives, 6 true grand-mothers, 10 daughters, and 7 uncles.

Seventh Rule

The seventh example is thus worked out by the author of the Sharifa.

A person leaves two wives, six true grand-mothers, ten daughters and seven uncles.

Two wives 1|8 3|24
Six Tr. gr.-mothers 1|6 4|24
Ten daughters 2|3 16|24
Seven uncles residue 1|24
The *musla* here is 24.

The number of wives two and the shares 3 are *mutabayin*, thus we retain 2. Similarly 6 and 4 are *tawafuq* by 2 so we retain 3 i.e., half of 6. Similarly 10 and 16 are *tawafuq* by 2 and we thus retain 5, and we see that 7 and 1 are *mutabayin*. Thus we get 2, 3, 5 and 7, and all these are *mutabayin* and we multiply all these and get 210 and multiply the last product by 24 we get 5040 shares which are distributed as follows. To 2 wives 630 shares, each 315, to 6 Tr. grand-mothers 840 shares, each 140 and to 10 daughters 3360 shares, each 336, and to 7 uncles 210 shares, each 30 shares.

Two wives 1|8 3|24.
Six Tr. gr.-mothers 1|6 4|24.
Ten daughters 2|3 16|24.
Seven uncles residue 1|24.
The *musla* here is 24.

The same result is obtained if we find out the L. C. M. of 2, 6, 10 and 7, and we get 210 and multiplying this with the *musla* 24 we obtain 5040, which is distributed as follows:

Two wives 630 shares each 315, 6 true grand-mothers 840 shares each 140, 10 daughters 3360 shares, each 336, and 7 uncles 210 shares each 30 shares.

The above problem may also be worked out thus by ordinary arithmetical process.

Two wives 1|8 3|24 each 3|48
in all 6|48 630|5040.
Six Tr. gr.-mothers 1|6 4|24 each 4|144
in all 24|144 840|5040.
Ten daughters 2|3 16|24 each 16|240
in all 160|240 3360|5040.
Seven uncles residue 1|24 each 1|168
in all 7|168 210|5040.

The L. C. M. of 48, 144, 240, 168=5040.

```
2 | 48, 144, 240, 168
  2 | 24, 72, 120, 84
    2 | 12, 36, 60, 42
      3 | 6, 18, 30, 21
        2 | 2, 6, 10, 7
              1, 3, 5, 7
```

$2\times2\times2\times2\times3\times3\times5\times7=5040$.

Here is an example of the doctrine of return. A person leaves 4 wives, 9 daughters and 6 true grand-mothers.

By the ordinary arithmetical process.

Wives take 1|8, and the residue 7|8 is to be divided between daughters, and true grand-mother in the ratio of 2|3: 1|6 or 4:1.

Four wives	1|8				5|40.
Nine daughters	2|3	4|6	4|5	of 7|8 residue	28|40.
Six true gr.-mothers	1|6	1|6	1|5	of 7|8 residue	7|40.

continuing:

Four wives each 5|160 in all 20|160 180|1440 each 45|1440.

Nine daughters each 28|360 in all 252|360 1008|1440 each 112|1440.

Six true gr.-mothers each 7|240 in all 42|240 252|1440 each 42|1440.

The L. C. M. of 160, 360, 240=1440.

```
2 | 160, 360, 240
  2 | 80, 180, 120
    2 | 40, 90, 60
      2 | 20, 45, 30
        5 | 10, 45, 15
          3 | 2, 9, 3
              2, 3, 1
```

$$2\times2\times2\times2\times2\times5\times3\times3=1440.$$

By the Arabian method the *musla* is 40. We find that the number of heirs is 4, 9 and 6 and they are *mutabayin* with respect to the shares assigned viz., 5, 28 and 7 respectively and 4, 6 are *tawafuq* by 2; hence we multiply 2 by 6 and get 12; 12 and 9 are *tawafuq* by 3 thus we multiply 12 and 3 and get 36; multiply the product 36 by the *musla* 40 and we get 1440 which is distributed as above. In other words the L. C. M. of 4, 9 and 6 is 36 which is multiplied by the *musla* 40 and we get 1440, which is distributed to four wives 180 shares or 45 shares each; to nine daughters 1008 shares or 112 shares each, and to 6 true grand-mothers 252 shares or 42 shares each.

Reprint from Allahabad Law Journal, No. 17 of April 28, 1933.

السراجيه

Al-Sirajiyyah

بسم الله الرحمن الرحيم

In the name of Allah, the Beneficient, the Merciful.

١ - الحمد لله رب العالمين حمد الشاكرين والصلوة والسلام على خير البريه محمد وآله الطيبين الطاهرين قال رسول الله صلى الله عليه وسلم تعلموا الفرائض وعلموها الناس فانها نصف العلم -

1. All praise be to God, the Lord of the Worlds and His blessings and peace be upon the best of the created, Muhammad and His Holy and Sacred Family. The Prophet of Allah (on whom be peace) said, "Yea learn the laws of Inheritance and teach them to men ; they consist of half of the knowledge."

٢ - قال علماؤنا رحمهم الله تعالى تتعلق بتركة الميت حقوق اربعة مرتبة الاول يبدأ بتكفينه وتجهيزه من غير تبذير ولا تقتير ثم تقضى ديونه من جميع ما بقي من

2. Our learned jurists (peace be on them) said :—There are four successive duties concerning the property of a deceased. The first[1] is to commence with the funeral and burial expenses without extravagance, yet without deficiency ; the second is to

[1] Ibrahim Nákhai, answering the question how the estate of a deceased should be dealt with, says, that it shall be commenced with the *kafan* shroud then pay the debts, and next the legacies :—Bukhari. (بخاري) يبدأ بالكفن ثم بالدين ثم بالوصية – هذا قول ابراهيم النخعي

The ordinary *kafan* for a man consists of three pieces of cloth, and if he dies in debts, then of two pieces of cloth only and for a woman it is five pieces of cloth and if she dies in debts, then of three pieces of cloth only. The quality of the shroud should be the same as a person puts on ordinarily, and according to some, the quality of cloth should be that which a man puts on *Id* occasions or on Fridays, and that a woman puts on when she visits her parents. The husband should provide *kafan* for his wife according to the view of Imam Abn Yusuf.

ماله ثم تنفذ وصاياه من
ثلث ما بقي بعد الدين
ثم يقسم الباقي بين ورثته
بالكتاب والسنة واجماع
الامة .

pay his debts[1] from the whole of his remaining property *mal*; the third is to pay legacies[2] out of the legal third of the remaining property, having already paid the debts; the fourth is to distribute the remaining property among the legal representatives of the deceased according to the Qoran, Hadis and Ijma of the Ummat.[3]

٣ - نبدء باصحاب
الفرائض وهم الذين لهم
سهام مقدرة في كتاب الله
تعالي ثم بالعصبات من
جهة النسب والعصبة كل
من ياخذ ما ابقته
اصحاب الفرائض وعند
الانفراد يحرز جميع المال
ثم بالعصبة من جهة السبب
وهو مولي العتاقة ثم عصبته
علي الترتيب ثم الرد علي
ذوي الفروض النسبية بقدر
حقوقهم ثم ذوي الارحام

3. Then we make a beginning with the *ashab faraiz*, the sharers, and they are those persons who have fixed shares assigned to them by the holy Qoran. Then we commence with the *asbat*, the residuaries, the relatives by reason of *nasab* consanguinity. And the *asbat* are those persons who take from the inheritance of what remains after satisfying *the ashab faraiz*, and if they exist alone they take the whole of the *mal*, property. Then comes the *asbat*

---

[1] As regards the debts the secured debts are to be paid first. If the debts exceed the estate they are rateably reduced.

[2] Legacies are to be paid from out of the legal third of the estate and if in excess of the legal third they shall abate in a manner fixed by the Muslim jurists.

[3] The term *ijma ummat* is an elastic term. It is understood by some jurists to mean *ijma* of the people of Medina, by some as *ijma* of the Companions of the Prophet, by some as *ijma* of the descendants of the Prophet, however according to the Hanafi School it means agreement among the learned jurists in a particular age on a question of Law. The term *ummat* means the followers of the Prophet and in this sense it would mean an agreement among all Muslims or at least by the majority of the Muslims.

ثم مولي الموالاة ثم المقرله
بالنسب علي الغير بحيث
لم يثبت نسبه باقراره من
ذالك الغير اذامات المقر
علي اقراره ثم الموصي له
بجميع المال ثم بيت
المال -

by some special reason and that is called *maula-al-ataqa*, the master of an emancipated slave and his residuaries in order. Thereafter we begin with *radd* (that is to return the surplus to sharers in accordance with their rights of inheritance). Thereafter to the *zawil arham*, the distant kindred then to the *maula-i-mawalat*,[1] the successor by contract then to the *Muqirlhu*, kinsman acknowledged through another, not proving his *nasab* (consanguinity) subject to the deceased maintaining his acknowledgement unto his death ;[2] thereafter to the *Musi*, the universal legatee, and lastly to *Bait-ul-mal*, the State Treasury.[3]

---

[1] A person of unknown descent says to another "You are my *maula*, when I die you will inherit my property," and this may be accepted by the other person. Similarly two persons of unknown descent may effect the contract of *mawalat inter se*.

[2] A Muslim acknowledges, a person of unknown descent as his brother or his uncle that is in the former case he assigns the *nasab* of this person towards his father and in the latter to his grandfather. Now the requisite conditions for the person of unknown descent to inherit from the deceased are as follows. The acknowledgment must be as in this case through another person and not through himself and the father or the grandfather must not acknowledge the *nasab* relationship for if they do so the person would inherit not in the capacity of *Muqirlhu* acknowledged kinsman but in the capacity of real brother or uncle, and the next condition is that acknowledgment should not be repudiated but upheld unto the death of the deceased. For if it is repudiated then the acknowledged kinsman can not participate in the inheritance. It may also be noted that in the above example the acknowledged kinsman as brother or uncle can not inherit from the father or grandfather at all. He can only inherit from the person who acknowledged him.

[3] In British India it would escheats to the Crown.

SECTION I

فصل في الموانع

On Impediments

۴ - المانع من الارث اربعة الرق وافرا كان اوناقصا والقتل الذي يتعلق به وجوب القصاص او الكفارة

4. There are four impediments to the right of succession ; (i) Slavery, whether perfect or imperfect ; (ii) and that homicide[1] which is punishable

---

[1] *Homicide.*

The Muslim jurists have classified various kinds of culpable homicide amounting to murder and culpable homicide not amounting to murder. Thus (1) intentional homicide or homicide with malice is known as *qatl-i-amad, e.g.,* a person kills another with a dangerous weapon so that a part of his body is severed from the body, in which case the punishment is death and it also can be compounded on payment of *diyat,* blood-money to his representatives. (2) *Shubh-i-qatl* : this is culpable homicide not amounting to murder or culpable homicide simple (also known as unintentional death) *e.g.,* a person kills another by giving him a slight blow on the head. Here also the case may be compounded on payment of blood-money. (3) *khata,* that is, accidental death: *e g.,* a person shoots an arrow to kill an animal and by chance he kills another man ; here also the case may be compounded on payment of blood-money. (4) ***Jari, majrai-khata*** : it is also a kind of accidental death; *e.g.,* a person falls on another person who is sleeping and kills him. In this case also it may be compounded on payment of blood-money. (5) ***qatl-i-sabab***; this is a case where a person is the indirect cause of another's death, *e.g.,* a person digs a pit and some person falls into it and dies: in this case also there is payment of blood-money. The first four kinds of murders are known as ***Qatl-i-Mubsherat*** direct cases of murder, and in these cases the murderer

واختلاف الدينين واختلاف
الدارين اما حقيقة
كالحربي والامي او حكما

by retaliation or expiation; (iii) difference of religion;[1] (iv) difference of domicile,[2] whether actual as in the

---

cannot inherit but in the fifth case *qatl-i-sabab* under the Hanafi Law (but not the Shafi Law) he can inherit.

In the case of culpable homicide not amounting to murder besides the heavy fine the punishment is expiation, that is, emancipation of a slave or fasting for two months. The prescribed *diyat* consists of one hundred female camels of different ages and it is recoverable from the tribe of the slayer. In the case of intentional homicide the *diyat* is 30 she-camels in the fourth year, 30 she-camels in the fifth year, and 40 pregnant she-camels. In the case of *Khata* the *diyat* is 20 she-camels in the first year, 20 she-camels in the second year, and 20 she-camels in the third year and 20 she-camels in the fourth year and 20 she-camels in the fifth year.

[1] *Difference of Religion.*

A Muslim cannot inherit from a non-Muslim and a non-Muslim cannot inherit from a Muslim. Apostates are capable of inheriting from no one not even from apostates like themselves. The Muslim heirs of an apostate are not deprived of their right of inheritance; but husband and wife cannot inherit from one another in the case of apostacy. But if the wife has apostatised in *mara-zul-maut,* then the husband is not excluded from inheriting from her. Similarly a wife would succeed to her husband, if the husband who has apostatised dies before the expiration of her *iddat,* or he is put to death for his apostaey or he retires into *dar-ul-harab.*

In the British India there is, however no bar to such inheritance since the passing of the Caste Disabilities Removal Act (XXI of 1850).

[2] *Difference of country.*

Zimmis are those state subjects who are non-Muslim and pay a *jazia* tax and are protected by the law. *Harbis* are

كالمستامن والذمي لوالحربيين من دارين مختلفين والدار انما تختلف باختلاف المنعة والملك لانقطاع العصمة فيما بينهم ◦

case of *harbi* (alien enemy) and *zimmi* (non-Muslim subjets), or constructive as in the case of *mustamin* and *zimmi*; or, two *harbis* of different countries; the difference of country arises by reason of allegiance to different powers and kings there being no alliance between them.

---

non-Muslims in general, *i.e*, enemies. *Mustamins* are persons residing in *Da-rul-Islam*, for purposes of trade and commerce, with the permission of the Government of the State (and they would become *Zimmis* after one years residence.)

The question of the right of inheritance of *Zimmis*, *Mustamins* and *Harabis* is interesting purely from an academic point of view. *e.g.* If there is an alien *harabi*, in *Dar-ul-harab* a non-Muslim state, who has his father or son in *Dar-ul-Islam* a Muslim State, then in this case there is difference of country so there is no right of inheritance betecwn the father and son *inter se*.

Similarly if there are two *harabis* of two different states or a *zimmi* and a *mustamin* are related to one another and reside in *Dar-ul-Islam*, yet they have no right of inheritance *inter se* because the *zimmi* is considered by the law to belong to *Dar-ul-Islam* and the *Mustamin* is considered by law to be a member of *Dar-ul-harab* inspite of his actual residence, since he can migrate to to *Dar-ul-harab* at his will. When a *mustamin* dies then his property situated in *Dar-ul-Islam* is given to his relations in *Dar-ul-harab* and will not go to the Public Treasury, *Bait-ul-mal.* On the other hand if a *zimmi* dies leaving no heirs his property is taken by the Treasury. However, there is a right of inheritance *inter se* among *zimmis*, and also between two *mustamins* who have come from one and the same non-Muslim State and are residing in *Dar-ul-Islam*.

CHAPTER I

باب معرفة الفروض
ومستحقيها

On the Rules of Distribution of Shares and persons entitled to it.

٥ - الفروض المقدرة
في كتاب الله تعالي ستة
النصف والربع والثمن
والثلثان والثلث والسدس
علي التضعيف والتنصيف
واصحاب هذه السهام اثنا
عشر نفرا اربعة من الرجال
وهم الاب والجد الصحيح
وهو اب الاب وان علا والاخ
لام والزوج وثمان من
النساء وهن الزوجة والبنت
وبنت الابن وان سفلت
والاخت لاب وام
والاخت لاب والاخت لام
والام والجدة الصحيحة
وهي التي لا يدخل في
نسبتها الي الميت جد
فاسد ـ

5. The holy Koran has fixed six shares: $\frac{1}{2}$, $\frac{1}{4}$, $\frac{1}{8}$, $\frac{2}{3}$, $\frac{1}{3}$ and $\frac{1}{6}$, formed by doubling and halving. These shares are assigned to twelve persons, out of them there are four males, *viz.*, father, true grandfather, that is, father of the father, how high so ever, half-brother by mother, (uterine brother) and the husband; and there are eight females, *viz.*, wife daughter, son's daughter, how low so ever, sister by the same father and mother, and half-sister by father (consanguine sister), half-sister by mother (uterine sister), mother, and true grandmother, that is a female ancestor between whom and the deceased no false grandfather intervenes.

٦ - اما الاب فله احوال
ثلث الفرض المطلق وهو
السدس وذالک مع الابن
او ابن الابن وان سفل
والفرض والتعصيب معا

6. For the father there are three cases[1]: (i) He takes a mere share of one sixth, along with the son or son's son how low so ever; (ii) he is a sharer and a residuary both

[1] Father is excluded by none.

وذالک مع الابنة اوابنة الابن وان سلفت والتعصيب المحض وذالک عند عدم الولد وولد الابن وان سفل -

when he exists with the daughter or son's daughter how low so ever ; (iii) he becomes a pure residuary in case there is no child or sons child, how low so ever.

٧ - و الجد الصحيح كالاب الا في اربع مسائل وسنذكرها في مواضعها ان شاء الله تعالي ويسقط الجد بالاب لان الاب اصل في قرابة الجد الي الميت والجد الصحيح هو الذي لاتدخل في نسبته الي الميت ام -

7. The true grandfather inherits like the father except in four cases ; God willing we shall speak about them later on. The grandfather is excluded by the father, because the father is the mean of relationship between the grandfather and the deceased. And the true grandfather is that male ancestor between whom and the deceased no female intervenes.[1]

٨ - واما لاولاد الام فاحوال ثلث السدس للواحد والثلث للاثنين فصاعدا ذكورهم واناثهم في القسمة والاستحقاق سواء ويسقطون بالولد وولد الابن وان سفل وبالاب والجد بالاتفاق -

8. For the mother's children (uterine brothers and sisters) there are three cases, (i) the share of one of them is one-sixth only, (ii) when two or more it is one-third, the male and female having equal right of inheritence and inheriting equally, (iii) they are excluded by the child, son's children, how so ever, and also by the father, and grandfather according to all jurists.

٩ - واما للزوج فحالتان النصف عند عدم الولد وولد الابن وان سفل والربع مع الولد او ولد الابن وان سفل -

9. For the husband there are two cases : (i) He takes one-half share when there are no children or son's children how low so ever, and (ii) he takes one-fourth share with children or son's children how low so ever.

---

[1] This definition is not found in Sir William Jone's translation of the Sirajiyyah.

CHAPTER II

On Women

فصل في النساء

١٠ - اما الزوجات فحالتان الربع للواحدة فصاعدة عند عدم الولد وولد الابن وان سفل والثمن مع الولد او ولد الابن وان سفل

10. For the wives there are **two** cases : (i) the share of one or **more** of them is one-fourth in the absence of children, how low so ever, (ii) and she or they take one-eighth with children or son's children how low so ever.

١١ - واما البنات الصلب فاحوال ثلث النصف للواحدة والثلثان للاثنتين فصاعدة ومع الابن للذكر مثل حظ الانثيين وهو يعصبهن -

11. For the daughters of the deceased there are three cases :—(i) if alone, one-half ; (ii) for two or more, two-thirds ; (iii) if there is a son, the male will take the share of two females and will convert them into residuaries.

١٢ - وبنات الابن كبنات الصلب ولهن احوال ست النصف للواحدة والثلثان للاثنتين فصاعدة عند عدم بنات الصلب ولهن السدس مع الواحدة الصلبية تكملة للثلثين ولا يرثن مع الصلبيتين إلا ان يكون بحذائهن او اسفل منهن غلام فيعصبهن والباقي بينهم للذكر مثل حظ الانثيين ويسقطن بالابن ولو ترك ثلث بنات ابن بعضهن اسفل من بعض

12. Son's daughters are treated like the deceased's own daughters and for them there are six cases :—(i) if alone, one-half, (ii) if two or more, two-thirds, provided there are no daughters of the deceased ; (iii) for the son's daughters the share is one-sixth if they exist with a single daughter of the deceased, (iv) they are excluded by two daughters of the deceased, (v) except when a son's son, how low so ever converts them into residuaries. In that case the male takes the double share of a female,

2

وثلث بنات ابن ابن
آخر بعضهن اسفل من
بعض وثلث بنات ابن
ابن ابن اخر بعضهن
اسفل من بعض بهذه الصورة -

(vi) and they are excluded by the son. Suppose a person leaves three son's daughters, some of them in lower degrees than the other, and he also leaves three son's daughters of another son, some in lower degrees than the others, and also leaves three son's daughters of another son's son, as in the following illustration.

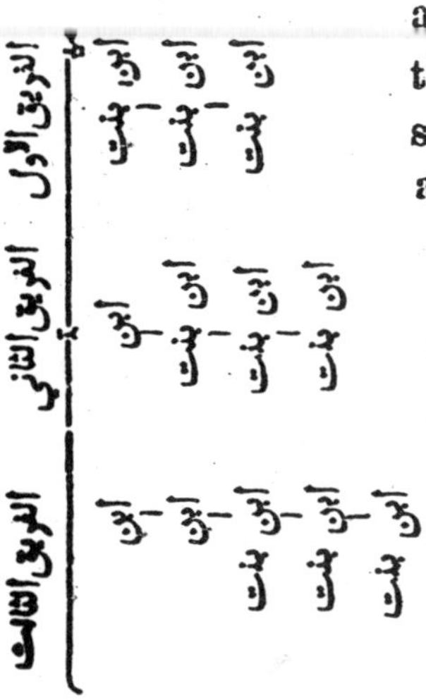

DIAGRAM

First Group	Second Group	Third Group
Son, daughter (A)	Son	Son
Son, daughter (B)	Son, daughter (C)	Son
Son, daughter (D)	Son, daughter (E)	Son, daughter (F)
	Son, daughter (G)	Son, daughter (H)
		Son, daughter (I)

١٣ - العليا من
الفريق الاول لايوازيها احد
والوسطي من الفريق الاول
توازيها العليا من الفريق
الثاني والسفلي من الفريق
الاول توازيها الوسطي من
الفريق الثاني والعليا من
الفريق الثالث والسفلي من
الفريق الثاني توازيها الوسطي
من الفريق الثالث
والسفلي من الفريق
الثالث لايوازيها احد
اذا عرفت هذا
فنقول للعليا من الفريق
الاول النصف وللوسطي
من الفريق الاول مع من
يوازيها السدس تكملة للثلثين

13. In the above example, the first daughter, A, in the first group has none equal in degree; the middle daughter, B, of the first group is equal in degree to the first daughter, C, of the second group; and the last daughter, D, of the first group is equal to the middle daughter, E, of the second group and also to the first daughter, F, of the third group; the last daughter, G, of the second group is equal to the middle daughter, H, of the third group; and the last daughter, I, of the third group has no equal in degree at all. When you have understood this then we observe that the first daughter, A,

ولشي للسافلات الا ان
يكون معهن غلام فيعصبهن
من كانت بحذائه ومن
كانت فوقه ممن لم تكن
ذات سهم ويسقط من
دونه -

will receive one-half share; and the middle one B of the first group has one-sixth share together with her equal in degree C, thus making up two-thirds; but those in lower degrees would take nothing unless there is a son with them who would convert them and all those daughters who are above him (who have got no share otherwise) into residuaries; but those daughters who are below him would be excluded.

١٤ - واما الاخوات لاب
وام فاحوال خمس النصف
للواحدة والثلثان للاثنتين
فصاعدة ومع الاخ لاب وام
للذكر مثل حظ الانثيين
يصرن به عصبة لستوائهم
في القرابة الى الميت ولهن
الباقي مع البنات او بنات
الابن لقوله عليه السلام
اجعلوا الاخوات مع البنات
عصبة -

14. For sisters by the same father and mother there are five cases:[1] (i) half is the share of one; (ii) two-thirds for two or more and (iii) if there is brother by the same father and mother, the male will take the share of two females, *i.e.*, the sister would become a residuary along with the brother by reason of being equal in degree in relationship to the deceased; (iv) and the residue is for them if they co-exist with daughters or with son's daughters; as held by the Prophet (on Him be peace) "Make sisters residuaries with daughters."[2]

---

[1] The author of the Sirajiyyah has only mentioned here four cases, he has mentioned the fifth case in the seventh case of consanguine sisters *vide* para 15.

[2] This tradition, " make sisters residuaries with daughters " is supported by a case decided by Huzail and Ibn Masud separately,

١٥ - ه. والاخوات
لاب كالاخوات لاب وام
ولهن احوال سبع النصف
للواحدة والثلثان للاثنتين
فصاعدة عند عدم الاخوات
لاب وام ولهن السدس
مع الاخت لاب وام تكملة
للثلثين ولا يرثن مع الاختين
لاب وام الا ان يكون
معهن اخ لاب فيعصبهن
والباقي بينهم للذكر مثل
حظ الانثيين والسادسة ان
يصرن عصبة مع البنات
او بنات الابن لما ذكرنا -
وبنوا الاعيان والعلات
كلهم يسقطون بالابن
وابن الابن وان سفل
وبالاب بالاتفاق وبالجد
عند ابي حنيفة رحمه الله
ويسقط بنو العلات ايضا
بالاخ لاب وام وبالاخت
لاب وام اذا صارت
عصبة -

15. Sisters by the same father are like sisters by the same father and mother and there are seven cases for them: (i) half is the share of one (ii) two-thirds for two or more provided there are no sisters by the same father and mother (full sisters), (iii) if they co-exist with one sister by the same father and mother they have a sixth to make up the maximum two-thirds, (iv) they are excluded by the existence of two sisters by the same father and mother (v) unless they co-exist with a consanguine brother who would convert them into residuaries; and then the residue will be distributed among them, the male member taking the share of two females, and (vi) the consanguine sisters will be residuaries with daughters or with son's daughters as stated above. (vii) Full brothers and sisters and consanguine brothers and sisters are all excluded by the son and the son's son how low so ever, and by the father as agreed by all the jurists and also by the grandfather as held by Imam Abu Hanifa[1] and

---

in confirmity with it. This is also the view of Zaid, Umar and Ali but Ibn-i-Abbas differs from it.

A person leaves the following heirs.

Daughter	=	1/2 — 3/6
Son's daughter	=	1/6 — 1/6
Sister	=	... 2/6 as residuary

[1] For full discussion *vide* p. 19.

consangiune brothers and sisters are excluded by full brothers and also by full sisters provided the latter take as residuaries.[1]

١٦ - واما للام فاحوال
ثلث السدس مع الولد او
ولد الابن وان سفل او
مع الاثنين من الاخوة
والاخوات فصاعداً من اي
جهة كانا وثلث الكل عند
عدم هؤلاء المذكورين وثلث
ما يبقى بعد فرض احد
الزوجين وذالك في
مسألتين زوج وابوين
وزوجة وابوين ولوكان
مكان الاب جد فللام ثلث
جميع المال الا عند ابي
يوسف رحمه الله فان لها
ثلث الباقي -

16. And for the mother there are three cases: (i) She takes one-sixth with a child or with son's child how low so ever or with two or[2] more brothers or sisters whether full or half-blood, (ii) and one-third of the whole property if the above mentioned relations do not exist [3], (iii) after giving shares to the husband or wife for the mother there is a third of the residue in the following two cases, when there co-exists a husband with both parents or the wife with both parents. And if there exists a grandfather instead of a father the mother takes a third of the whole property; but according to Imam Abu Yusuf (peace be on him) mother takes one-third of the residue.[4]

---

[1] The last sentence is not found in Sir William Jones translation of the Sirajiyyah.

[2] And whether the full brothers and sisters inherit or are excluded.

[3] *i.e.*, when there is no child or son's child how low so ever or two or more brothers and sisters.

[4]

I.	Widow	...	1/4		1/4
	Mother	...	1/4 (1/3 of 3/4)	(as residuary)	1/4
	Father	...	1/2 (2/3 of 3/4)	(as residuary)	2/4
II.	Husband	...	1/2		3/6
	Mother	...	1/6 (1/3 of 1/2)	(as residuary)	1/6
	Father	...	1/3 (2/3 of 1/2)	(as residuary)	2/6
III.	Widow	...	1/4		3/12
	Mother	...	1/3		4/12
	Father's father	...	5/12 (as residuary)		5/12

١٧ - وللجدة السدس لام كانت اولاب واحدة كانت اواكثر اذاكن ثابتات متحاذيات في الدرجة ويسقطن كلهن بالام و الابويات ايضاً بالاب وكذالك بالجد الا ام الاب وان علت فانها ترث مع الجد لانها ليست من قبله والقربي من اي جهة كانت تحجب البعدي من اي جهة كانت وارثة كانت القربي او محجوبة واذا كانت الجدة ذات قرابة واحدة كام ام الاب والاخري ذات قرابتين اواكثر كام ام الام وهي ايضاً ام اب الاب بهذه الصورة

17. For the grandmother there is a sixth whether she is related to the mother or to the father and whether alone or two or more provided they are true grandmothers of equal degree, and they shall be excluded by the mother, and the paternal grandmothers are excluded by the father and similarly they will be excluded by the grandfather; but the father's mother how high so ever would inherit with the grandfather since she is not connected through him; and the nearest true grandmother, whether paternal or maternal, would exclude the distant grandmother paternal or maternal, whether she (the nearer true grandmother) was entitled to inherit or is excluded. When the true grandmother has a single rela-

---

IV.	Husband	...	1/2	3/6
	Mother	...	1/3	2/6
	Father's father	...	1/6 (as residuary)	1/6

The above two cases (III and IV) of the mother co-existing with the father's father, in one case with the widow and in the other case with the husband are decided in accordance with the opinion of Abu Bakr, the first Khalifa and as finally held by Imam Abu Hanifa and Imam Muhammad. But comparing the first two cases with the last two it will be seen that the grandfather has not been treated like the father as is the general rule. The share of the mother when she co-exists with the father is half of the share of the father; but when she co-exists with the grandfather she takes her legal share one-third.

tionship *e.g.*, father's mother's mother and the other grandmother has two or more such relationship *e.g.*, as the mother's mother's mother, and also as father's father's mother as in the following case.

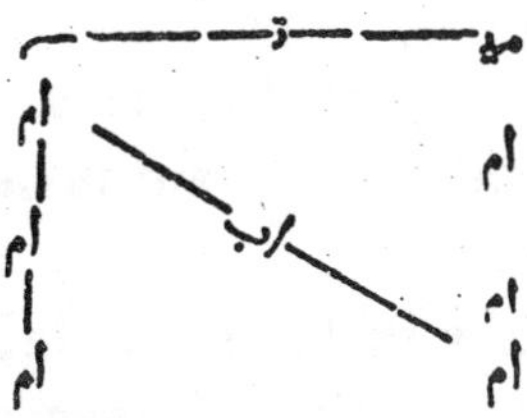

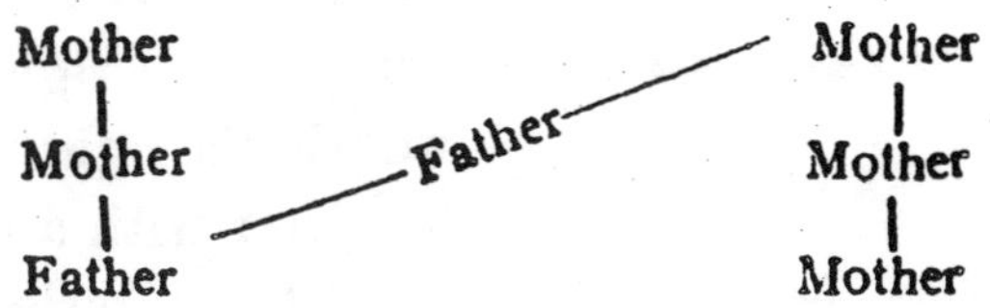

يقسم السدس بينهما عند ابي يوسف رحمه الله انصافا باعتبار الابدان وعند محمد رحمه الله اثلاثا باعتبار الجهات ۔

Here one-sixth is divided between them as stated by Imam Abu Yusuf (peace be on him) equally by reason of their persons, *abdan*, but according to Imam Muhammad (peace be on him), division will be in thirds by reason of their sides *jihat*.[1]

---

[1] The Fatawa accords with the view of Abu Yusuf.

[2] In a case of cousins' marriage, the same grandmother may be the wife's maternal grandmother and the husband's paternal grandmother and *vice versa*. The double relationship may be seen from the following example given in the Sharifa.

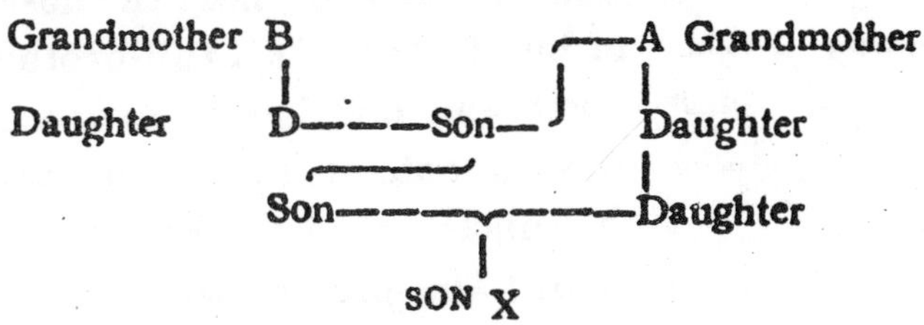

A's daughter's daughter marries A's Son's Son and they have a child X, and previously B's daughter had married A's Son. Here A is the paternal grandmother of X, and maternal grandmother of X and so is doubly related. B is X's paternal grandmother's mother and has a single relationship.

CHAPTER III

باب العصبات

On Residuaries

١٨ - العصبات النسبية ثلثة عصبة بنفسه وعصبة بغيره وعصبة مع غيره -

18. There are three kinds of residuaries by *nasb*: (i) residuaries in their own right, (ii) residuaries in another's right, and (iii) residuaries together with another.

١٩ - اما العصبة بنفسه فكل ذكر لا تدخل في نسبته الي الميت انثي وهم اربعة اصناف جزء الميت و اصله وجزء ابيه وجزء جده الاقرب فالاقرب يرجحون بقرب الدرجة اعني اولهم بالميراث جزء الميت اي البنون ثم بنوهم وان سفلوا ثم اصله اي الاب ثم الجد اي اب الاب وان علا ثم جزء ابيه اي الاخوة ثم بنوهم وان سفلوا ثم جزء جده اي الاعمام ثم بنوهم وان سفلوا ثم يرجحون بقوة القرابة اعني به ان ذا القرابتين اولي من ذي قرابة واحدة ذكراً كان او انثي لقوله عليه السلام ان اعيان بني الام يتوارثون دون بني العلات كالاخ لاب وام او الاخت لاب وام اذا صارت عصبة

19. A residuary in his own right is every male in whose line of descent to the deceased no female intervenes and there are four classes of these: (*a*) the descendents of the deceased, (*b*) and his "root", (*c*) and descendents of his father (*d*) and that of the grandfather, preference being given to the nearer in degree. In short, first come the deceased's descendents, *i.e*, his sons, then his grandsons how low so ever, then his root *i.e.*, his father, then his paternal grandfather *i e.*, his father's father how high so ever; next the descendents of his father, *i.e.*, full-brothers then their sons how low so ever; next the descendents of the grandfather, *i.e.*, his uncles, then their sons how low so ever; the preference shall be given by the strength of relationship, that is preference is given to one having double relationship over one having single relationship, whether male or

مع البنت اولى من الاخ
لاب و ابن الاخ لاب وام
لاب وام اولى من ابن الاخ
لاب وكذالك الحكم في
اعمام الميت ثم في اعمام
ابيه ثم في اعمام جده ٥

female as observed by the Prophet (on whom be peace): "Relations by the same father and mother shall be preferred to relations by the same father only.[1]" A sister by the same father and mother, as a residuary with the daughter will be preferred to a brother or sister by the father only; and the son of the brother by the same father and mother will be preferred to the son of the consanguine brother and same is applicable in the case of paternal uncles of the deceased and also in the case of the paternal uncles of grandfather of the deceased

٢٠ - واما العصبة بغيره
فاربع من النسوة وهن
اللاتي فرضهن النصف
والثلثان يصرن عصبة
باخوتهن كما ذكرنا في
حالاتهن ومن لا فرض لها
من الاناث واخوها عصبة
لا تصير عصبة باخيها كالعم
والعمة المال كله للعم دون
العمة

20. Residuaries in another's right are four females:[2] they are those whose shares are half and two-thirds; and they become residuaries along with the brothers as stated in their cases. But when she takes no share among females and her brother is a residuary, then she can not become a residuary in his right, *i.e.* in the case of paternal uncle and paternal aunt, the whole property is for the uncle and there is nothing for the aunt.[3]

---

1 *i.e.* A full brother is preferred to a consanguine brother.

2 Namely daughter, son's daughter, full sister, and consanguine sister.

3 The last line is not found in Sir William Jones' translation of the Sirajiyyah. Similarly the daughter of the full uncle or

٢١ - واما العصبة مع غيره فكل انثي تصير عصبة مع انثي اخري كالاخت مع البنت لما ذكرنا

21. Residuaries together with another is a female who becomes a residuary with another female, *e.g.* a sister[1] with a daughter as stated above.

٢٢ وآخر العصبات مولي العتاقة ثم عصبته علي الترتيب الذي ذكرنا لقوله عليه السلام الولاء لحمة كلحمة النسب

22. The last residuary is *maula atuqa*,[2] and then his heirs in a fixed order as stated before, as held by the Prophet (on him be peace and blessings) "The master has a relationship similar to that of blood relationship."

N.B.—Some subsequent passages of this chapter deal with the right of inheritance of the master and the slave, so they have been omitted. The institution of slavery was abolished in British India by Act V of 1843, hence the Muslim law has become obsolete.

---

consanguine uncle will take nothing when co-existing with the son of the full uncle, as also in the case of the brother's daughter co-existing with the brother's son.

[1] Full sister and half sister by the father.

[2] Maula-i-Ataqa is the master of an emancipated slave.

باب الحجب

CHAPTER IV

Exclusion

٢٣ - الحجب على
نوعين حجب نقصان وهو
عن سهم الى سهم
آخر وذالك لخمسة نفر
للزوجين والام وبنت الابن
والاخت لاب وقد مربيانه

23. There are two kinds of exclusions : *Hajab nuqsan*; partial exclusion, that is an exclusion from a share, *siham* and an admission to a smaller *siham*; it appertains to five persons, namely, husband, wife, mother, son's daughter and consanguine sister, and we have discussed it.

٢٤ - وحجب حرمان
والورثة فيه فريقان فريق
لا يحجبون بحال البتة
وهم ستة الابن والاب والزوج
والبنت والام والزوجة و
فريق يرثون بحال و
يحجبون بحال وهذا
مبني على اصلين احدهما
هو ان كل من يدلي
الى الميت بشخص لايرث
مع وجود ذالك الشخص
سوى اولاد الام فانهم يرثون
معها لانعدام استحقاقها
جميع التركة والثاني الاقرب
فالاقرب كما ذكرنا في

24. *Hajab hirman*, absolute exclusion: there are two classes of heirs, one of which is not excluded at all, and they are six in number, *viz.*, son, father, husband, daughter, mother, and wife, and the other class is such that under certain circumstances they inherit and under certain circumstances they are excluded.[1] The law of exclusion is based on two rules, one of which is that a person who is related to the deceased through another person shall not inherit while that person is alive, one exception is that the children of the

1 Sharers liable to be excluded are: true grandmother, true grandfather, son's daughter, full sister, consanguine sister, uterine brother, and uterine sister.

العصبات والمحروم
لايحجب عندنا وعند ابن
مسعود رضي الله عنه
يحجب حجب النقصان
كالكافر والقاتل والرقيق
والمحجوب يحجب
بالاتفاق كالاثنين من الاخوة
والاخوات فصاعداً من اي
جهة كانا فانهما لايرثان مع
الاب ولكن يحجبان الام
من الثلث الي السدس -

mother may inherit along with her, because she is not entitled to the whole inheritance. The second rule is that the nearer in blood succeeds in preference, and we have already discussed it in the chapter on residuaries. A person who is *mahroom*, incapable of inheriting, cannot exclude another as held by our jurists; but according to *Ibn Masood* (peace be on him) he can exclude partially *e.g.*, a non-Muslim, a murderer, and *raqiq* (slave).[1] But a person excluded may exclude other heirs according to all jurists *e.g.*, two or more brothers, and sisters whether full or consanguine cannot inherit with the father of the deceased, yet they partially exclude the mother from a third share to a sixth.[2]

---

[1] Wife 1/4
Father 3/4 as residuary

Son (non-Muslim) excluded under the Muslim Law, so the wife take 1/4 instead of 1/8. Under Anglo-Muslim Law the non-Muslim son cannot be excluded on account of Act XXI of 1850.

[2] Mother = 1/6
Father = 5/6 as residuary
Two sisters = excluded by the father, but they reduce the share of the mother from 1/3 to 1/6. If there were no sisters the mother would take 1/3 and the father 2/3.

CHAPTER V

Common Denominator of Fractions of Shares

باب مخارج الفروض

25. Learn yea, that the sharers[1] stated in the Qoran are of two kinds: of the first 1/2, 1/4, and 1/8 and of the second 2/3, 1/3, and 1/6, by

٢٥ - اعلم ان الفروض
المذكورة فى كتاب الله
تعالي نوعان الاول النصف
والربع والثمن والثاني

[1] The fixed shares are 1/2 1/4, 1/8 ; 2/3 1/3 1/6. They may come one by one or jointly, in the first case *asl i masala* is their denominator; when they come jointly *asl i masala* will be the least common multiple of the denominators. Therefore all the possible denominators of the shares into which the property is actually or at least is originally divisible are: 2, 3, 4, 6, 8, 12, and 24.

ILLUSTRATIONS

Makhraj 2	*Makhraj 4*	*Makhraj 8*
Husband = 1/2	Husband = 1/4	Wife = 1/8
Sister = 1/2	Son = 3/4	Son = 7/8

Makhraj 3	*Makhraj 3* Share 2/3	*Makhraj 6*
Mother = 1/3	2 Sisters = 2/3	Father = 1/6
Brother = 2/3	Uncle = 1/3	Mother = 1/6
		Son = 4/6

way of doubling and halving.[1] Thus if these shares occur in any case one by one then the *makhraj*, denominator, is that by which the share derives its name *e.g.*, a half[1] whose *makhraj* is 2 and a fourth whose *makhraj* is 4, and an eighth whose *makhraj* is 8 and a third whose

الثلثان والثلث والسدس
على التضعيف والتنصيف
فاذا جاء في المسائل من
هذه الفروض احاد احاد
فمخرج كل فرض سميه
الا النصف وهو من اثنين
كالربع من اربعة والثمن
من ثمانية والثلث من

Now it is possible to have combination of any of these fractions *inter se* with one another, *e.g.*, 1/2, and 1/4, 1/2 and 1/8, 1/2 and 1/6, 1/2 and 1/3, etc.

The following chart represent the *makhraj* in various cases.

Makhraj	2	4	8	3	6
2	2	4	8	6	6
4	4	4	8	12	12
8	8	8	8	24*	24
3	6	12	24	3	6
6	6	12	24	6	6

*This case is not possible under the Hanafi Law with 1/3 share but is possible with 2/3 shares.

1 The Arabic phrase is, "الا النصف وهو من اثنين" that is excepting half; the expression is due to the peculiarity of the language, that the denominator of 2 is called *isnain* and not *nisf*. The literal translation becomes ambiguous *vide* Sir William Jones' translation of Al-Sirajiyyah.

ثلثة واذاجاء مثني او ثلث وهما من نوع واحد *makhraj* is 3, but if these fractions occur by two or three, at a time[1] and

[1] Similarly it is possible to have the combination of 1/2, 1/4 and 1/8 with 2/3, 1/3 and 1/6, or with any two of these, the following chart illustrates all these cases, and some of these cases are subject to the doctrine of Increase *'awl*, which is discussed in the next chapter.

When with	1/2	*Makhraj*	1/4	*Makh raj*	1/8	*Makh-raj.*
1/3, 2/3 and 1/6	Husband =1/2=3/6=3/10 Mother =1/6=1/6=1/10 2 full sisters =2/3=4/6=4/6 2 uterine sisters =1/3=2/6=2/10 —— 10/6	6 increased by *'awl* to 10.	Wife =1/4=3/12=3/17 Mother =1/6=2/12=2/17 2 full sisters =2/3=8/12=8/17 2 uterine sisters =1/3=4/12=4/17 —— 17/12	12 increased by *'awl* to 17.	Such a case is not possible under the Hanafi Law.*	24
1/3 and 2/3	Husband =1/2=3/6=3/9 2 full sisters =2/3=4/6=4/9 2 uterine sisters =1/3=2/6=2/9 —— 9/6	6 increased by *'awl* to 7.	Wife =1/4=3/12=3/15 2 full sisters =2/3=8/12=8/15 2 uterine sisters =1/3=4/12=4/15 —— 15/12	12 increased by *'awl* to 15.	Case is not possible under the Hanafi Law.*	24

*According to Ibn Masud such cases are possible as he holds that 'mahrum,' absolute excluder, can partially exclude an heir. (vide, p 135 f. n.)

فكل عدد يكون مخرجاً they happen to be of the same kind
لجزء فذالك العدد ايضاً then the denominator of one is the

[1] Similarly it is possible to have the combination of 1/2, 1/4 and 1/8 with 2/3, 1/3 and 1/6, or with any two of these, the following chart illustrates all these cases, and some of these cases are subject to the doctrine of Increase *'awl*, which is discussed in the next chapter.—*concld.*

When with	1/2	*Makhraj*	1/4	*Makhraj*	1/8	*Makhraj.*
2/3 and 1/6	Husband =1/2=3/6=3/8 Mother =1/6=1/6=1/8 2 full sisters =2/3=4/6=4/8 —— 8/6	6 increased by *'awl* to 8.	Wife =1/4=3/12=3/13 Mother =1/6=2/12=2/13 2 full sisters =2/3=8/12=8/13 —— 13/12	12 increased by *'awl* to 13.	Wife =1/8=3/24 Mother =1/6=4/24 2 Daughters =2/3=16/24 Brother =1/24	24
1/3 and 1/6	Husband =1/2=3/6 2 uterine sisters =1/3=2/6 True grand-mother =1/6=1/6	6	Wife =1/4=3/12 2 uterine sisters =1/3=6/12 True grand-mother =1/6=3/12 Residue 2/6, 2/3 of 3/4=6/12=2/4 1/6, 1/3 of 3/4=3/12=1/4	12 or in this case it is 4.	Case is not possible under the Hanafi Law.*	24

*This case is possible according to Ibn Masud.

يكون مخرجاً لضعف ذالك
الجزء ولضعف ضعفه
كالستة هي مخرج السدس
ولضعفه ولضعف ضعفه واذا
اختلط النصف من الاول
بكل الثاني اوببعضه فهو
من ستة واذا اختلط الربع
بكل الثاني اوببعضه فهو
من اثني عشر واذا
اختلط الثمن بكل الثاني
او ببعضه فهو من اربعة
وعشرين -

denominator of its twice and thrice the number, *e.g.*, 6 is the denominator of 1/6 and so is of its double *i.e.* 1/3 and also of the double of that *i.e.* 2/3; but if half belonging to the first class is mixed with all or some of the second class then the denominator must be 6, and when a fourth is mixed with all or some of the second class then the denominator must be 12, and when a eighth is mixed with all or some of the second class then the denominator must be 24.[1]

---

1 The following diagram illustrates the combination of various fractions.

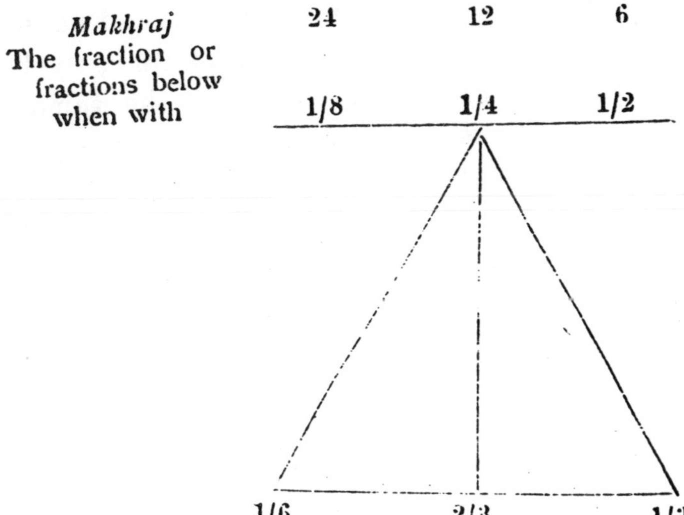

i.e., 1/6, 1/8 ... *Makhraj* 24
1/6, 2/3, 1/8 ... „ 24
1/6, 2/3, 1/3, 1/8 ... „ 24 (case actually not possible *vide*, p. 131.)

etc., etc etc.,

CHAPTER VI

Increase, *'awl*

باب العول

26. The doctrine of *awl* is to increase the *makhraj*, denominator, when it fails to admit the shares.[1] Learn yea that the denominators are seven, and four of which are not liable to be increased *viz.*, 2, 3, 4 and 8, and three of them are liable to be increased: thus the denominator 6 may be increased upto 10, by odd or even numbers;[2] 12 is increased up to 17 by odd and not by even numbers; and 24 can only be increased to 27 as in the famous example known as *mimbariya*,[3] where a man left a wife, two daughters and his both parents. In

٦٢ - العول لن يزاد علي المخرج من اجزائه اذا ضاق عن فرض اعلم ان مجموع المخارج سبعة اربعة منها لاتعول وهي الاثنان و الثلثة و الاربعة و الثمانية و ثلثة منها قد تعول اما الستة فانها تعول الى عشرة وتراً و شفعاً و اما اثنا عشر فهي تعول الى سبعة عشر وترا لا شفعا و اما اربعة و عشرون فانها تعول الى سبعة و عشرين عولاً واحداً كما في

---

1 When the sum total of numerators exceed the denominator. The doctrine of increase operates by increasing the denominator of the fractions to the sum total of all the numerators, thus each share is reduced.

2 6 is increased to 7, 8, 9, 10; 12 is increased to 13, 15, or 17; For illustrations *vide* pp. 34-35.

3 The case is known as *mimbariya* as it was answered by Ali from the pulpit.

Wife ...	1/8	=	3/24	reduced to	3/27
2 Daughters...	2/3	=	16/24	„	16/27
Father ...	1/6	=	4/24	„	4/27
Mother ...	1/6	=	4/24	„	4/27
			27/24		1

المسئلة المنبرية وهي امراة و بنتان و ابوان و لا يزاد على هذا الا عند ابن مسعود رضي الله عنه فان عنده تعول الي احد و ثلثين -

no case 24 can be increased beyond 27 except according to the view of Ibn masud it can be increased to 31.[1]

فصل في معرفة التماثل و التداخل و التوافق و التباين بين العددين

SECTION II

Numbers, equal, multiple, having common factor, and prime to one another

٢٧ - تماثل العددين كون احدهما مساويا للاخر و تداخل العددين المختلفين ان يعد اقلهما الاكثر اي يفنيه

27. The *tamasul* or equality of two numbers denotes, the actual equality of one to the other;[2] the *tadakhul* or concordant of two numbers means that the smaller of the

---

[1] *e.g.*, a man leaves a wife, his mother, 2 full sisters, 2 uterine sisters and a *mahrum* son (incapable of inheriting for some reasons). In this problem the difference between Ibn Masud and other jurists is this, that according to the former the *mahrum* son reduces the share of the wife from 1/4 to 1/8 and so *makhraj* is increased to 31.

Wife	... 1/8 =	3/24	reduced to	3/31
Mother	... 1/6 =	4/24		4/31
2 Full sisters	... 2/3 =	16/24		16/31
2 Uterine sisters	... 1/3 =	8/24		8/31
		31/24		1

[2] *e.g.*, 3=3, 4=4. The *tamasul addadain* are equal numbers, so called because they agree and leave no fraction when one is divided by the other.

او نقول هو ان يكون اكثر العددين منقسماً على الاقل قسمة صحيحة او نقول هو ان يزيد على الاقل مثله او امثاله فيساوي الاكثر او نقول هو ان يكون الاقل جزء الاكثر مثل ثلثة و تسعة و توافق العددين ان لايعد اقلهما الاكثر ولكن يعدها عدد ثالث كالثمانية مع العشرين تعد هما اربعة فهما متوافقان بالربع لان العدد العاد لهما مخرج لجزء الوفق و تباين العددين ان لايعد العددين معاً عدد ثالث كالتسعة مع العشرة -

two exactly divides the other,[1] or we may say *tadakhul* implies that if we multiply the smaller number by a certain number it will become the greater number.[2] *e.g.* 3 and 9. The *tawafuq* (composite) of two numbers denotes that the smaller can not divide the greater but that the smaller and greater are both divisible by a third common factor;[3] *e.g.* 8 and 20 are divisable by four. The *Tabayun*[4] of two numbers denotes that no number divides such two different numbers *e.g.*, 9 and 10.

---

[1] *e.g.*, 2 and 4; 3 and 6; 2 divides 4 and 3 divides 6 equally.

[2] *e.g.*, 3 can be increased to 6; 3 can be increased to 12 and so on.

[3] *e.g.* Such numbers as 8 and 12 are called *mutawafiq*. $8=4\times2$ and $12=4\times3$. In these equations 4 is termed as *juz mushtamil* (common factor) and the number 2 in the first equation and the number 3 in the second are termed *wafq*, factors. Similaly in the case of 8, and 20, $4\times2=8$ and $4\times5=20$; here 4 is the common factor.

[4] They have no common factor nor can one divide the other. That is we find there is no greatest common measure except if at all, it is the number one, then such numbers are *mutabyin*.

٢٨ و طريق معرفة الموافقة و المباينة بين العددين المختلفين ان ينقص من الاكثر بمقدار الاقل من الجانبين مرة او مرارا حتى اتفقا في درجة واحدة فان اتفقا في واحد فلا وفق بينهما و ان اتفقا في عدد فهما متوافقان بذلك العدد ففي الاثنين بالنصف و في الثلاثة بالثلث و في الاربعة بالربع هكذا الي العشرة وفي ماوراء العشرة يتوافقان بجزء منه اعني في احد عشر بجزء من احد عشروفي خمسة عشر بجزء من خمسة عشر فاعتبر هذا –

28. The mode of distinguishing *tawafuq* between two different numbers is that the greater number is diminished by the smaller number once or more often until there remains the number one then such numbers are not *mutawafiq*; however if there remains any other number then they are said to be *mutawafiq* to that number, *e.g.*, 2 in 1/2, 3 in 1/3, 4 in 1/4, and so on till 10 and above 10 they would agree in a fraction *i.e.*, in 11 by the fraction of 11 and in 15 by the fraction of 15 and you may use this rule accordingly.[1]

---

[1] *E.g.*, $2 \times 2 = 4$ and $2 \times 5 = 10$; the common factor 2 divides both of them hence they are known as *tawafuq* by 2. Similarly in the case of 8 and 18; $2 \times 9 = 18$, and $2 \times 4 = 8$; so it is *tawafuq* by 2. As regards 8, and 12 they will be *tawafuq* by 4 and so on.

Tawafuq by 11 would be in the case of 22 and 33 as 11 divides them equally; *tawafuq* by 13 would be in the case of 26 and 39 as 13 divides them equally; 12 would divide 24 and 36 and so on. *Tawafuq* by 15 would be in the case of 30 and 45, it divides them equally.

The *wafq* factor is the factor other than the common factor in respect of any 2 numbers, *e.g.*, in the case of 8 and 20 $2 \times 4 = 8$ and $5 \times 4 = 20$, here 4 is the common factor and the *wafq* factors are 2 and 5 respectively.

CHAPTER VII

باب التصحيح

Tashih Process of Distribution[1]

٢٩ يحتاج في تصحيح المسائل الى سبعة اصول ثلثة بين السهام و الرؤس و اربعة بين الرؤس و الرؤس –

29. For *tashih*, process of distribution of shares without fraction there are seven rules: Three of these rules appertain to *siham*, and *rous*, (the shares and the number of heirs) and four rules are related to *rous* and *rous* (the number of heirs and heirs.)

٣٠ اما الثلثة فاحدها ان كانت سهام كل فريق منقسمة عليهم بلا كسر فلا حاجة الي الضرب كابوين و بنتين –

30. One of the three rules is that if the shares are equally distributed among the heirs without leaving fraction then there is no necessity of applying the rule of *zarb* multiplication, *e.g.*, a person leaves his both parents and two daughters[2]

٣١ و الثاني أن انكسر على طائفة واحدة ولكن بين سهامهم ورؤسهم موافقة فيضرب وفق عدد رؤس من انكسرت عليهم السهام في اصل

31. The second rule is that if the share of one class, when distributed leaves fraction, and the number of shares and the number of heirs are *mutawafiq*, then the *wafq* of the disagreeing numbers of the heirs is

---

[1] For the working out of shares according to modern arithmetical process *vide* pp. 95—108 where the subject has been discussed more thoroughly.

[2] Father 1/6
Mother 1/6
2 Daughters 2/3=4/6 (2/6 each)

It is a case of perfect distribution, the *asl masla* is 6. Father receives one share, mother receives one share and daughters get two shares each.

المسئلة وعولها ان كانت
عائلة كابوين و عشر بنات
اوزوج و ابوين وست
بنات –

to be multiplied by the *asl masala* common denominator or in case of *awl*, by the increased denominator, for example, a man leaves both parents, and ten daughters;[1] or a woman leaves her husband, both parents and 6 daughters.[2]

۳۲ و الثالث ان
لاتكون . بين سهامهم
ورؤسهم موافقة فيضرب كل

32. The third rule is that if there is no *tawafuq* between the shares and the number of heirs, then the number

---

[1]

Mother	1/6
Father	1/6
10 Daughters	2/3=4/6

Here 4 *sihams* are not divisible among ten daughters without fraction; and the *wafq* factor of 10 is 5, for 2×2=4 and 2×5=10, the common factor being 2. According to the rule we multiply 6 by 5 and we get 30 thus the distribution will be into 30 shares; father 5 shares, mother 5 shares, daughters in all 20 shares (2 shares each).

Asl-Masala 6, *Mazrub* 5, *Tashih* 30. (6×5).

Mother	Father	10 Sisters
1	1	4
5	5	20 (2 each)

[2]

Husband	...	1/4	= 3/12	Applying the	3/15
Father	...	1/6	= 2/12	doctrine of	2/15
Mother	...	1/6	= 2/12	increase and	2/15
6 Daughters	...	2/3	= 8/12	reducing	8/15
				shares we get	
			15/12		1

The *awl* here is 15. And 8 shares are not divisible among 6 daughters without fraction; the *wafq* factor of 6 and 8 is 3, the common factor being 2. Applying the rule we multiply 15×3=45 hence the husband is entitled to 9 shares, father 6 shares, mother 6 shares, and 24 shares are given to the six daughters (4 shares each).

Asl-Masala 12, *Awl* 15, *Mazrub* 3, *Tashih* 45. (15×3).

Husband	Mother	Father	6 daughters
3	2	2	8
9	6	6	24 (4 each)

عدد رؤس من انكسرت
عليهم السهام في اصل
المسئلة و عولها ان كانت
عائلة كاب وام و خمس
بنات اوزوج و خمس
اخوات لاب وام –

of heirs (which is not divisible by the *siham* without fraction) should be multiplied by the *asl masala* common denominotor and in case of *awl* by the increased denominator *e.g.*, a man leaves his father and mother, and five daughters;[1] or a woman leaves her husband and five full sisters.[2]

٣٣ - واما ا لا ربعة
فاحدها ان يكون الكسرعلي
طائفتين او اكثر ولكن
بين اعداد رؤسهم مماثلة
فالحكم فيها ان يضرب
احدالاعداد في اصل
المسئلة مثل ست بنات
و ثلث جدات و ثلثة
اعمام –

33. Of the four remaining rules the first is that when on division (of shares) between the numbers of the heirs of two classes or more a fraction is left and the numbers of heirs are *mutamasil*, then any *mutamasil* number may be multiplied by the common denominator *asl masala. e.g.*, a person leaves 6 daughters, 3 true grandmothers, 3 uncles.[3]

---

[1] Father		=	1/6
Mother		=	1/6
5 Daughters	2/3	=	4/6

The *asl masala* is 6, but 4 *sihams* cannot be distributed among the five daughters without fraction and 4 and 5 have no common factor. Applying the rule we multiply the number of heirs by the common denominator that is 6 × 5 = 30. Therefore father receives 5, mother 5, and 5 daughters receive 20 shares.

[2] Husband	1/2 = 3/6	Applying the doctrine	3/7
5 Full sisters	2/3 = 4/6	of *awl* we get	4/7

Here 4 shares cannot be distributed among the five full sisters without fraction and 4 and 5 have no common factor, so according to the rule, the denominator increased *awl*, *i.e.*, 7 is to be multiplied by 5, we get 35 thus the husband takes 15 shares, and 5 sisters 20 shares, that is each sister 4 shares.

[3] 6 Daughters	2/3 = 4/6
3 True grandmothers	1/6
3 Uncles	1/6

The *asl masala* here is 6. It will be noticed that 4 shares are not divisible among 6 daughters without fraction, and the *wafq*

۳۴ و الثاني ان يكون بعض الاعداد متداخلة في البعض فالحكم فيها ان يضرب اكثر الاعداد في اصل المسئلة مثل اربع زوجات و ثلث جدات و اثنا عشر عما ۔

34. And the second rule (of this class, which is really the fifth) is that if the numbers of some classes of heir are *mutadakhul* to (multiple of) the number of other classes, then the largest number of heirs should be multiplied by the *asl masala*, common denominator *e.g.*, a person leaves 4 wives, 3 true grandmothers and 12 uncles.[1]

۳۵ - والثالث ان يوافق بعض الاعداد بعضا فالحكم فيها ان يضرب وفق احد الاعداد في جميع الثاني ثم ما بلغ في وفق الثالث ان وافق المبلغ الثالث والا فالمبلغ في جميع الثالث ثم المبلغ في الرابع كذالك ثم المبلغ في

35. The third rule (of this class which is really the sixth) is that if some of the numbers of the heirs are *mutawafiq*, (that is, have a common factor) then one should multiply the *wafq* of the first number by the second number and multiply the product by the *wafq* of the third and if the resulting product is *mutawafiq* with the third otherwise by the whole, then

---

factor of 6 is 3. $2 \times 3 = 6$; $2 \times 2 = 4$, 2 being the common factor. All numbers become *mutamasil*. Hence multiplying 6 by 3 we get 18 and the distribution is as follows: 6 daughters receive 12 shares, 3 true grandmothers 3 shares, that is, one each, and 3 uncles 3 shares, that is, one each.

1	4 Wives	1/4 = 3/12
	3 Grandmother	1/6 = 2/12
	12 Uncles	7/12 residue

The *asl masala* here is 12, and the largest number among the classes of heirs is 12 uncles, the numbers 4, 3 and 12 are *mutadakhul*, hence we multiply 12 by 12 and get 144, and the distribution is to 4 wives 36 shares, each 9 shares, 3 true grandmothers 24 shares, each 8 shares; 12 uncles 84 shares, each 7 shares.

اصل المسئلة كاربع
زوجات و ثماني عشرة
بنتاً و خمس عشرة
جدة و ستة اعمام ـ

multiply by the fourth; and finally multiply the resulting product by the *asl masala* common denominator. *e.g.*, a person leaves 4 wives, 18 daughters 15 true grandmothers and 6 uncles.[1]

٣٦ و الرابع ان
تكون الاعداد متباينة
لا يوافق بعضها بعضاً
فالحكم فيها ان يضرب
احد الاعداد في جميع
الثاني ثم ما بلغ
في جميع الثالث ثم
ما بلغ في جميع
الرابع ثم ما اجتمع
في اصل المسئلة

36. The fourth rule (of this class which is really the seventh) is that if the number of heirs is *mutabayin* *i.e.*, prime to one another and have no common factor one should multiply the first number by the whole of the second, and multiply the product by the whole of the fourth and the resulting product by *asl masala* common denominator itself, *e.g.*, a person leaves

---

[1] The author of the Sharifa works out the sixth and the seventh rules in a different manner, *vide* pp. 105—107.

4 Wives	1/8	=	3/24
18 Daughters	2/3	=	16/24
15 True grandmothers	1/6	=	4/24
6 Uncles	residue	=	1/24

The *asl masala* here is 24. As regards number 4 and 18 the *wafq* of 4 and 18 is 2. The rule is to multiply *wafq* of the first by the second number. Therefore 2 × 18 = 36. Now as regards the product 36 and 15 the *wafq* of 15 is 5; so we multiply 36 by 5 and get 180. As regards 180 and 6 the numbers there is *tadakul*, so there is no need of multiplication. The final multiplication is by the product into the *asl masala* that is 24 × 180 and we get 4320 shares which are distributed as follows :—

4 Wives	... RECEIVE	540	shares,	each	135	shares
18 Daughters	... ,,	2880	,,	,,	160	,,
15 True grandmother...	,,	720	,,	,,	48	,,
6 Uncles	... ,,	180	,,	,,	30	,,

كمراتين وست جدات وعشر بنات وسبعة اعمام ۔ 2 wives, 6 true grandmothers, 10 daughters and 7 uncles.[1]

---

[1]

2 Wives	...	1/8	3/24
6 True grandmothers	...	1/6	4/24
10 Daughters	...	2/3	16/24
7 Uncles		residue	1/24

The *asl masala* here is 24. The number of wives two and the shares 3 are *mutabayin*, thus we retain 2, similarly 6 and 4 are *tawafuq* by 2 so we retain 3, half of 6, similarly 10 and 16 are *tawafuq by* 2, so we retain 5, and we see that 7 and 1 are *mutabayin*. We multiply all these $2 \times 3 \times 5 \times 7 = 210$, we get 210 and multiplying it with *asl masala* 24 we get 5040 shares distributed as follows.

2 Wives	...	630	shares,	315	shares each
6 True grandmothers		840	„	140	„ „
10 Daughters	...	3360	„	336	„ „
7 Uncles	...	210	„	30	„ „

The following is the Arabian method of representing these problems in a diagram.

(vi) *Asl-Masala* 24, *Masrub* 180, *Tashih* 4320.

4 Wives	18 Daughters	15 Grandmothers	6 Uncles
3	16	4	1
540	2880	720	180
(135 each)	(160 each)	(48 each)	(30 each)

(vii) *Asl-Masala* 24, *Masrub* 210, *Tashih* 5040.

2 Wives	10 Daughters	6 Grandmothers	7 Uncles
3	16	4	1
630	3360	840	210
(315 each)	(336 each)	(140 each)	(30 each)

فصل

SECTION I

٣٧ - و اذا اردت ان تعرف نصيب كل فريق من التصحيح فاضرب ما كان لكل فريق من اصل المسألة في ما ضربته في اصل المسألة فما حصل كان نصيب ذلك الفريق و اذا اردت ان تعرف نصيب كل واحد من احاد ذلك الفريق فاقسم ما كان لكل فريق من اصل المسألة على عدد رؤسهم ثم اضرب الخارج في المضروب فالحاصل نصيب كل واحد من احاد ذلك الفريق ووجه اخر و هو ان تقسم المضروب على اي فريق شئت ثم اضرب الخارج في نصيب الفريق الذي قسمت عليهم المضروب فالحاصل نصيب كل

37. And if ye require to find out the share of each class of sharers by the process of *tashih*, then multiply the share assigned by the *mazrub* product, which you had multiplied with the *asl masala* and what ye shall obtain will be the share assigned to that class. And when ye require to find out the share of each member of that class, then ye must divide that number which was assigned to each class, in terms of the *masala* by the number of the heirs, then multiply the quotient by the *mazrub*, the resulting product will be the share of each member of the class. Another mtehod is to divide the *mazrub*, product, by any class that you desire, then multiply the quotient by the share assigned to that class, and the answer would be the share of each member of the class.[1] Another method is to employ

---

[1] To illustrate we take the example from the (Sirajiyyah vii rule).

Two Wives ...	$\frac{1}{8}=\frac{3}{24}$	each	$\frac{3}{48}$	in all	$\frac{6}{48}=\frac{630}{5040}=$	$\frac{315}{5040}$	each
Six True grand-mothers	$\frac{1}{6}=\frac{4}{24}$	"	$\frac{4}{144}$	"	$\frac{24}{144}=\frac{840}{5040}=$	$\frac{140}{5040}$	each
Ten Daughters	$\frac{2}{3}=\frac{16}{24}$	"	$\frac{16}{240}$	"	$\frac{160}{240}=\frac{3360}{5040}=$	$\frac{336}{5040}$	each
Seven Uncles... residue	$\frac{1}{24}$	"	$\frac{1}{168}$	"	$\frac{7}{168}=\frac{210}{5040}=$	$\frac{30}{5040}$	each

Masala=24, *Mazrub*=210, *Tashih*=5040 (24×210).

واحد من احاد
ذلك الفريق ووجه
اخرو هو طريق النسبة
وهواًلا وضح وهوان
تنسب سهام كل فريق
من اصل المسئلة الى عدد
رؤسهم مفردا ثم تعطي
بمثل تلك النسبة من
المضروب لكل واحد من
احاد ذلك الفريق -

the rule of *nisbat* (the rule of ratio and proportion); and it is a clear method, that is first ascertain the ratio of the shares of each class with reference to the number of shares and then according to the method of ratio and proportion the share may be given from the *mazrub*.[1]

The Sirajiyyah says: Multiply the share assigned which is 3 in the case of the wives by the product *mazrub* 210 and we get 630, and similarly multiplying 4 by 210, we get 840, the shares of six true grandmothers and so on; in order to obtain the share of each member of the class the Sirajiyyah suggests that we divide the product which was assigned to that class by the number of heirs, *e.g.*, divide 630 by 2 and we get 315 shares assigned to each daughter, and by dividing 840 by 6 we get shares assigned to each true grandmother 140, and so on.

Again the *mazrub*, product, 210 in the above example is to be divided by 2 the number of the heirs and multiplying it by 3, the share assigned we get $210/2 \times 3 = 315$, the share of each wife; and similarly $210/6 \times 4 = 140$, the share of each grandmother.

1 In the seventh example which we have taken, the *mazrub* is 210 and the ratio of the number of wives to shares is 2 : 3.

i.e., 2: 210 : : 3: ?

i.e., $\frac{210 \times 3}{2} = 315$ shares each.

Taking the seventh example, the following method of ratio and proportion may also be suggested:

Wife	True grandmothers	Daughters	Uncles
3/24	4/24	16/24	1/24

The total shares by *tashih* are 5040.

Now 24:5040 : : 3: ?

i.e., $\frac{5040 \times 3}{24} = 630$, the share of wives, each wife getting 315.

24 : 5040 : : 4 : ?

$\frac{5040 \times 4}{24} = 840$, each true grandmother receiving 140,

etc., etc.

SECTION II

فصل في قسمة التركات بين الورثة والغرماء

THE

Rules of Distribution of the Property among Heirs and Creditors

٣٨ - اذا كان بين التصحيح و التركة مباينة فاضرب سهام كل وارث من التصحيح في جميع التركة ثم اقسم المبلغ على التصحيح مثاله بنتان و ابوان و التركة سبعة دنانير .

38. If the *tashih* and *tarka*, the inheritance, are *mutabayin*[1] then multiply the share of each heir received by *tashih* by the *tarka* and divide the product by the *tashih* e.g., a person leaves two daughters and both his parents and a *tarka*, property, consisting of 7 dinars.[2]

---

1 The Sirajiyyah has not dealt the case of *tamassul*, because it is a simple case, *e.g.* a person leaves his both parents, and four daughters and a *tarka* of 6 dinars.

Father = 1/6 ; Mother = 1/6 ; Four daughters 2/3 = 4/6

The *asl masala* is 6 and *tarka* is also 6, there is no difficulty since they both are *tamassul*.

2 This example is not found in several editions of the Sirajiyyah and it has not been translated by Sir William Jones whose translation of the whole section is not clear.

Two Daughters	2/3 =	4/6
Father	...	1/6
Mother	...	1/6
		6/6

The *asl masala* here is 6, and the *tarka* is 7 ; 6 and 7 are *mutabayin* the rule is $\frac{\text{SHARE OF AN HEIR} \times \text{TARKA}}{\text{TASHIH}}$.

i.e., Two Daughters $= \frac{7 \times 4}{6} = 4\frac{4}{6}$

Mother $= \frac{1 \times 7}{6} = 1\frac{1}{6}$

Father $= \frac{1 \times 7}{6} = 1\frac{1}{6}$

7

٣٩ - ان كان بين
التصحيح و التركة موافقة
فاضرب سهام كل وارث
من التصحيح علي وفق
التركة ثم اقسم المبلغ علي
وفق التصحيح فالخارج
نصيب ذلك الوارث في

39. Now if the ***tarka*** and ***tashih*** are ***mutawafiq*** the rule is to multiply the share of each heir received by ***tashih*** by the ***wafq*** of the ***tarka*** and divide the resulting product by the ***wafq*** of the ***tashih***, the answer would be the required share. The

---

The Sharifa gives the following example to illustrate this rule subject to *awl*:—

A women leaves her husband, her mother and two full sisters and a *tarka* of 25 dinars

Husband...	1/2	3/6	Applying the doctrine of *Awl* and reducing the shares we get	3/8
Mother ...	1/6	1/6		1/8
Two Sisters	2/3	4/4		4/8
		8/6		1

The *awl* here is 8 and the *tarka* 25, are ***mutabayin***,

Hence the rule is $\frac{\text{SHARE OF AN HEIR} \times \text{TARKA}}{\text{TASHIH}}$

i.e., Husband $= \frac{3 \times 25}{8} = 9\frac{3}{8}$

Mother $= \frac{1 \times 25}{8} = 3\frac{1}{8}$

Two sisters $= \frac{4 \times 25}{8} = 12\frac{4}{8} \left(6\frac{1}{4} \text{ each.} \right)$

According to the modern method it would be as follows :—

$3/8$ of $25 = 9\frac{3}{8}$

$1/8$ of $25 = 3\frac{1}{8}$

$4/8$ of $25 = 12\frac{4}{8}$

Asl Masala 6, Awl, 8. tarka 25

Husband	Mother	Two Sisters
3	1	4
$9\frac{3}{8}$	$3\frac{1}{8}$	$12\frac{4}{8}$
		[each $6\frac{2}{8}$]

في الوجهين هذالمعرفة
نصيب كل فرد -

rule has been suggested with a view to find out the portion of each heir.[1]

٤٠ - اما المعرفة نصيب
كل فريق منهم فاضرب
ما كان لكل فريق من
اصل المسألة في وفق
التركة ثم اقسم المبلغ
على وفق المسألة ان كان
بين التركة والمسألة موافقة
وان كان بينهما مباينة
فاضرب في كل التركة ثم
اقسم الحاصل على
جميع المسألة فالخارج
ذلك ذلك الفريق
في الوجهين -

40. But in order to know the portion of each class of heirs, the rule is to multiply the share of each class of heirs received per *masala* by the *wafq* of the *tarka* and then divide the product by the *wafq* of *masala* common denominator provided there was *tawafuq* between the *tarka* and *masala*; and if they were *mutabayin*, the rule is to multiply the share of each class of heirs by the whole of the *tarka* and divide the resulting product by the *masala* and

---

[1] Taking the same example of husband, mother and two sisters let us suppose that the *tarka* consists of 50 dinars, so there is *tawafuq* between 8 and 50 by 2 ; $2 \times 4 = 8$ and $2 \times 25 = 50$; *wafq* factor of 8 is 4 and the *wafq* factor of 50 is 25. Now the rule is

$$\frac{\text{SHARE OF AN HEIR} \times \textit{wafq} \text{ OF TARKA}}{\textit{wafq} \text{ OF TASHIH}}$$

Therefore

Husband $= \frac{3 \times 25}{4} = 18\frac{3}{4}$

Mother $= \frac{1 \times 25}{4} = 6\frac{1}{4}$

Two Sisters $= \frac{4 \times 25}{4} = 25$ $\left(\text{each sister } 12\frac{1}{2}\right)$

According to modern method it would be as follows:

3/8 of $50 = 18\frac{3}{4}$

1/8 of $50 = 6\frac{1}{4}$

4/8 of $50 = 25$.

the answer would be the share of the class in both cases.[1]

۴۱ - امالي قضاء الديون فدين كل غريم بمنزلة سهام كل وارث

41. As regards payment of debts, the debt of each creditor is to be treated like the share of each heir in

---

[1] The principle governing the rule to ascertain the share of an heir or class of heirs is necessarily the same that is if the *masala taskih* and *Tarka* are *mutawafiq* the rule is

$$\frac{\text{SHARES OF THE CLASS} \times \textit{wafq} \text{ OF } \textit{Tarka}}{\textit{wafk} \text{ OF } \textit{Tashih} \ (\textit{masala})}$$ or if they are *mutabayin*

the rule is $$\frac{\text{SHARES OF CLASS} \times \textit{Tarka}}{(\textit{masala}) \ \textit{Tashih}}$$ *e.g.* a woman leaves her husband 4 uterine sisters and 2 consanguine sisters, and she leaves Rs. 30. (or Rs. 32).

Husband	1/2	3/6	Applying Increase, reduce the shares	3/9
4 Uterine Sisters	1/3	2/6		2/9
2 Consanguine Sisters	2/3	4/6		4/9
		9/6		1

The *awl* here is 9 and suppose the *tarka* is Rs. 30; therefore there is *tawafuq* by 3 between 9 and 30 and the *wafq* factors are 3 and 10 respectively.

The rule is $$\frac{\text{SHARES OF CLASS} \times \textit{wafq} \text{ OF TARKA}}{\textit{Wafq} \text{ OF } \textit{Tashih}}$$

Husband $\frac{3 \times 10}{3}$ = Rs. 10, 4 Uterine Sisters $\frac{2 \times 10}{3}$ = Rs. $6\frac{2}{3}$

2 Consanguine Sisters $\frac{4 \times 10}{3}$ = Rs. $13\frac{1}{3}$

According to ordinary method it would be

3/9 of 30 = Rs. 10; 2/9 of 30 = Rs. $6\frac{2}{3}$; 4/9 of 30 = Rs. $13\frac{1}{3}$

In the same example suppose that the *Tarka* is 32. Now the *masala awl* 9 and *Tarka* 32 are *mutabayin* thus the husband receives $\frac{3 \times 32}{9} = 10\frac{6}{9}$; 4 uterine sisters $\frac{2 \times 32}{9} = 7\frac{1}{9}$

2 consanguine sisters $\frac{4 \times 32}{9} = 14\frac{2}{9}$

في العمل و مجموع الديون بمنزلة التصحيح و ان كان في التركة كسور فابسط التركة والمسألة كلتيهما اي اجعلهما من جنس الكسر ثم اعمل فيه مارسمناه -

working out the problem and the sum total of debts are to be treated as the *tashih*; and if there is any fraction in the *tarka*, then first apply the method of *tashih* and thereafter proceed as above mentioned.

---

[1] The Muslim Law insists that the debts must be paid first and if the property is sufficient to pay all debts there would be no difficulty. In case the amount of debts exceeds the property the payment to each creditor will have to be rateably reduced. Discussing this topic the author of the Sharifa suggests this example: that a person dies leaving 9 dinars as his property and he owes to one creditor 10 dinars and to another creditor 5 dinars. It is obvious that debts cannot be paid in full from this estate as the total amount of debt is 15 dinars.

The author states the following rule with a view to reduce debts proportionately.

$$\frac{\text{ANY DEBT} \times \textit{wafq} \text{ OF TARKA}}{\textit{wafq} \text{ OF DEBTS}}$$

As regards the *tarka* 9 and debts 15 they are *mutawafiq* $3 \times 3 = 9$ $3 \times 5 = 15$ *wafq* factors are 3 and 5 respectively.

i.e. $\frac{10 \times 3}{5} = 6$ and $\frac{5 \times 3}{5} = 3$.

The modern method would be as follows :

15 : 9 : 10: ?

$$\frac{9 \times 10}{15} = 6$$

and 15 : 9 : : 5 : ?

$$\frac{9 \times 5}{15} = 3.$$

Thus one creditor will be paid 6 and the other creditor will be paid 3.

If the numbers are *muta-bayin* different rule will be applicable *e.g.*, a person leaves 13 dinars. Here *tarka* and the sum

SECTION III

ON

Deduction

42. If any person is prepared to compromise and take some particular thing out of the *tarka* then the share of that person would be reduced in the *tashih* and the residue will be distributed among the other heirs in terms of their shares, *e.g.* a woman leaves her husband, her mother and her patornal uncle, and husband is prepared to compromise in what was the dower due from him to the wife; then he would not be counted among the heirs and the balance of the *tarka* would be distributed between the mother and the uncle, mother

فصل في التخارج

٤٢ - من صالح على
شيء من التركة فاطرح
سهامه من التصحيح
ثم اقسم ما بقي من
التركة علي سهام الباقين
كزوج وام وعم فصالح الزوج
علي ما في ذمته من المهر
وخرج من البين فتقسم
باقي التركة بين الام والعم
اثلاثا بقدر سهامهما
سهمان للام وسهم للعم
اوزوجة واربعة بنين
فصالح احد البنين علي
شي وخرج من البين
فيقسم باقي التركة علي

---

total of debts 15 are *mutabayin*. The rule of the Sharifa is as follows:

$$\frac{\text{TARKA} \times \text{ANY DEBT}}{\text{SUM TOTAL OF DEBTS}}$$

i.e. $\frac{13 \times 10}{15} = 8\frac{2}{3}$

and $\frac{13 \times 5}{15} = 4\frac{1}{3}$

And according to the modern method the same rule would be applicable thus:

15: 13 : : 10 : ?

i.e. $\frac{13 \times 10}{15} = 8\frac{2}{3}$

and 15 : 13 : : 5 : ?

i.e. $\frac{13 \times 5}{15} = 4\frac{1}{3}$

خمسة وعشرين سهما للمرأة اربعة اسهم ولكل ابن سبعة اسهم -

receiving 2 shares and the uncle one share.[1] If a person leaves his wife, four sons, and one of the sons compromises in lieu of something, then he would be excluded and the remaining *tarka* will be divided into 25 shares, the woman receiving 4, and the sons 7 each.[2]

---

[1] If the uncle and mother were the only heirs the distribution would be 1/3 to the mother and the residue to the uncle. But the Sirajiyyah assigns contrary shares and the Sharifa explains that the procedure has been adopted with the consensus of the jurists.

The distribution takes place in this manner :—

Husband	1/2	3/6
Mother	1/3	2/6
Uncle (residue)		1/6

Therefore in this case the mother takes twice as much as the uncle and this proportion ought to be maintained although the husband actually takes nothing since he has compromised not to take his share and is not to pay the dower.

Similarly if the uncle compromise even then the distribution would be 3 shares to the husband and 2 for the mother; and if the mother compromises, then 3 for the husband, and 1 for the uncle.

If a person leaves his wife, mother, and an uncle

Wife	1/4	3/12
Mother	1/3	4/12
Uncle residue		5/12

If the wife were to compromise on something, say, she takes some valuable jewellery, then we shall take away her share 3 and the division of the balance of the property would be given to the mother 4 shares and the uncle 5 shares.

[2]

Wife	1/8	4/32
4 Sons	7/8	28/32, each 7/32.

In this case the fact of one son going out would make the property divisible into 25 shares instead of 32, *i.e.*, 32—7—25.

Some editions of the Sirajiyyah do not contain this example.

CHAPTER VIII

باب الرد

The Doctrine of Return, *Radd*

٤٣ - الرد ضد العول
ما فضل عن فرض ذوي
الفروض ولا مستحق له
يرد علي ذوي الفروض
بقدر حقوقهم الا علي
الزوجين وهو قول عامة
الصحابة رضي الله تعالي
عنهم وبه اخذ اصحابنا
رحمهم الله وقال زيد بن
ثابت الفاضل لبيت المال
وبه اخذ مالك والشافعي
رحمهما الله .

43. The doctrine of return, *radd*, is the opposite of the doctrine of increase. If some residue is left over and above the shares of the sharers entitled, and there is no claimant to it, the surplus is returned to the sharers except to the husband and wife,[1] in proportion, to their share of the inheritance. And this is the view of our jurists in conformity with the opinion of the general companions of the Prophet.[2] However Zaid is of the opinion that the residue is to be given to the *Bait-ul-mal*, Public treasury, and his opinion is adopted by Imam Malik and Imam Shafi'i.[3]

---

[1] Ibn Abbas takes the view that the husband, wife and true grandmothers are not entitled to the return, but the Hanafi jurists speak about the husband and wife only, so if there are no other sharers, or residuaries, or distant kindred then the husband or wife take the residue by return. There are eight sharers entitled to the return, one male and seven females, namely uterine brother, and uterine sister, daughter, son's daughter, full sister, consanguine sister, mother and true grandmother.

The father and true grandfather are sharers as well as residuaries so when they co-exist with sharers there is no return at all.

[2] Sir William Jone says "Ali and his followers," but these words do not occur in the Arabic text, and he also mentions Urwah and Alzuhuri as supporters of the view adopted by Zaid, again these names do not occur in the text of the Sirajyyah but the statements are correct.

[3] However in the absence of the public treasury even under the Shafi law the sharers will be entitled to the return.

٤٤ - ثم مسائل الباب
على اقسام اربعة احدها
ان يكون في المسئلة
جنس واحد ممن يرد
عليه عند عدم من لا يرد
عليه فاجعل المسئلة من
رؤسهم كما لو ترك بنتين
او اختين او جدتين فاجعل
المسئلة من اثنين والثاني
اذا اجتمع في المسئلة
جنسان او ثلثة اجناس
ممن يرد عليه عند عدم
من لا يرد عليه فاجعل
المسئلة من سهامهم اعني
من اثنين اذا كان في
المسئلة سدسان او من
ثلثة اذا كان فيها ثلث
وسدس او من اربعة اذا
كان فيها نصف وسدس
او من خمسة اذا كان
فيها ثلثان وسدس او

44. The doctrine of return has four cases. The first case is when there are one kind of heirs who are entitled to the return there being none who is not entitled to the return, then solve the case according to number of the heirs, *e.g.* A person leaves two daughters, or two full sisters or two true grandmothers. Here *masala*, the solution is in division by two. The second case is when there are heirs of two or three kinds entitled to the return there being no others who are so entitled[1] then the *masala*, solution, of the case is according to their shares. That is the *masala* is two if there be 2/6, or by three when there are 1/3 and 1/6, or by four when there are 1/2 and 1/6, or by 5 five when there are 2/3 and 1/6 or 1/2 and 2/6 or 1/2 and 1/3.[2] The third

---

[1] In case of the Return there may be one, two or three classes of heirs but there cannot be more than three classes.

[2] Cases of *masala*, 2, 3, 4, 5, are as follows :—

(i) Two daughters 1/2 each by return and as sharer.

(ii) Mother........................1/6............1/6......1/3
Two uterine brothers......1/3............2/6......2/3

The *masala* here is 6 but there being residue, the distribution will be 1/3 : 2/3 that is 3 as *masala radd* by reason of return.

Masala 6,	*Masala radd* 3
Mother	2 uterine brothers
1	2

(iii) Daughter......1/2......3/6
Mother....................1/6

نصف وسدسان او نصف
وثلث والثالث ان يكون
مع الاول من لا يرد عليه
فاعط فرض من لا يرد عليه
من اقل مخارجه فان
استقام الباقى على رؤس من
يرد عليه فيها كزوج وثلث
بنات وان لم يستقم
فاضرب وفق رؤسهم في
مخرج فرض من لا يرد
عليه ان وافق رؤسهم الباقي
كزوج وست بنات و الا
فاضرب كل رؤسهم في
مخرج فرض من لا يرد
عليه فالمبلغ تصحيح المسألة
كزوج وخمس بنات
والربع ان يكون مع الثاني

case is when there is with first case co-existing some one not entitled to the return, in this case first assign the share to this person, not so entitled, in terms of the lowest denominator *makhraj*, and it is well if the residue is distributed exactly with the number of heirs, as in the case of a woman who leaves her husband and three daughters.[1] However if the residue is not so divisible then multiply *wafq* of the number of heirs by the *makhraj* denominator of the persons not entitled to the return provided the number of the heirs and the residue are *mutawafiq*, *e.g.* a woman leaves her husband and six daughters.[2]

Here the *masala* is 6 and there being residue the distribution will be 1/4 : 3/4 that is *masala radd* is 4.

(iv) Two daughters....2/3...4/6...increased to by return....4/5
Mother....................1/6....................................1/5.

Here the *masala* is 5.

[1] Husband.........1/4.
Three daughters.....3/4 as sharers and by return.

[2] Husband................1/4..2/8
Six daughters............3/4......each 1/8,...............in all 6/8

The *masala* here is 4, but 3 shares cannot be distributed among 6 daughters, however 6 and 4 are *tawafuq* by 3. The rule is *wafq* of number of heirs multiplied by the denominator, 2 × 4 = 8 and the distribution will be 2 shares to the husband and 6 shares to the daughters, one each. The problem may also be solved as indicated above by ordinary arithmetical process.

Masala radd 4, *Masrub* 2, *Tashih* 8. (2 × 4).

Husband	6 daughters
1	3
2	6

من لا يرد عليه فاقسم
ما بقي من مخرج فرض
من لا يرد عليه على مسألة
من يرد عليه فان استقام
فيها وهذا في صورة واحدة
وهي ان يكون للزوجات
الربع والباقي بين اهل
الرد اثلاثا كزوجة واربع
جدات وست اخوات لام
وان لم يستقم فاضرب
جميع مسألة من يرد عليه
في مخرج فرض من
لا يرد عليه فالمبلغ مخرج
فروض الفريقين كاربع

if the number of heirs entitled to the return and that of the residue are not *mutawafiq* then multiply the total number of the heirs by the *makhraj* denominator of the shares of those not entitled to the return, and the answer is the required solution *masala*, *e.g.* a woman leaves her husband and five daughters.[1] . The fourth case is when there is with second case co-existing some one not entitled to the return, then divide the residue (that is what remains from the *makhraj* denominator of the person not entitled to the return) among the sharers, if it is divisible exactly so much the better and that is possible only in the following case, that is when wives take 1/4, and the residue 3/4 is distributed in thirds among the rest of the sharers, *e.g.* a person leaves his wife, four true grandmothers, and

---

[1] Husband ....1/4..5/20

Five daughters......3/4......3/20 each...................in all 15/20

Here 3 and 5 are *mutabayin.*

The rule is to multiply 5 × 4 = 20 distributed as above.

Masala radd 4, *Mazrub* 5, *Tashih* 20 (4 × 5)

Husband	5 daughters
1	3
5	15

زوجات وتسع بنات وست جدات ثم اضرب سهام من لا يرد عليه في مسألة من يرد عليه وسهام من يرد عليه فيما بقي من

six uterine sisters.[1] However if the residue is not divisible then multiply the number of persons entitled to the return by the *makhraj* denominator of the person not entitled to the return, and the product will be the *makhraj* denominator of both classes, *e.g.*, a person leaves 4 wives, 9

---

[1] Sir William Jones in his translation gives an example thus "if there be a wife, and a grandmother, and two sisters by the mother's side" but the Arabic text of the Sirajiyyah gives the above example. In the former case the distribution will be

(i) Wife ... 1/4
Grandmother ... 1/4
Two uterine sisters ... 2/4

(ii) Wife.........1/4..............................1/4
Four true grandmothers...1/6.........1/3 of 3/4 Residue...1/4
Six uterine sisters...1/3...2/6.......2/3 of 3/4 Residue...2/4
1/4....................................12/48
each 1/16 in all 4/16.................12/48 each 3/48
each 2/24 in all 12/24..............24/48 each 4/48

The above is worked by ordinary arithmetical process.

The arabian method is as follows :

The *masala* is 4 and the number 4 of true grandmothers and 1 the share are *mutabayin* so we reserve 4. The number 6 of uterine sisters and 3 of the shares assigned are *tawafuq* by 2 so we reserve 3 (half of six) and 3 by 4=12 and multiplying it with *masala* that is 4×12 we get 48 shares distributed as follows to the wife 12 shares, to the true grandmothers 12 shares, 3 each, and to 4 uterine sisters 24 shares 4 each.

Masla radd 4, *Mazrub* 12, *Tashih* 48 (4×12)

Wife	4 True grandmothers	6 Uterine sisters
1	1	2
12	12	24

مخرج فرض من لا يرد
عليه وان انكسر علي البعض
فتصحيح المسائل بالاصول
المذكورة

daughters 6 true grandmothers.[1] And multiply the share of those not entitled to the return, by the denominator of persons entitled to return and the shares of persons entitled to return by residue *makhraj* in the share of those not entitled to the return, thereafter if there is a fraction in respect of some or all then adjust it by the rules discussed previously.

---

[1] By the oridinary arithmetical process.

Wives take 1/8, and the residue 7/8 is to be divided between daughters, and true grandmother in the ratio of 2/3 : 1/6 or 4 : 1

4 wives	1/8			5/40
9 daughters	2/3	4/6	4/5 of 7/8 residue	28/40
6 true grand mothers	1/6	1/6	1/5 of 7/8 residue	7/40

continuing :

4 wives	each	5/160	in all 20/160	180/1440	each	45/14440
9 daughters	"	28/360	" 252/360	1008/1440	"	112/1440
6 true grand mothers		7/240	" 42/240	252/1440	"	42/1440

L.C.M.—160, 360, 240 = 1440

By the Arabian method the *tashih* is 40. We find that the number of heirs are 4, 9 and 6 and they are *mutabayin* with respect to the shares assigned, *viz.* 5, 28 and 7 respectively, but 4, 6 are *mutawafiq* by 2 hence we multiply 2 by 6 and get 12 ; 12 and 9 are *mutawafiq* by 3 thus we multiply 12 and 3 and get 36 ; multiply the product 36 by the *tashih masala* 40 and we get 1440 which is distributed as above.

In other words the L.C.M. of 4, 9 and 6 is 36 which is multiplied by the *masala* 40 and we get 1440.

It is thus distributed : to four wives 45 shares or 9 shares each, to nine daughters 1008 shares or 112 shares each, and to 6 true grandmothers 252 shares or 42 shares each.

Masala radd 8, *Tashih* 40, *Final Tashih* 1440 (36 × 40)

4 Wives	9 Daughters	6 True grandmothers
5	28	7
180	1008	252
(each 45)	(each 112)	(each 42)

باب مقاسمة الجد

CHAPTER IX

THE

Division concerning the Right of the Paternal Grandfather

۴۵ - قال ابو بكر الصديق رضي الله عنه ومن تابعه من الصحابة بنو الاعيان و بنو العلات لا يرثون مع الجد و هذا قول ابي حنيفة رحمه الله و به يفتي وقال زيد بن ثابت رضي الله عنه يرثون مع الجد وهو قولهما وقول مالك والشافعي رحمهما الله وعند زيد بن ثابت للجد مع بني الاعيان وبني العلات افضل الامرين من المقاسمة ومن ثلث جميع المال وتفسير المقاسمة ان يجعل الجد في القسمة كاحد الاخوة وبنو العلات يدخلون في

45. Abu Bakr Siddiq (peace be on him) and those who have adopted his views among the companions of the Prophet say, "full blood brothers and consanguine brothers do not inherit along with the grandfather." And this is also the view of Imam Abu Hanifa and the *fatwa* is given according to this view.[1] However according to Zaid bin Sabit the grandfather and the full brothers or consanguine brothers inherit with the grandfather and this is the opinion of them (the Sahiban, Imam Abu Yusuf, and Muham mad) as well as of Imam Malik and Imam Shafi'i, (peace be on them). The grandfather takes the best share

[1] Among those who adopt the view of Sayyadna Abu Bakr we may mention among the companions of the Prophet, Ibn Abbas, Ibn Zubair, Ibn Umar, Hazifa'a binul Yaman, Abi Saeed Hazri, Abi bin Kab, Maaz bin Jabal, Abi Musa Ashari, and Hazrat Aisha Siddiqa. Among jurists we may mention Hazrat Sharih, 'Ata, Urwah bin Zubair, Amar bin Abdul Aziz, Hasan Basri and Ibn Sirin.

القسمة مع بني الاعيان
اضرارا للجد فاذا اخذ
الجد نصيبه فبنو العلات
يخرجون من البين خائبين
بغير شي والباقي لبني
الاعيان الا اذا كانت من
بني الاعيان اخت واحدة
فانها اذا اخذت فرضها
نصف الكل بعد نصيب الجد
فان بقي شي فلبني العلات
والا فلا شي لهم كجد واخت
لاب وام واختين لاب فبقي
للاختين لاب عشر المال
وتصح من عشرين ولو كانت
في هذه المسألة اخت لاب
لم يبق لها شي

in *muqasima* the actual distribution of shares or a third of the whole estate. The *muqasima* is this: that the grandfather will be counted as a brother among the brothers and the consanguine brothers will enter into the inheritance along with the full blood brothers with a view to prejudice the share of the grandfather, and when the grandfather has taken his share, the consanguine brothers will be excluded, the whole residue being given to the full brothers, except when there is a full blood sister who will receive her legal share, that is, half of the whole property after assigning the share to the grandfather and if there is residue that would go to the brothers of the half blood and if no residue remains, nothing will be taken by the half-brothers. Such would be the case when a man leaves a grandfather, a sister by the same father and mother and two sisters by the same father. [1]

---

[1] Is we work out the problem according to Zaid, the grandfather taking in the capacity of a brother we have :

Grandfather	... 2/5	4/10	8/20
Full sister	... 1/2	5/10	10/20
Two consanguine sisters (residue)		1/10	2/24

Grandfather equal to 2 sisters; therefore there are five sharers and the share of a male would be 2/5 and the residue is for females:

But if, in the above example, there was one consanguine sister only, then nothing would remain for her.[1]

٤٦ - وان اختلط بهم
ذو سهم فللجد هنا افضل
الامور الثلثة بعد فرض ذي
سهم اما المقاسمة كزوج
وجد واخ واما ثلث مابقي
كجد وجدة واخوين
واخت واما سدس جميع
المال كجد وجدة وبنت
واخوين واذا كان ثلث الباقي
خيرا للجد وليس للباقي

46. If some one entitled to a fixed legal share is mixed with them then after assigning share to him the grandfather is entitled to the best of the three courses. See the case of the division in the case of a woman who leaves her husband, a grandfather, and a brother,[2] or a third of the residue is given when a man leaves a grandfather, a grandmother, two

---

since the full sister must take half it will be 3/5 – 1/2, that is, leaving 1/10 for the 2 consanguine sisters. The primary distribution *masala* is 10 but since 1 share cannot be divided between 2 sisters without leaving a fraction we raise the denominator by *Tashih* to 20.

[1] *e.g.*

Grandfather	1/2
Sister	1/2

consanguine sister (no residue left over).

The grandfather is equal to 2 sisters; so there are four sharers; male taking the double share, grandfather would receive 1/2; and since the sister must receive her legal share of 1/2, the estate is exhausted leaving nothing for the consanguine sister; in the first example, there being 2 consanguine sisters, there were 5 shares, hence some residue was left over for the consanguine sisters; the share of the grandfather was reduced, but here there is no residue left over at all.

[2]

Husband	1/2	2/4
Grandfather }	residue	1/4
Brother }		1/4

(The Husband takes 1/2, and the grandfather and brother would take the residue 1/2 equal by *i.e.*, 1/4 each). Here the grandfather takes 1/4 in the supposed capacity as a brother.

ثلث صحيح فاضرب مخرج
الثلث في اصل المسألة فان
تركت جدا وزوجاً وبنتاً
واما واختاً لاب وام اولاب
فالسدس خير للجد وتعول
المسألة الي ثلثة
عشر وللاخت شي

brothers and a full sister[1] and a sixth of the whole estate is given when a person leaves a grandfather, a grandmother and a daughter and two brothers[2] and when a third of the residue is the best share for the grandfather and out of the residue the third cannot be deducted then multiply the denominator of the third

---

[1] Grandmother	1/6		3/18
Grandfather	5/18		5/18
Two brothers	residue 10/18	4/5 of 10/18	8/18
Full sister		1/5 of 10/18	2/18

(Grandmother takes 1/6 ; here the rule suggests that the best share is 1/3 of the residue ; it is 1/3 of 5/6 *i.e.* 5/18. The other course would be that grandfather takes as a brother among the brothers, in which case his share would be 2/7 of 5/6 or 5/21, there being 7 sharers (1 grandfather is equal to 2 sisters, 2 brothers are equal to 4 sisters, and 1 sister thus the whole is equal to 7 shares). Now 5/18 is better than 5/21, and the third alternative is that the grandfather may take 1/6 as a sharer. Now 5/18 is better than 1/6 also ; therefore the best course is 1/3 of the residue.

[2] Grandmother	1/6		2/12
Grandfather	1/6		2/12
Daughter	1/2	or 3/6	6/12
Two brothers	residue	or 1/6 (each 1/12)	2/12

The Sirajiyyah suggests that the best course for the grandfather would be to take 1/6 his legal share and this is obvious because the grandmother takes 1/6 and the daughter takes 3/6, the residue is 2/6 and if he shares along with the two brothers as a brother he would take 2/3 of 1/6 which would be 1/9 and 1/9 is less than 1/6. Similarly 1/3 of the residue would also be 1/9 which is less than 1/6. Therefore the best share is 1/6.

واعلم ان زيد بن
ثابت رضي الله عنه لايجعل
الاخت لاب وام اولاب
صاحبة فرض مع الجد الا
في المسئلة الاكدرية وهي
زوج وام وجد واخت لاب
وام اولاب فالزوج النصف
وللام الثلث وللجد السدس
وللاخت النصف ثم يضم الجد
نصيبه الي نصيب الاخت
فيقتسمان للذكر مثل حظ
الانثيين لان المقاسمة خير
للجد اصلها من ستة
وتعول الي تسعة وتصح
من سعبة وعشترين وسميت
اكدرية لانها واقعة امراة
من بني اكدر وقال بعضهم
سميت اكدرية لانها كدرت

by the *masala*.[1] If a woman leaves her grandfather, her husband, a daughter, and her mother and her full sister or consanguine sister[2], then in this case also 1/6 is the best share for the grandfather and the doctrine of Increase becomes applicable and the sister takes nothing. Learn ye, Zayad bin Sabit (peace be on him) has not put the sister by the same father and mother or the sister by the same father to share with the grandfather except in the case of famous *masala* known as *Akdarya*, that is a person leaves a husband, mother, grandfather, sister by the same father and mother or consanguine sister.[3] If instead of

---

1 This simply explains the rule. In the preceding example of the grandmother and grandfather and two brothers and sisters the grandmother had taken 1/6 and grandfather took 1/3 of 5/6 =5/18 ; so the rule is to multiply 3 by the *masala* 6 and we get 18 shares as we have already solved.

2

Husband	1/4	3/12	reduced	3/13
Grandfather	1/6	2/12	shares	2/13
Mother	1/6	2/12	*'awl*	2/13
Daughter	1/2	6/12	becomes applicable	6/13
Full sister or Consanguine sister			get nothing.	
				1

3

Husband	1/2	3/6	shares are reduced :	3/9
Mother	1/3	2/6	Doctrine of Increase	2/9
Grandfather	1/6	1/6	becomes applicable ;	1/9
Full sister or Consanguine sister	1/2	3/6		3/9
		9/6		1

علي زيدبن ثابت مذهبه ولوكان مكان الاخت اخ او اختان فلاعول ولا اكدرية -	the sister there were a brother or two sisters then the doctrine of Increase will not be applicable and the case would not be *Akdarya.*[1]

Here the husband will take 1/2, the mother 1/3, and grandfather 1/6, and the sister 1/2; The *masala* here is 6, the doctrine of Increase becomes applicable it will be increased to 9.

The Sirajiyyah says the best course for the grandfather is to take as a brother. Therefore the share of the grandfather and sister 1/9 and 3/9 would be mixed up and the grandfather would take as brother 2/3 of 4/9 or 8/27 and the sister would get 1/3 of 4/9 or 4/27 : thus denominator is increased to 27 and the final distribution would be in terms of the denominator 27 :—

Husband	9/27
Mother	6/27
Grandfather	8/27
Sister	4/27

This case is known as *Akdarya* because it is a case appertaining to a woman of Bani Akdar.

[1] Husband	1/2	3/6
Mother	1/3	2/6
Grandfather (residue)		1/6
Brother or 2 sisters		

(Here the grandfather will take as a sharer 1/6 of the estate which is the best course for him; if he were to take in the capacity of a brother he would take less. The result is brother or sisters would be excluded.

Under the *Hanafi* Law, we may point out the grandfather would take and always would exclude brothers and sisters, whether half blood or full. The author of the Sirajiyyah has written so much in this chapter out of respect for the eminent jurist Zaid and Imam Abu Yusuf and Imam Mohammad. The Muslim jurists are agreed that the share of the grandfather can never be less than 1/6.

Foot-note continued :—

The following Chart represents cases under which according to the disciples Imam Abu Yusuf and Imam Muhammad the Grandfather is to take the best share in the *Muqasima* of 1/3 and 1/6. The solutions are of not much importance since the *Fatwa* accords with the view of Imam Abu Hanifa.

Masala 2.	
G. F.	B.
1/2	1/2
1	1

Masala 3, *Tashih* 9.	
G. F.	3 B.
1/3	2/3
3	6

Masala 3.	
G. F.	2 B.
1/3	2/3
1	2

Masala 2, *Tashih* 4.		
H.	B.	G. F.
1/2	1/4	1/4
2	1	1

Masala 6, *Tashih* 12.			
G. M.	G. F.	2 B.	D.
1/6	1/6	1/6	3/6
2	2	2	6

Masala 6, *Tashih* 12.			
2 D	G. F.	B.	S.
4/6	1/6	2/6	
8	2	1	1

Masala 6.		
D.	G. F.	2 B.
3/6	1/6	2/6
3	1	2

Masala 6, *Tashih* 18.		
H.	G. F.	3 B
3/6	3	
9	3	6

Masala 4, *Tashih* 8.			
W.	G. F.	B.	2 S.
1/4	1/4	2	
2	2	2	2

Masala 6.		
2 D	G. F.	B.
4/6	1/6	1/6
4	1	1

Masala 6, *Awl* 9, *Tashih* 27. The *Akdarya* case.			
H.	M.	G. F.	S.
3/6	2/6	1/6	3/6
9	6	8	4

G. F.=True grandfather, G. M.=True grandmother, B.=Brother, S.=Sister, H.=Husband, W.=Wife, D.=Daughter, M.=Mother.

CHAPTER X

باب المناسخة

ON THE

Devolution of Vested Inheritance

٤٨ - ولو صار بعض الانصباء ميراثا قبل القسمة كزوج و بنت و ام فمات الزوج قبل القسمة عن امرأة و ابوين ثم

48. Some shares may devolve as vested inheritance before the distribution of the estate, for example,[1] a woman leaves her husband, her daughter and her mother and the husband dies before the distribution of the estate, leaving a wife and both his

---

[1] The Sirajiyyah has tackled one of the most difficult illustrations, and instead of working it out by the Arabian system we first represent the actual distribution in the following chart from which at a glance we can make out the distribution of shares :

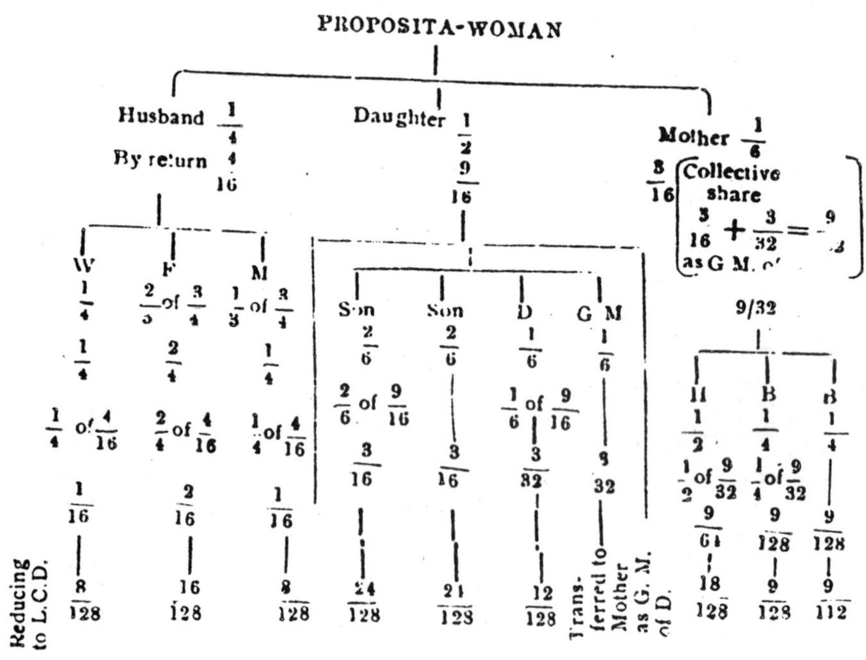

ماتت البنت عن ابنين و
بنت و جدة ثم ماتت
الجدة عن زوج و اخوين
فالعمل فيه ان تصحح
مسئلة الميت الاول وتعطي
سهام كل وارث من
التصحيح ثم تصحح مسئلة
الميت الثاني و تنظر بين

parents; and the daughter dies before distribution of the estate leaving 2 sons and a daughter and a grandmother (the mother of the *Proposita*), and the grandmother also dies leaving her husband and 2 brothers. The principle in this case is this[1]: first arrange by *tashih* the case of the deceased *i.e.*, assign share to each heir according to the *masala* then arrange the case of the second deceased on what he has received under the first distribution and if as the result

---

[1] According to the Arabian method in working out the problem wherever fractions occur with a view to avoid it the principle of *tashih* is applied. That is as noted previously we multiply the *masala* either by the concerned *wafq* or concerned *mutabayin* number as the case may be, so that no fraction remains in any share under the *masala*. Hence if a fraction occurs in the first immediate distribution the first *masala* is adjusted by multiplication and is called the first *tashih* of the first distribution. Again if the fraction is to be avoided in the second distribution, then not only the *masala* of the second distribution is multiplied by the concerned *wafq* or concerned *mutabayin* number as the case may be but the first *tashih* of the first distribution itself is multiplied and this is technically know as the second *tashih* of the first distribution, and hence redistribution is effected in the first stage. Finally if in the third distribution this procedure is found to be necessary the second *tashih* of the first distribution will again be adjusted, and the new *tashih* will be called the third *tashih* of the first distribution, and hence redistribution of the first as well as the second stages will be effected, and so on until the last final *tashih* is obtained. This principle is worked out in an admirable manner in the classical example selected by the Sirajiyyah. In the end of this chapter I have also worked out two easy examples to illustrate the same principle so

ماني يده من التصحيح
الاول و بين التصحيح
الثاني ثلثة احوال فان
استقام ما في يده من
التصحيح الاول علي الثاني

of the second distribution; the first distribution is *mustaqim*, fits in, then there is no need to multiply; but if it does not fit in then see whether these two

---

if the reader finds any difficulty it will be better for him to go first through those easy examples.

The following is the Arabian Method of working out the same example.

First Distribution—

Wife deceased

Husband	Daughter	Mother
4	9	3

Husband	... 1/4	...		... 3/12
Daughter	... 1/2	...	3/6	... 6/12
Mother	... 1/6	...	1/6	... 2/12
				11/12

Since the husband receives 1/4, daughter 1/2, mother 1/6 the *masala* is 12 leaving 1 to be disposed of by return, and the rule is to multiply the denominator (which is 4) of the person not entitled to return by the *masala* of the person entitled to the return which is also 4. Hence multiplying 4 by 4 we get 16 by *tashih* which is distributed as above to the husband 4 shares, to the daughter 9 shares, and to the mother 3 shares.

Second distribution—

Masala 4, Husband deceased (in hand 4)

Wife	Father	Mother
1	2	1

As here the *masala* 4 of the distribution and 4 shares of the deceased in hand are *mutamasil* (equal, same) no multiplication is required.

فلاحاجة الى الضرب و
و ان لم يستقم فانظر ان
كان بينهما موافقة فاضرب
وفق التصحيح الثاني في
التصحيح الأول و ان كان

are *mutawafiq* if so, multiply the *wafq* of the second *tashih* by the whole of the first *tashih*; but if these two are *mutabayin*, then multiply the whole of the

---

Third distribution—

Masala 6, Daughter deceased (in hand 9)

Son	Son	Daughter	True grandmother
2	2	1	1

The *masala* here is 6 and we have in hand 9 shares of the deceased which cannot be distributed without leaving fraction. So it is to be adjusted. We see that the number 9 and 6 are *mutawafiq* and *wafq* of 6 is 2. So by multiplying 9 by 2 we get 18 which would be distributed without leaving fraction. This really means that we should adjust the first *tashih* of the first distribution, namely 16 is to be multiplied by 2 the *wafq* number by which we have just multiplied, and we get 32 shares. In other words the rule is to multiply the first *tashih* by the *wafq* of the second *masala viz*, $16 \times 2 = 32$.

Now on the basis of the second *tashih* of the first distribution namely 32 the distribution is as follows :

Masala 32, Wife deceased.

Husband	Daughter	Mother
8	18	6

And *second distribution* will be :—

Masala 8, Husband deceased (in hand now 8).

Wife	Father	Mother
2	4	2

Masala 8 is the second *tashih* of the second distribution.

And the shares of the *third distribution* are :—

Masala 18, Daughter deceased, (in hand now 18).

Son	Son	Daughter	True grandmother
6	6	3	3

18 is the first *tashih* of the third distribution.

بينهما مباينة. فاضرب كل
التصحيح الثاني في كل
التصحيح الاول فالمبلغ

second *tashih* by the first *tashih*, the resulting product will be the *makhraj* (denominator) of both

---

***Fourth distribution*—**

Masala 4, Mother (True grandmother) deceased. (3+6=9 in hand).

Husband	Brother	Brother
2	1	1

The *Masala* 4 and the number of shares 9 are *mutabayin* so we must multiply 4 to avoid fraction. That is multiply 9 by 4 and we get 36, consequently second *tashih* of the first distribution will again be adjusted, that is we multiply 32 by 4 and we get 128 as the third *tashih* of the first distribution. Finally we shall have to work the whole problem on basis of 128 as the final *tashih*. Hence the ***First distribution*** will be as follows :—

Tashih 128, Wife deceased.

Husband	Daughter	Mother
32	72	24

***Second distribution*—**

Husband deceased (in hand 32.)

Wife	Father	Mother
8	16	8

***Third distribution*—**

Daughter deceased (in hand 72.)

Son	Son	Daughter	True grandmother
24	24	12	12

***Fourth distribution*—**

Mother, true grandmother deceased (in hand 24+12=36.)

Husband	Brother	Brother
18	9	9

مخرج المسئلتين فسهام these *masalas.* If you desire to find out the share of each heir then
ورثة الميت الاول تضرب multiply the share of the heirs of

The following diagram represents the solution explained in the last two pages.

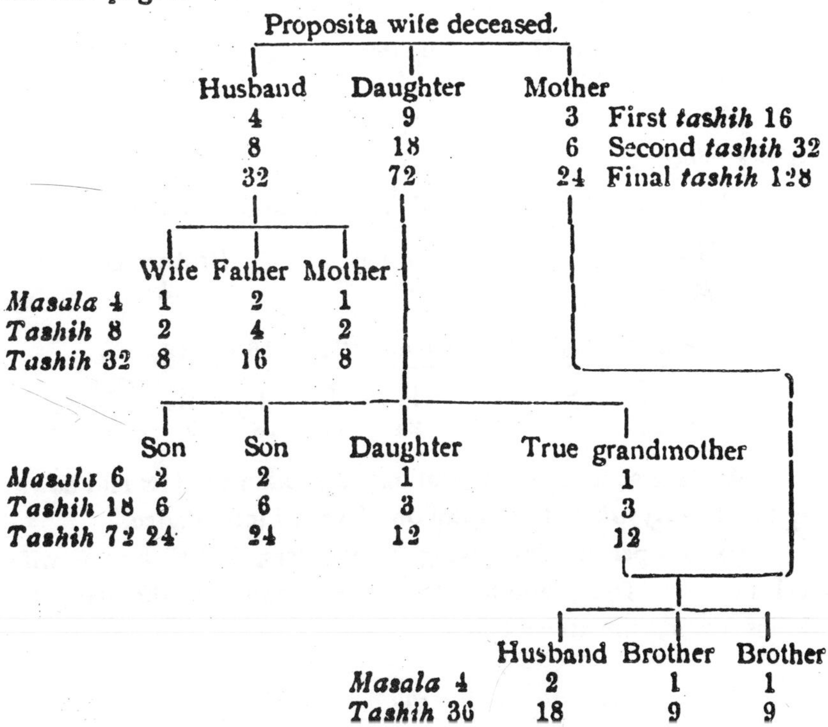

This diagram represents the Arabian method of representing the same problem.

***Masala* 12, by *Radd* (4×4), *First Tashih* 16, (i) *Mazrub* 2,**

***Second Tashih* 32, (ii) *Mazrub* 4, *Final Tashih* 128.**

Husband A	Daughter B	Mother C
4	9	3

Re A's estate.

Masala* 4, in hand 4, *Mustaqim.

Mother D	Father E	Wife F
1	2	1

في المضروب اعني في التصحيح الثاني أو في the first deceased by the *mazrub* that is by the *tashih* of the second

---

Re B's estate.

Masala 6, in hand 9, *tawafuq* by 3.

Son G	Son H	Daughter I	Grandmother C
2	2	1	1

Re C's estate.

Masala 2, *Mazrub* 2, *Tashih* 4, in hand 9, *Tabayin.*

Husband J	Brother K	Brother L
2	1	1

Final Distribution *Tashih* 128. (16×2×4).

D	E	F	G	H	I	J	K	L
8	16	8	24	24	12	18	9	9

We take some easy illustrations to explain the law laid down by the *Sirajiyyah* as to devolution of vested inheritance.

(i) *X* a person dies leaving 3 daughters, A.B.C. by one wife and one son. D, by another wife. Subsequently the daughter C dies leaving the above heirs.

Masala 5, *Mazrub* 3, *Tashih* 15.

A	B	C	D
1	1	1	2

C's estate.

Masala 3, in hand 1, *Tabayin.*

A	B	D
1	1	1

Tashih 15.

A	B	D
4	4	7

Since 3 and 1 are *Tabayin* we muliply second *Tashih* by first *Masala i.e.* 3×5=15 Final *Tashih.*

ونقه و سهام ورثةالميت
الثاني نضرب في كل ماني
يده او في ونقه و ان
مات ثالث او رابع او
خامس فاجعل المبلغ
مقام الاولى والثالثة مقام
الثانية في العمل ثم في

distribution or by its *wafq* and multiply the heirs of the second distribution by the whole of what is in the hands or by the *wafq* of it; and if the third or fourth or fifth die then you should treat the product in place of the first distribution and put the third in place of the second and

---

By ordinary arithmetical process.

PROPOSITUS

A	B	C	D
1/5	1/5	1/5	2/5

C's share (1/5) goes to:

A	B	D
1/3	1/3	1/3
1/3 × 1/5	1/3 × 1/5	1/3 × 1/5
1/15	1/15	1/15

Finally :

A receives 1/5 + 1/15 = 4/15

B ,, 1/5 + 1/15 = 4/15

D ,, 2/5 + 1/15 = 7/15

(ii) A person leaves two sons A and B, and two daughters C and D.

Subsequently A dies leaving his wife E, his son F and his daughter G.

Masala 6, *Final Mazrub* 12, *Final Tashih* 72.

A	B	C	D
2	2	1	1

الرابعة والخامسة كذالك الى غير النهاية ـ	similarly in the case of fourth and fifth and so on.

A's estate.

Masala 8, *Mazrub* 3, *Tashih* 24, In hand 2.

E	F	G
1	7 (F and G together)	
3	14	7

Tashih 72.

B	C	D	E	F	G
24	12	12	3	14	7

In the second distribution of A's estate, since 7 could not be distributed without leaving fraction between F and G, we multiply 3 by 8 and get by *Tashih* 24. Now 24 and 2 in hand are *tawafuq* by 2. Hence we multiply *wafq* of 24 *i.e.*, 12 by 6 original *masala* and we get 72 shares which are distributed as above.

By ordinary arithmetical process.

PROPOSITUS

A	B	C	D
2/6	2/6	1/6	1/6
	24/72	12/72	12/72

(A's heirs:)

E	F	G
1/8	2/3 of 7/8	1/3 of 7/8
3/24	14/24	7/24
3/24 of 2/6	14/24 of 2/6	7/24 of 2/6
3/72	14/72	7/72

CHAPTER XI

ON

Zuvil Arham, Distant Kindred.

باب ذوي الارحام

۴۹ - ذوالرحم هو كل
قريب ليس بذي سهم
و لا عصبة و كانت عامة
الصحابة رضي الله تعالى
عنهم يرون توريث ذوي
الارحام و به قال اصحابنا
رحمهم الله و قال زيد بن
ثابت رضي الله تعالى عنه
لا ميراث لذوي الارحام و
يوضع المال في بيت المال
و به قال مالك والشافعي
رحمهما الله و ذووالارحام
اصناف اربعة -

49. *Zuvil Arham* or distant kindred are those relations who are neither sharers nor residuaries. Majority of the companions of the Prophet (on whom be peace)[1] hold that *Zuvil Arham* are entitled to inheritance, and our Hanafi jurists have accepted their view. But Zaid bin Sabit says " *Zuvil Arham* are not entitled to inheritance, the property is to be given to *The Bait-ul-mal*," and this is the view of Imam Malik and Imam Shafii. There are four classes of distant kindred.

۵۰ - الصنف الاول
ينتمي الي الميت و هم
اولاد البنات و اولاد بنات
الابن والصنف الثاني ينتمي
اليهم الميت و هم الاجداد
الساقطون و الجدات

50. The first class is descended from the deceased (*i.e.* descendants of the deceased) and they consist of the children of daughters and the children of son's daughters. The second class consists of those from

---

[1] Majority of the companions consist of Umar, Ali, *ibn* Masood, Abu Ubaid bin Jarah, Maaz bin Jabal, Abu Obaida, *ibn* Abbas. The Hanafi jurists who have adopted their view are Alqama, Ibrahim, Sharih, Hasan Basri, *ibn* Sirin, Attar and Mujahid. This is also the opinion of Imam Abu Hanifa, Imam Mohammad, Imam Yusuf, and Imam Zafar.

السّاقطات والصنف الثالث
ينتمي الى ابوى الميت
و هم اولاد الاخوات وبنات
الاخوة و بنو الاخوة لام
والصنف الرابع ينتمي الى
جدي الميت او جدتيه
و هم العمات والاعمام
لام والاخوال والخالات
فهؤلاء وكل من يدلى بهم
من ذوي الارحام

whom the deceased descended (ascendants of the deceased) and they are false grandfathers and grandmothers. The third class consists of those who are descended from the mother and father of the deceased and they are the children of sisters and brothers' daughters and also of uterine brothers. The fourth class consists of those persons who are descended from the two grandfathers and the two grandmothers of the deceased *i.e.*, their paternal aunts, and uterine uncles by the same mother and maternal uncles and maternal aunts. These persons and all those who are related to the deceased through them belong to the distant kindred class.[1]

٥١ - روي ابو سليمان
عن محمد بن الحسن
عن ابي حنيفة رحمهم الله
تعالى ان اقرب الاصناف
الصنف الثاني و ان
علوا ثم الاول و ان سفلوا
ثم الثالث وان نزلوا ثم
الرابع وان بعدوا وروي ابو
يوسف والحسن بن زياد
عن ابي حنيفة و ابن
سماعة عن محمد بن
الحسن عن ابي حنيفة
رحمهم الله ان اقرب
الاصناف الصنف الاول

51. Abu Sulaiman reports from Muhammad bin Hasan, who reports from Imam Abu Hanifa that among those classes preference is given to the second class, how high so ever, then to the first class how high so ever, then to the first class how low so ever ; then to the third class even how remote so ever ; then to the fourth class, how distant so ever. And Abu Yusuf and Hasan bin Ziyad report from Imam Abu Hanifa and Muhammad Ibn Sama[2] reports from bin Hasan who reports from Imam

[1] For a list of Distant Kindred see p. 41 and also the charts relating to Distant Kindred in the appendix.

[2] Sir William Jones' Translation of the Sirajiyyah omits the name of ibn Sama.

ثم الثاني ثم الثالث ثم الرابع كترتيب العصبات و هو الماخوذ به عند هما الصنف الثالث مقدم على الجد اب الام -

Abu Hanifa that preference is given to the first class, then the second, then the third, and then the fourth, just as in the arrangement of residuaries, and this view is accepted, but according to them, the Sahiban (Imam Yusuf and Imam Muhammad) the third class is preferred to the maternal grandfather.[1]

SECTION 1

ON

The First Class

فصل في الصنف الاول

٥٢ - اولهم بالميراث اقربهم الي الميت كبنت البنت فانها اولي من بنت بنت

52 Preference among them in the right of succession is given to the nearest heir in degree, to the deceased, *i.e.* the daughter's daughter

---

[1] Some texts of the Sirajiyyah contain an additional passage which according to the author of the Sharifa is an interpolation as its sense is not clear. The passage is this :—

لان عند هما كل واحد منهم اولى من فرعه و فروعه وان سفل اولى من اصله

The literal translation is :—"because according to both of them (*i.e.* Imam Abu Yusuf and Imam Muhammad) each of them is preferably entitled to inheritance than his descendants, and his (?) descendants are preferably entitled to inheritance than his (?) ancestors." Apparently the pronoun 'them' seems to refer to the members of the third class and the pronoun 'his' in all the three places appears to refer to 'each of them.' But then there are two difficulties. In the first place it is wrong to say that the descendants of a man are preferred to his ancestors as the Muslim Law does not recognise such a view ; according to which ancestors inherit along with descendant, and the second difficulty is that such a principle is out of place here. Some other commentators have tried to explain the passage by suggesting different antecedents for the pronouns used in the passage. This passage is not found in Sir William Jones' translation of the Sirajiyyah.

الابن وان استووا في الدرجة فولد الوارث اولى من ولد ذوي الارحام كبنت بنت الابن فانها اولى من ابن بنت البنت و ان استوت درجاتهم ولم يكن فيهم ولد الوارث او كان كلهم يدلون بوارث فعند ابي يوسف رحمه الله تعالى و الحسن بن زياد يعتبر ابدان الفروع و يقسم المال عليهم سواء اتفقت صفة الاصول في الذكورة والانوثة اواختلفت و محمد رحمه الله تعالى يعتبر ابدان الفروع ان اتفقت صفة الاصول موافقا لهما و يعتبر الاصول ان اختلفت صفاتهم و يعطي الفروع ميراث الاصول مخالفا لهما كما اذا ترك ابن بنت و بنت بنت عندهما يكون المال بينهما للذكر مثل حظ الانثيين باعتبار الابدان و عند محمد رحمه الله كذالك لان صفة الاصول متفقة ولو ترك

is preferred to the daughter of son's daughter; but if they are equal in degree then the descendants of heir are preferred to the descendants of *Zuvil Arham*, *e.g.* daughter of a son's daughter is preferred to the son of a daughter's daughter; and if they are equal in degree and there is no child of an heir among them or if all of them are the descendants of the heirs, then according to Abu Yusuf (peace be on him) and Hasan ibn Ziyad attention will be given to *abdan-ulfaru* (the actual persons in the branches) and the property will be distributed equally among them whether the roots of these are of the same sex or different sexes; but Imam Muhammad would pay attention to *ablanulfaru* (the persons of the branches) if the sex of the roots is the same and in that he agrees with Abu Yusuf and Hasan bin Ziyad; but if the sex of the rootis is different then he would pay attention to the persons of the root and he would give to the descendants (the branches) the actual inheritance assigned to the root and in this he is opposed to both the above mentioned jurists, *e.g.* a person leaves a son of the daughter and a daughter of the daughter, then according to Abu Yusuf and Hasan, the property will be distributed between them by the

بنت ابن بنت و ابن
بنت بنت عندهما المال
بين الفروع اثلاثاً باعتبار
الابدان ثلثاه للذكر و
ثلثه للانثي و عند محمد
رحمه الله المال بين
الاصول اعني في البطن
الثاني اثلاثاً ثلثاه لبنت
ابن البنت نصيب ابيها
و ثلثه لابن بنت البنت
نصيب امه -

rule, "double share to the male and a single share to female according to the *abdan* (the sex of the claimant) and the same will be the distribution according to Imam Muhammad because the nature of the ancestor (*sifatal asul*) is the same. And if a person leaves a daughter's son's daughter and a son of a daughter's daughter, then according to both the Imams (Imam Abu Yusuf and Hasan bin Ziyad) the estate will be distributed according to the sex of the actuals claimant, that is 2/3 to the male, 1/3 to the female; but according to Imam Muhammad the distribution would take effect in the second degree and 2/3 would descend to the daughter of the son's daughter, which is the share of her father, and 1/3 would descend to the son of the daughter's daughter the share of her mother.[1]

٥٣ - و كذلك عند
محمد رحمه الله اذا كان
في اولاد البنات بطون
مختلفة يقسم المال علي
اول بطن اختلف في
الاصول ثم يجعل الذكور

53. And similarly, according to Imam Muhammad when the children of the daughter are of different sexes then the distribution would take effect according to the first *batn* (degree) where the sexes of the ancestor (the

	P	
	D	D
	S 2/3	D 1/3
According to Imam Muhammad	D 2/3	S 1/3
........to Imam Abu Yusuf ...	1/3	2/3

طائفة والاناث طائفة بعد
القسمة فما اصاب الذكور
يجمع و يقسم على اعلى
الخلاف الذي وقع في
اولادهم و كذالك ما
اصاب الاناث ، هكذا يعمل
الى ان ينتهى بهذه الصورة ٠

roots) are different; then all the males will be put together in one class and all the females would be put together in another. Whatever has been given to the males will be collected together and will be distributed among their own descendants and similarly whatever has been assigned to the females would be distributed among their own descendants as in the following scheme :[1]

---

[1] The following is the famous illustration given in the Sirajiyyah. It has been worked out by the author of the Sharifa. It will be seen that there are nine daughters and three sons hence three sons are equal to 6 daughters so there are 15 sharers and the property will be distributed 2/15 to each son and 1/15 to each daughter. In fact that would be the distribution according to the method of Imam Abu Yusuf. According to Imam Muhammad we see there is no dfference of sexes in the second root, there being all daughters. In the third root the sexes differ and they are the descendants of three sons and nine daughters. As regards the descendants of nine daughters we see that they contain three sons and six daughters, *i.e.*, 12 sharers in all. Now 9 shares assigned on top cannot be distributed among the 12 sharers, and the number 9 and 12 are *mutawafiq* by 3 ; thus according to the rule we multiply the *wafq* of the number of heirs which is 4 by the *masala* which is 15 and we get 60, *tashih-i-masala*, according to which no fraction occurs in any share. Thus the *masala* is 15 and the *tashih* is 60. The division will be into 60 shares. On this basis the nine daughters will take 36 shares (36/60) and 3 sons 24 shares (24/60). Further in working out this example we follow the general principle "double share to the male and a single to the female."

ابن	ابن	ابن	بنت	بنت	بنت	بنت	بنت	بنت	بنت	بنت	بنت
	۲۴						۳۶				
بنت	بنت	بنت	بنت	بنت	بنت	بنت	بنت	بنت	بنت	بنت	بنت
ابن	بنت	بنت	ابن	ابن	ابن	بنت	بنت	بنت	بنت	بنت	بنت
۱۲	۱۲			۱۸				۱۸			
بنت	بنت	بنت	ابن	بنت	بنت	ابن	ان	ابن	بنت	بنت	بنت
۱۲	۱۲		۹	۹			۱۲			۶	
بنت	ابن	بنت	بنت	بنت	بنت	ابن	بنت	بنت	ابن	بنت	بنت
۱۲	۸	۴	۹	۹		۶	۶		۳	۳	
بنت	بنت	بنت	بنت	بنت	ابن	بنت	بنت	ابن	بنت	ابن	بنت
۱۲	۸	۴	۹	۳	۶	۶	۲	۴	۳	۲	۱

THE DECEASED

S	S	S	D	D	D	D	D	D	D	D	D
	24						36				
D	D	D	D	D	D	D	D	D	D	D	D
S	D	D	S	S	S	D	D	D	D	D	D
12	12			18				18			
D	D	D	S	D	D	S	S	S	D	D	D
12	12		9	9			12			6	
D	S	D	D	D	D	S	D	D	S	D	D
12	8	4	9	9		6	6		3	3	
D	D	D	D	D	S	D	D	S	D	S	D
12	8	4	9	3	6	6	2	4	3	2	1

The distribution on the basis of 60 as *tashih* would be as follows :—

PROPOSITUS

		24/60							36/60			
I	S	S	S	D	D	D	D	D	D	D	D	D
	8/60	8/60	8/60	4/60	4/60	4/60	4/60	4/60	4/60	4/60	4/60	4/60
II	D	D	D	D	D	D	D	D	D	D	D	D
		12/60			18/60				18/60			
III	S_1	D	D	S	S	S	D	D	D	D	D	D
	12/60	6/50	6 60	6/66	6/60	6/60	3/60	3/60	3/60	3/60	3/60	3/60
					9'60			12/60				
IV	D	D	D	S	D	D	S	S	S	D	D	D
				9/60			4/60	4/60	4/60	2/60	2/60	2/60
V	D	S	D	D	D	D	S	D	D	S	D	D
		8/60	4/60				6/60	6/60		3/60	8/60	
VI	D	D	D	D	D	S	D	D	S	D	S	D
	12/60	8/60	4/60	9/60	3/60	6/60	6/60	2/60	4/60	3/60	2/60	1/6

S=Son, D=Daughter.

۵۴ - و كذالك محمد
رحمه الله تعالى ياخذ
الصفة من الاصل حال
القسمة عليه والعدد من
الفروع كما اذا ترك ...
بنت بنت ... و بنت
ابن بنت بنت و بنتي

54. Similarly Imam Mohammad, when distributing pays attention to the sexes of the roots and to the number of the descendants *e.g.*, a person leaves two sons from daughter's daughter's daughter and one daughter from son's daughter's daughter and two daughters from daughter's

---

In the above illustration I have made an attempt to arrange the shares in such a way that at a glance the distribution of shares may be seen.

In column II there is no difference of sex at all.

In column III the ancestors differ in their sexes.

S_1 takes 1/2 of 24/60 or 12/60 which descends to D_1 there being no change of sex in this line of descent.

D and D take 1/4 of 24/60 or each 6/60.

And as regards the descendants of daughters, the three sons take 18/60 and six daughters take 18/60.

In column IV the ancestors differ in their sexes in cases of some of the heirs, and the descendants of sons and daughters are again dealt with separately, the result is as indicated in the chart.

In column V the distribution is similarly effected and finally the result is stated in column VI *viz.* 12, 8, 4, 9, 3, 6, 6, 2, 4, 3, 2, 1 respectively.

The general rule of double share to male members applies throughout.

The distribution on the basis of 2/15 and 1/15 is as follows:—

2/15	2/15	2/15	1/15	1/15	1/1	1/15	1/15	1/15	1/15	1/15	1/15
1/5	1/10	1/10	1/10	1/10	1/10	1/20	1/20	1/20	1/20	1/20	1/20
1/5	1/10	1/10	3/20	3/40	3/40	1/15	1/15	1/15	1/30	1/30	1·30
1/5	2/15	1/15	3/20	3/40	3/40	1/10	1/20	1/20	1/20	1/40	1/40
1/5	2/15	1/15	3/20	1/20	1/10	1/10	2/60	4/60	1/20	2/60	1/60

According to Imam Abu Yusuf the distribution would be 2/15 to each son and 1/15 to each daughter.

بنت ابن بنت بهذه الصورة

son's daughter as in the following example[1] :—

مو

		THE DECEASED	
١ - بنت بنت بنت	1. Daughter	Daughter	Daughter
٢ - بنت بنت ابن	2. Daughter	Daughter	Son
٣ - بنت ابن بنت	3. Daughter	Son	Daughter
٤ - ابني بنت بنتي	4. Two sons	Daughter	2 daughters

1

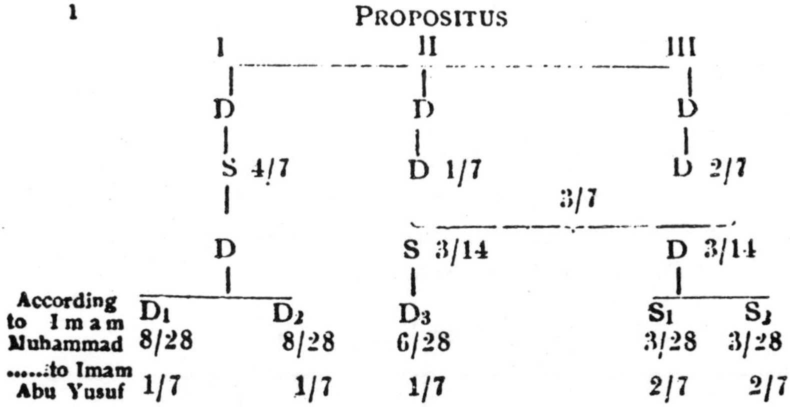

Here the ancestors differ in their sexes in the second *batn* and their being two claimants in the first line of descent they would count as two males and the two claimants in the third line of descent would count as two females, the distribution in the second *batn* would be DS=4/7 ; DD=1/7 ; DD=2/7.

Now 4/7 is inherited by the descendants in the first line equally. D_1 = 2/7=8/28 ; D_2 =2/7=8/28.

The collective share of DD of the second line II and DD of the third line III is (2/7+1/7=3/7), and this is to be redistributed to their descendants. There is a further difference of sex between the roots in this collective group in the third *batn*. The above operation is again to be repeated. There are two male claimants in the second line, but they are to be counted as two females, and the only one claimant in the third line would be counted as a male.

Thus DDS gets 1/2 of 3/7=3/14 and DDD gets 1/2 of 3/7 =3/14. And the final distribution to their respective descendants would be. D_3 gets 3/14=6/28; S_1 gets 1/2 of 3/14=3/28; S_2 gets 1/2of 3/14=3/28.

According to Imam Abu Yusuf:—

D_1 gets 1/7, D_2 gets 1/7, D_3 gets 1/7, S_1 gets 2/7 S_2 gets 2/7.

عند ابي يوسف رحمه‌الله تعالى يقسم المال بين — According to Imam Abu Yusuf the property will be distributed

---

According to the Arabian method we see that the sex of the ancestors differ in the second *batn* and the distribution is 4/7 and 3/7., that is 4 parts and 3 parts, now 3 cannot be divided between the two heirs therefore we multiply 2 by the *masala* 7=14 and the distribution in terms of 14 shares will be 8 and 3, 3, that is,

D	D	D
S	D	D
D=8	S=3	D=3

Now again 3 cannot be divided between 2 sons, hence we multiply 2 by 14 and we get *tashih-i-masala* 28, hence the whole distribution would be 6 to two sons (3 each) S_1 and S_2 ; and 6 to D_3 ; and D_1 and D_2 take 8 shares each.

Masala 7, *Mazrub* 4, *Tashih* 28

Batn 1	D	D	D	
„ 2	S 4	D	D	(3)
„ 3	D 3 16	S 3 6	D 3 6	
„ 4	D_1 D_2	D_3	S_1	S_2
According to Imam Muhammad.	16 (each 8.)	6	6 (each 3)	
According to Imam Abu Yusuf.	2	1	4	

الفروع اسباعاً باعتبار ابدانهم و عند محمد رحمه الله تعالى يقسم المال على اعلى الخلاف اعني في البطن الثاني اسباعا باعتبار عدد الفروع في الاصول اربعة اسباعه لبنتي بنت ابن البنت نصيب جدهما و ثلثة اسباعه و هو نصيب البنتين يقسم على ولديهما اعني في البطن الثالث انصافا نصفه لبنت ابن بنت البنت نصيب ابيها والنصيب الآخر لابني بنت بنت البنت نصيب امهما وتصح المسئلة من ثمانية و عشرين و قول محمد رحمه الله تعالى اشهر الروايتين عن ابي حنيفة رحمه الله تعالى في جميع ذوي الارحام و عليه الفتوى۔

among the descendants by considering their persons in seven parts. But according to Imam Muhammad the distribution will take effect in the first *batn* descent, where the sexes of the ancestors differ, and in this case in the second *batn* by considering the number of the descendants, the distribution would be in seven parts: 4 parts shall be given to the daughters of the son's daughter, because that is the share of their grandfather and 3 parts, which is the share of 2 daughters will be distributed among their descendants, that is, in the third *batn* in equal shares half to daughter of the daughter's son that is the share of father and the other half will be given to the two sons of the daughter's daughter, that is the share of their mother; and the *tashih* in this case is by 28. The opinion of Imam Muhammad is the better of the two views narrated from Imam Abu Hanifa concerning the *Zuvil arham* and the fatwa accords with his view.[1]

---

[1] Sir William Jones incorporates the following passage in his translation of the Sirajiyyah, which is not found in the Arabic text:—"and this was the first opinion of Abu Yusuf; then he departed from it, and said that the roots were by no means to be considered."

فصل

SECTION II

٥٥ - علماؤنا رحمهم الله
تعالى يعتبرون الجهات
في التوريث غير ان ابا
يوسف رحمه الله تعالي
يعتبر الجهات في ابدان
الفروع و محمد رحمه
الله تعالى يعتبر الجهات
في الاصول كما اذا ترک
بنتي بنت بنت و هما
ايضا بنتا ابن بنت و ابن
بنت بنت بهذه الصورة -

55. Our jurists consider the *jihat* (stock) of the heirs in distribution with this difference that Abu Yusuf considers the *jihat* (stock) with reference to the branches and Imam Muhammad considers *jihat* (stock) in the roots *e.g.*, a person leaves two daughters of a daughter's daughter who are also two daughters of a daughter's son and the son of a daughter's daughter according to this example :-

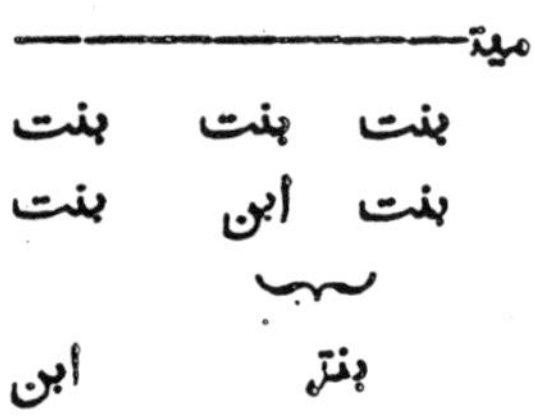

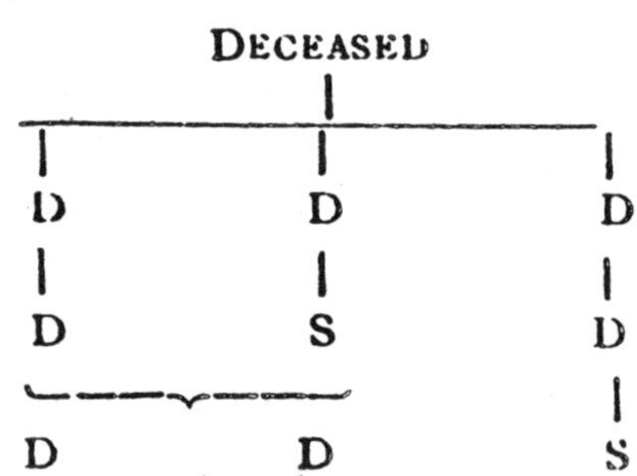

عند ابي يوسف رحمه
الله تعالي يكون المال
بينهم اثلاثا و صار كانه
ترک اربع بنات و ابنا
ثلثاه للبنتين و ثلثه للابن
و عند محمد رحمه الله
تعالى يقسم المال بينهم
على ثمانية و عشرين سهما

According to Abu Yusuf the property will be divided among them in thirds as if the deceased leaves 4 daughters and a son, 2/3 will go to the two daughters and 1/3 to the son; but according to Imam Mohammad, the distribution will be in 28 shares, namely 22 shares being given to two

للبنتين أثنان و عشرون
سهما ستة عشر سهما من

daughters[1], 16 shares on behalf of their father and 6 shares on behalf of

---

1

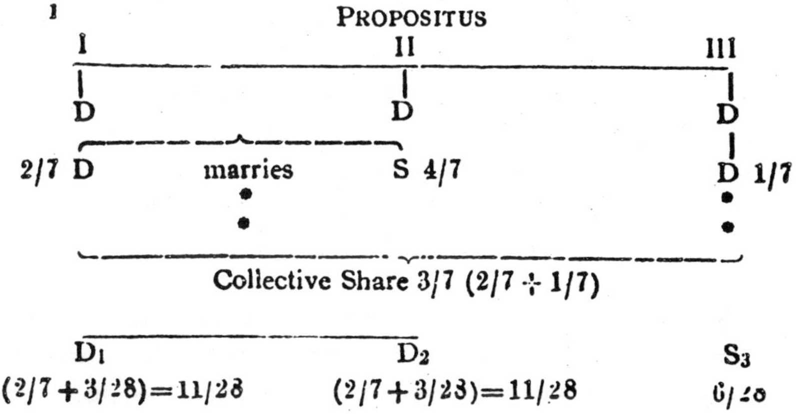

Here the ancestors differ in their sexes in the second *batn*, descent, and there are two claimants in the first line I of pedigree and two in the second line II of pedigree, but in the former capacity they count as females and in the latter as male members. Hence, the distribution at this stage is as follows :—

I D D = 2/7
II D S = 4/7
III D D = 1/7

Now the share of D S, 4/7 is inherited by his heirs directly 2/7 each, *i.e.*, D_1 = 2/7 ; D_2 = 2/7.

The share of DD (I) and DD (III) is collected together *i.e.*, 2/7 + 1/7 = 3/7 and is redistributed to their descendants as follows :

I D_1 = 1/4 of 3/7 = 3/28
II D_2 = 1/4 of 3/7 = 3/28
III S_3 = 2/4 of 3/7 = 6/28

Thus finally because of the marriage of their parents the daughters in the first and second lines inherit in two different capacities, each taking 2/7 + 3/28 = 11/28 each.

D^1 gets 11/28
D^2 gets 11/28
S^3 gets 6/28.

من قبل ابيها و ستة
اسهم من قبل امهما و للابن
ستة اسهم من قبل امه .

their mother, and the son will receive 6 shares on behalf of his mother.[1]

---

[1] According to the Arabian method the distribution in second *batn* where the ancestors differ would be in 7 parts, 4 (4/7) being given to the son and 3 (3/7) is the collective share of the two daughters in that line ; [2 shares (2/7) given to the daughter which has two descendants] Now we separate the descendants of son and daughter ; 4 shares (4/7) which we have assigned to the son would go to his descendants daughters D_1 and D_2 ; *i.e.*, 2 shares (2/7) to each. But when we distribute 3 shares (3/7) among D_1 and D_2 and S_3 we see that it cannot be distributed because there are four heirs (son being equal to two daughters and D_1 and D_2 in all equal to 4 sharers) and 3 shares to be distributed between them. Now the numbers 3 and 4 are *mutabayin* thus we multiply the number of the heirs, that is 4 by the *masala* which is 7, and we get 28. The share will be distributed as follows :—

D_1	D_2	S_3
8+3=11	8+3=11	6

Masala 7, Mazrub 4, Tashih 28.

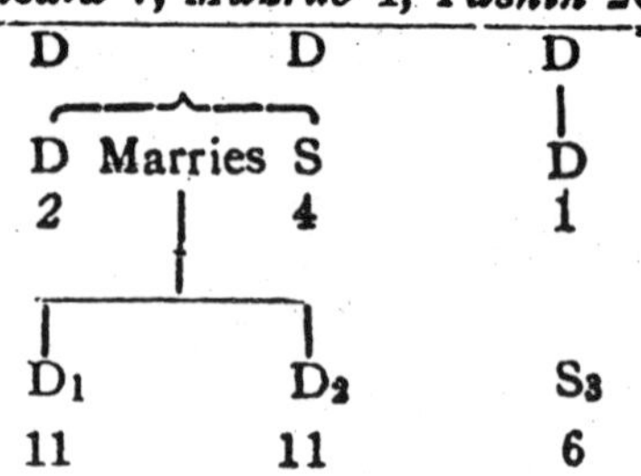

According to Imam Muhammad ...	22	6
According to Imam Abu Yusuf ...	2	1.

SECTION III

ON

The Second Class

فصل في الصنف الثاني

٥٦ - اولهم بالميراث
اقربهم الي الميت من اي
جهة كان و عند الاستواء
فمن كان يدلي بوارث فهو
اولى كاب ام الام اولى
من اب اب الام عند ابي
سهيل الفرائضي و ابي
فضل الخصاف و علي بن
عيسي البصري و لا تفضيل
له عند ابي سليمان
الجرجاني وابي علي البستي
و ان استوت منازلهم و
ليس فيهم من يدلي
بوارث اوكان كلهم يدلون
بوارث واتفقت صفة من
يدلون بهم واتحدت
قرابتهم فالقسمة حينئذ علي

56. Among this class that person would be preferred who is nearest to the deceased by reason of any *jihat*;[1] and if they are of the same *jihat* then that person will be preferred who is related to the deceased, through an heir, for example mother's mother's father is preferred to mother's father's father[2] This is the view of Abu Suhail-al-Faraizi, Abi Fazl-ul-Khassaf and Ali bin-Isa-al Basri. There is no preference for them according to Abi Sulaiman Jurjani and Abi Ali al-basti; and if the degree is equal and there is no one among them who is related through an heir or all of them are related through some heir and the

[1] Whether related on the side of the father or on the side of the mother.

[2] The mother's father is preferred to mother's mother's father or father's mother's father. Mother's mother's father is preferred to mother's father's father, although they belong to the same degree, for mother's mother's father is related to the deceased through mother's mother who is a true grandmother; and mother's father's father is related to the deceased through a false grandfather that is the mother's father; and mother's father does not take along with mother's mother that is mother's mother is preferred and similarly her father is preferred.

ابدانهم و ان اختلف اصفة
من يدلون بهم يقسم المال
علي اول بطن اختلف كمافي
الصنف الاول و ان اختلف
قرابتهم فالثلثان لقرابة الاب
و هو نصيب الاب والثلث
لقرابة الام و هو نصيب الام
ثم ما اصاب كل فريق
يقسم بينهم كما لو اتحدت
قرابتهم

sexes of those heirs through whom they are related are the same and the relationship is also the same then the distribution shall take place according to their *abdan*[1] their persons; but if the sex of the root through whom they are related is different then the distribution shall take place on the first line of descent where the sexes differ as in the case of the first class and if relationship is different then 2/3 is the share of those related on the father's side, for that is the share of the father and 1/3 is given to persons related on the mother's side for that is the share of the mother, thereafter what has been assigned will be distributed to each class as is done in the case of the same relations.

SECTION IV

ON

The Third Class.

فصل في الصنف الثالث

٥٧ - الحكم فيهم كالحكم
في الصنف الاول اعني

57. The principles concerning them are the same as in the first case,

---

Similarly Father's mother's father = 2/3 Father's father's mother = 1/3 FMFF=2/3 FMFM=1/3

[1] *e.g.*, FFMFM will get 2/3 as being related to the father and the MFFFM will get 1/3 the share of the mother.

اولهم بالميراث اقربهم الى
الميت و ان استووا في
القرب فولد العصبة اولى
من ولد ذوي الارحام كبنت
ابن الاخ وابن بنت الاخت
كلاهما لاب و ام اولاب
لو احدهما لاب و ام و
الآخر لاب المال كله لبنت
ابن الاخ لانها ولد العصبة
و لو كانا لام المال بينهما
للذكر مثل حظ الانثيين
عند ابي يوسف رحمه
الله تعالى باعتبار الابدان

that is, among them, preference will be given to the nearest relation of the deceased and if they are equal in degree then descendants of the residuaries will be preferred to the descendants of *Zuvil arham*, *e.g.*, a person leaves the daughter of a brother's son and the son of a sister's daughter, one by the same father and mother or by the same father only, or either by the same father and mother or the other by the same father only, then all the property will be given to the daughter of the brother's son because she is a descendant of a residuary and if both of them be by the same mother then distribution will be made between them according to the rule "double share for the male members" in accordance with the opinion of Abu Yusuf considering their *abdan*, persons.

٥٨ - و عند محمد
رحمه الله تعالى المال بينهما

58. But according to Imam Muhammad[1] it would be distributed equally between them according to

---

1 As regards distribution in the third class of the Distant Kindred there is great difference of opinion between Imam Abu Yusuf and Imam Muhammad. However the *Fatwa* accords with the opinion of Imam Muhammad as it does in all matters relating to the Distant Kindred.

انما نا باعتبار الاصول بهذه الصورة ۔

the *usul i.e.*, their ancestors as in the following example :—[1]

م	
الاخت لام	الاخ لام
بنت	ابن
ابن	بنت

PROPOSITUS

Uterine Brother	Uterine Sister
Son	Daughter
Daughter	Son

وان استووا في القرب وليس فيهم ولد عصبة او كان كلهم اولاد العصبات و بعضهم اولاد اصحاب الفرائض فابو يوسف رحمه الله تعالى يعتبر الاقوى و محمد رحمه الله تعالي يقسم المال على الاخوة والاخوات مع اعتبار عدد الفروع والجهات في الاصول فما اصاب كل فريق يقسم بين فروعهم كما في الصنف الاول كما اذا ترك ثلث بنات اخوة متفرقين و ثلثة

and if they be equal in degree and there is no child of a residuary among them or all of them are children of residuaries and some of them are children of sharers then according to Abu Yusuf attention will be paid to blood relationship and according to Imam Muhammad the distribution would be made among the brothers and sisters by reason of their descendants and their *jihat* (stock) and the *usul* (root) ;[3] and whatever has been given to class will be distributed among the descendants as has been done in the case of the first class *e.g.*, a person leaves 3 daughters of brothers of different kinds and 3

---

[1] According to Abu Yusuf the distribution is to daughter 1/3 and to son 1/2 and according to Imam Muhammad it would be half and half and the latter view is accepted.

[2] This is the accepted view of Imam Abu Hanifa.

sons, and 3 daughters of different sisters as in the following example :—

بنين و ثلث بنات اخوات متفرقات بهذه الصورة .

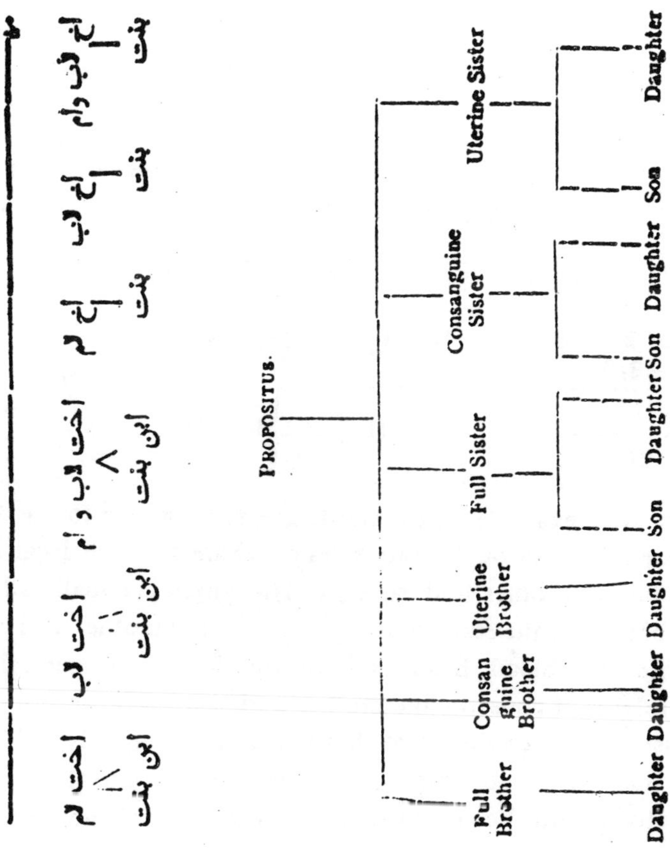

According to Abu Yusuf the distribution will take effect between descendants of full brothers and sisters, next between descendants of consanguine brothers and sisters and next between descendants of uterine brothers and sisters according to the rule "double share to the male" and in this case it will be in fourths in terms of their *abdan*, persons.

عند ابي يوسف رحمه الله يقسم كل المال بين فروع بني الاعيان ثم بين فروع بني العلات ثم بين فروع بني الاخياف للذكر مثل حظ الانثيين ارباعاً باعتبار الابدان

وعند محمد رحمه الله يقسم
ثلث المال بين فروع
بني الاخياف علي

But according to Imam Muhammad a third of the property will be distributed among the uterine relations in

---

[1] *e.g.*, descendants of full, consanguine and uterine brothers and sisters.

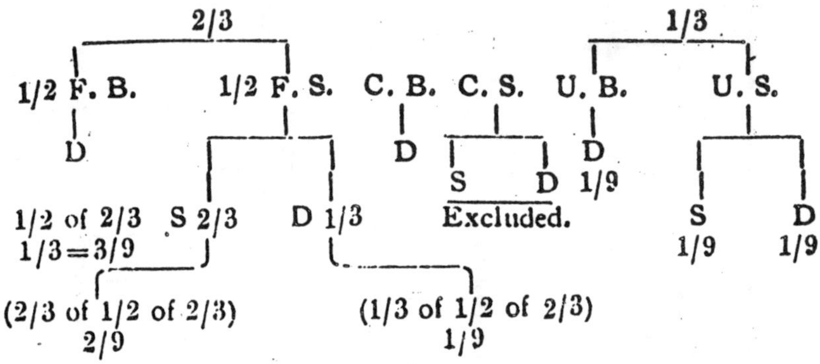

In this example all claimants are equally near to the deceased and are related through residuaries or sharers. The legal share of the uterine brother and sister is 1/3 which is equally allotted to their branches, the residue 2/3 goes to the full brother and sister.

The full blood heirs exclude the half-blood heirs, therefore, descendants of consanguine brother and sister take nothing. The full-sister F. S. having two branches takes equally with F. B. who has only one branch, and their shares go to their branches respectively and the rule of double portion to male applies.

F. B. D.	gets 1/2 of 2/3 or 1/3	= 3/9
F. S. S. =	2/3 of 1/2 of 2/3	= 2/9
F. S. D. =	1/3 of 1/2 of 2/3	= 1/9
U. B. D. =	1/3 of 1/3	= 1/9
U. S. S. =	1/3 of 1/3	= 1/9
U. S. D. =	1/3 of 1/3	= 1/9

According to Imam Abu Yusuf the descendants of consanguine brothers and uterine brothers and sisters would be excluded; consequently we have full-brother's and full sister's sons and daughter;

Son = 2 daughters; therefore the division will be in fourths, son taking 2/4; each daughter taking 1/4.

السوية اثلاثا لاستواء
اصولهم في القسمة و الباقي
بين فروع بني الاعيان
انصافا باعتبار عدد الفروع
في الاصول نصفه لبنت الاخ
نصيب ابيها والنصف الاخر
بين ولدي الاخت للذكر
مثل حظ الانثيين باعتبار
الابدان و تصح من تسعة

thirds in terms of the *usul* (the root) of their parents, and their shares are equal and the rest of the property will be distributed among the descendants of the full brother and sister in equal halves in terms of their descendants, half will be given to the daughter of the brother, share of her father and the other half will be distributed between the child of the sister, the male taking double share in terms of their persons and the distribution would be into 9 shares.[1] If a person leaves 3 daughters from 3 sons

---

[1] The following is the Arabian method of working the same example :—

Masala 3, Mazrub 3, *Tashih* 9.

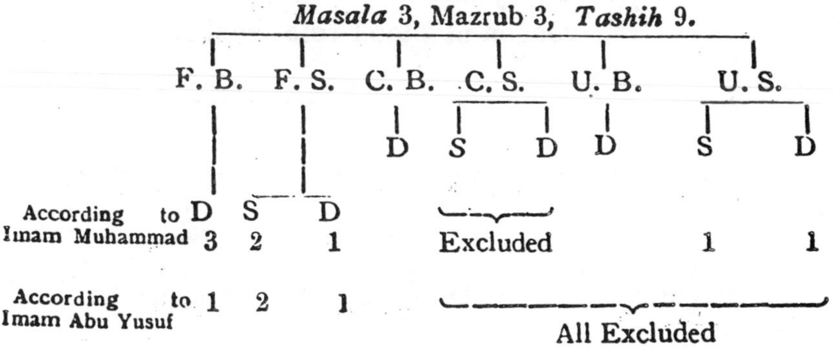

According to Imam Muhammad we first assign two shares to descendants of full brother and sister, and one share to uterine class thus the *Masala* is 3. Now we see that the number of shares and heirs are *Mutabayin.* Similarly the numbers 2 and 3 are *Mutabayin* and we further notice that 3 the number of heirs is same *i.e., Muta masal* thus we multiply 3 by 3 and get 9 as *Tashih-i-Masala.*

و لو ترك ثلث بنات بني أخوة متفرقين بهذه الصورة –

of different brothers as in the following example :—[1]

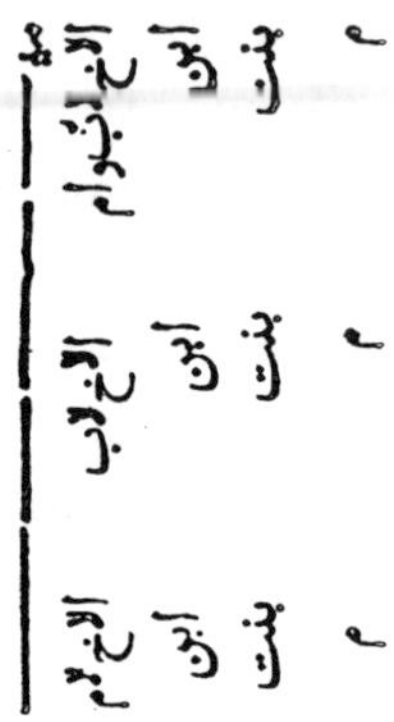

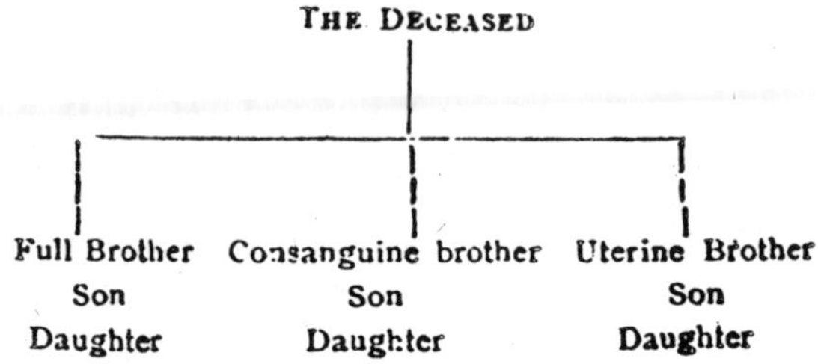

المال كله لبنت ابن الاخ لاب وام بالاتفاق لانها ولد العصبة و لها ايضا قوة القرابة .

In this case all the property will go to the daughter of full-brother because she is a descendant of a residuary and she would be preferred by reason of blood relationship.[2]

---

[1]

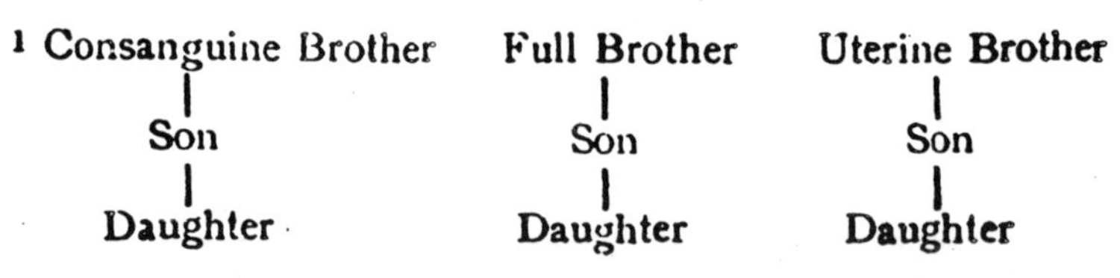

[2] In this example the full-brother's son's daughter excludes uterine brother's son's daughter according to the rule "among claimants of equal degree those related through a residuary exclude those related through a Distant Kindred." And further as the heirs of full-blood exclude those of half-blood on the father's side, consanguine brother's son's daughter is also excluded. Hence full brother's son's daughter is alone entitled to the whole property.

فصل فی الصنف الرابع

SECTION IV

ON

The Fourth Class

٥٩ - الحکم فیهم انه
اذا انفرد واحد منهم استحق
المال کله لعدم المزاحم و
وان اجتمعوا وکان حیز
قرابتهم متحداً کالعمات
والاعمام لام او الاخوال
والخالات فالاقوی منهم اولی
بالاجماع اعنی من کان
لاب و ام اولی ممن کان
لاب و من کان لاب اولی
ممن کان لام ذکوراً کانوا
او اناثاً و ان کانو ذکوراً و
اناثاً و استوت قرابتهم
فللذکر مثل حظ الانثیین
کعم و عمة کلاهما لام او

59. The rule concerning this class is this: if there is only one of them he will be entitled to the whole inheritance[1] by reason of there being none to prevent his taking and if there are many and their relationship is the same, *e.g.*, as paternal aunts, and uterine uncles by the same mother, or maternal uncles and maternal aunts, then preference is given by reason of consanguinity as agreed by all jurists, that is those related by the same father and mother are preferred to those related by the same father and those related by the same father are preferred to those related by the same mother irrespective of their being male or female; but if there are males and females of equal degrees then the male shall receive the double share *e.g.*, a person leaves father's uterine-brother and father's uterine-sister or maternal uncle and maternal aunt, whether by the same father and mother or by the same father or by

[1] *e.g.*, a person leaves a paternal aunt or a maternal uncle or maternal aunt, then all the property will be given to anyone of them, there being no one else to take it.

11

خال و خالة لهما لاب
و ام اولاب اولام و ان
كان حيز قرابتهم مختلفاً
فلا اعتبار لقوة القرابة كعمة
لاب و ام و خالة لام او
خالة لاب و ام و عمة
لام فالثلثان لقرابة الاب

the same mother; but if the stock of relationship be different then no attention will be paid to this fact, *e.g.*, if there is a paternal aunt by the same father and mother and a maternal aunt by the same mother or a maternal aunt by the same father and mother and a paternal aunt by the same mother then in this case two-thirds will be given to the relations on the father's side[1] which is the share of the father and 1/3 to the relation

---

1 The Table of Distant kindred Uncles and Aunts.

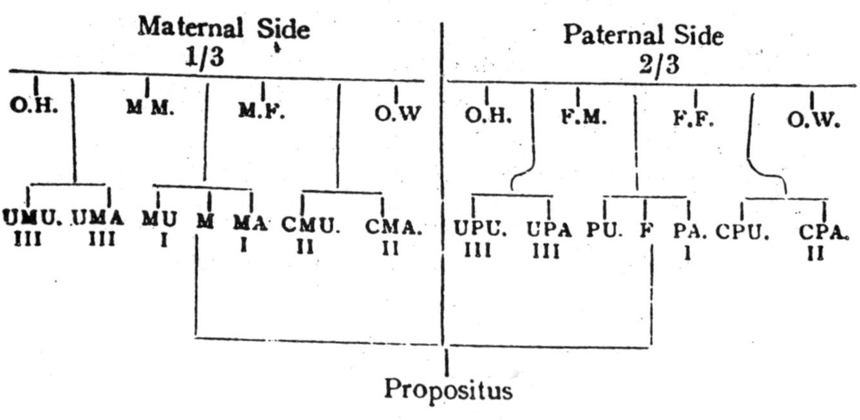

The numbers I, II, and III indicate the order of preference.

O.H. = other Husband
O.W. = other Wife
M.M. = Mother's mother
M.F. = Mother's Father
M. = Mother

F. = Father
F.M. = Father's Mother
F.F. = Father's Father
(*N.B.*—P.U. Paternal Uncle and C. P. U. Consanguine paternal Uncle do not belong to the class of Distant kindred.)

و هو نصيب الاب والثلث لقرابة الام و هو نصيب الام ثم ما اصاب كل فريق يقسم بينهم كما لو اتحد حيز قرابتهم ۔	on the mother side which is the share of the mother. Then whatever has been given will be distributed in this class as if the relationship were identical.

I. P. A (paternal Aunt) will take 2/3=6/9
M.U. (maternal Uncle) „ „ 2/3 of 1/3=2/9
M.A. („ aunt) „ „ 1/3 of 1/3=1/9
In absence of either of these the other will take the maternal portion 1/3

II. In default of P. A. C. P. A. (consanguine paternal uncle) will take 2/3 the paternal portion.
In default of M. U. and M. A. the maternal portion 1/3 will devolve upon :—
C.M.U. (Consanguine maternal uncle) 2/3 of 1/3=2/9
C.M.A. („ „ aunt) 1/3 of 1/3=1/9
In absence of either of these, the other will take the whole 1/3.

III. In default of P. A. and C. P. A.,
U.P.U. (uterine paternal uncle) will take 2/3 of 2/3=4/9
U.P.A. („ „ aunt) „ „ 1/3 of 2/3=2/9
In absence of either of these the other will take the whole 2/3.
In default of M. U., M. A., C. M. U. and C. M. A.,
U.M.U. (uterine maternal uncle)=2/3 of 1/3=2/9
U.M.A. („ „ aunt)=1/3 of 1/3=1/9
In absence of either of these the other will take 1/3

The following chart will show at a glance what each will get on the father's side and on the mother's side.

PATERNAL SIDE 2/3.		MATERNAL SIDE 1/3.	
Father's father's side 2/3 of 2/3	Father's mother's side 1/3 of 2/3	Mother's father's side 2/3 of 1/3	Mother's mother's side 1/3 of 1/3

SECTION VI

ON

Their Descendants

فصل في اولادهم ◦

60. The rule concerning them is similar to the rule concerning the first class that is preference is given to the nearest in relationship to the deceased by reason of any *jihat* (whichever side of relationship) and if they be equal in relationship and the *jihat* be the same then that will be preferred according to *Ijma*;[1] who has the strength of blood relationship and if they are equal in *qurb* and *qarabat* (that is, equal in degree and in blood) then the descendants of residuaries will be preferred *e.g.*, a person leaves the daughter of a paternal uncle and the son of paternal aunt, the whole property will be given to the son of the uncle because he is the descendant of the residuary; and if one of them is the descendant of the same father then all the property will go on the strength of blood

٦٠ - الحكم فيهم كالحكم في الصنف الاول اعني اولاهم بالميراث اقربهم الي الميت من اي جهة كان و ان استووا في القرب و كان حيز قرابتهم متحداً فمن كانت له قوة القرابة فهو اولي بالاجماع و ان استووا في القرب والقرابة و كان حيز قرابتهم متحداً فولد العصبة اولي كبنت العم و ابن العمة كلا هما لاب و ام اولاب المال كله لبنت العم لانها ولد العصبة و ان كان احد هما لاب و ام والآخر لاب المال كله لمن كان له قوة القرابة في ظاهر الرواية قياساً علي خالة لاب مع كونها ولد ذي رحم هي اولي بقوة القرابة من الخالة

[1] The agreement among the jurists on a question of Law.

Some illustrations as regards descendants of the Distant kindred and preference among them :—

Paternal aunt's daughter is preferred to paternal aunt's daughter's daughter, paternal aunt's descendants are preferred to consanguine aunts descendants, and the latter are preferred to uterine aunt's descendants,

الوارثة ولد كونها مع لام	relationship in accordance with the
لمعني الترجيح لان	accepted view; according to the
القرابة قوة هو ، فيه	doctrine of *qiyas*[1] the maternal aunt

Those related by the same father and mother would exclude those related by the same father.

In the case of a son of a paternal aunt and the son of a consanguine paternal uncle the whole propeity will be given to the son of the paternal aunt; and applying this case by analogy to the maternal aunt by the same father (that is mother's consanguine sister) she is the descendant of mother's father, she would be preferred to a maternal aunt by same mother (that is mother's uterine sister) who is the descendant of mother's mother, though mother's mother is an heir and is considered as a true grandmother as opposed to the mother's father who is not a sharer, but a distant kindred. And the reason for giving preference to mother's consanguine sister over the mother's uterine sister is simply by reason of relationship for mother's consanguine sister is related through father. That is in giving preference to the son of the paternal aunt, who is a descendant of distant kindred, the jurists are agreed that the daughter of the uncle by the same father and son of the full aunt are equal in degree and relationship, nevertheless the strength of blood-relationship does not favour the son of the paternal aunt.

Again in the following case:—

PATERNAL UNCLE	PATERNAL AUNT
DAUGHTER	SON

Here Daughter is preferred to Son.

Similarly Paternal Uncle's daughter is preferred to paternal aunt's daughter and the latter is preferred to consanguine aunt's daughter.

The descendants of full paternal aunt are preferred to the descendants of maternal uncle or maternal aunt by the same father or by the same mother. In the same manner the daughter of the full paternal uncle would be preferrea to the daughter of the full maternal uncle or full maternal aunt by the same father.

[1] Analogy, a process of deduction recognised by the jurists.

اولى من الترجيح لمعني في غيره و هو الادلاء بالوارث -

by the same father (that is mother's consanguine sister) although she is a descendant of *Zuvil arham* is preferred by reason of *qarabat* relationship to the maternal aunt by the same mother (that is mother's uterine sister) although the maternal aunt by the same mother is the descendant of an heir, since the cause of preference is the strength of relationship and it is considered as a perference to the fact of descent from an heir.

٦١ - و قال بعضهم المال كله لبنت العم لاب لانها ولد العصبة و ان استووا في القرب و لكن اختلف حيز قرابتهم فلا اعتبار لقوة القرابة و لا لولد العصبة في ظاهر الرواية قياساً علي عمة لاب و ام مع كونها ذات القرابتين و ولد الوارث من الجهتين هي ليست باولى من الخالة لاب او لام لكن الثلثين لمن يدلي بقرابة الاب فتعتبر فيهم قوة القرابة ثم ولد العصبة والثلث لمن يدلي بقرابة الام و تعتبر فيهم قوة القرابة ثم عند ابي يوسف رحمة الله تعالي ما اصاب كل فريق يقسم علي ابدان

61. Some of the jurists say that the whole property will be given to the daughter of the consanguine uncle as she is the descendant of the residuary; and if they are equal in degree, but different by reason of *(jihat)* side of relationship, then we shall not pay attention to the strength of blood-relationship nor by reason of their being the descendants of residuaries; this is so according to the accepted view. Now applying *qiyas* to the case of full paternal aunt by the same father and mother though she is doubly related and she is a descendant of an heir on two *jihats*, yet she is not preferred to the consanguiue maternal aunt or the uterine maternal aunt but inspite of *qiyas* two-thirds will be given to one who is related to the father, thus we shall pay attention to the strength of relationship and next to the fact of being descend-

فروعهم مع أعتبار عدد
الجهات في الفروع و عند
محمد رحمه الله تعالي
يقسم المال علي أول
بطن اختلف مع اعتبار
عدد الفروع والجهات في
الأصول كما في الصنف

ants of residuaries. And one-third will be given to those related to the mother and here we pay attention to the strength of relationship. Then according to Abu Yusuf whatever has been assigned to one class shall be distributed in terms of *abdan*, their persons taking into consideration the number of branches and according to

---

The following illustration is taken from the Sharifa :—

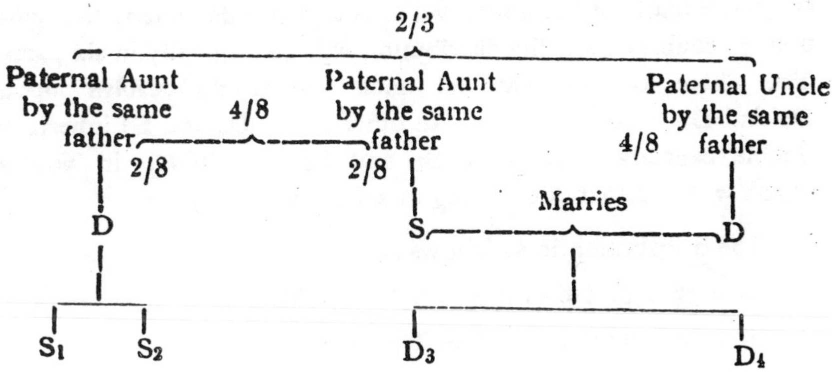

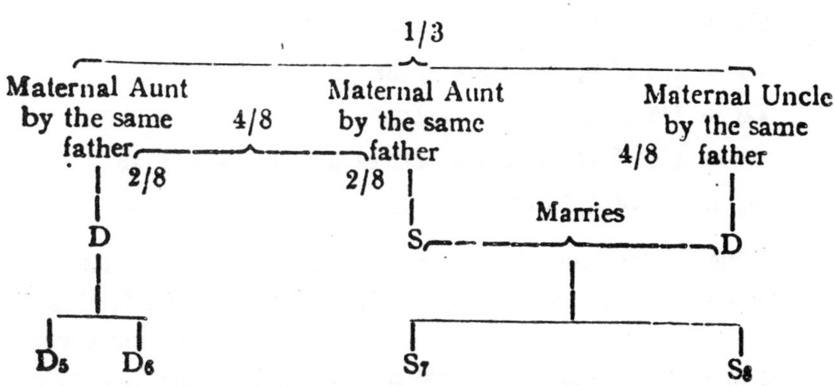

According to Imam Muhammad we shall first assign 2/3 on the paternal side and 1/3 on the maternal side. And in the

الاول ثم ينتقل هذا
الحكم الي جهة عمومة
ابويه و خوولتهما ثم الي
اولادهم ثم الي جهة
عمومة ابوي ابويه

Imam Muhammad the property will be distributed in the first line while the sexes of the ancestors differ by reason of the descendants and the sexes of the root as done in the case of first class of distant kindred: thus this rule become applicable as regards the paternal uncles of his

---

first line the sexes of ancestors differ, and in terms of their descendants the uncle would take 4/8 and the two aunts 2/8 each. The latter shares will be grouped together *i.e.*, 4/8 would devolve upon the descendants of the aunts two sons and two daughters, the sons taking double share, the distribution will be originally in six parts. The share of the paternal uncle 4/8 would devolve upon D_3 and D_4 in equal shares. In other words D_3 and D_4 inherit in double capacity. Similarly S_7 and S_8 will inherit in double capacity, the distribution being in six parts.

The distribution is as follows :—

S_1 = 2/6 of 4/8 of 2/3 = 1/9 = 4/36

S_2 = 2/6 of 4/8 of 2/3 = 1/9 = 4/36

D_3 = 1/6 of 4/8 of 2/3 + 1/2 of 4/8 of 2/3 = 8/36

D_4 = 1/6 of 4/8 of 2/3 + 1/2 of 4/8 of 2/3 = 8/36

D_5 = 1/6 of 4/8 of 1/3 = 1/36

D_6 = 1/6 of 4/8 of 1/3 = 1/36

S_7 = 2/6 of 4/8 of 1/3 + 1/2 of 4/8 of 1/3 = 5/36

S_8 = 2/6 of 4/8 of 1/3 + 1/2 of 4/8 of 1/3 = 5/36

This is the correct distribution the author of the Sharifa has assigned to S_1 3/36 shares, S_2 3/36 and to D_3 and D_4 9/36 shares each, apparently without following Imam Muhammad's system. The mistake is apparent, he has not grouped together two paternal aunt's descendants as he actually does when distributing the maternal aunt's descendants. After consulting some legal works.

وخو ولتهما ثم الي اولادهم
كما في العصبات

parents and also as regards the maternal uncles of the parents and next to their children, as in the case of residuaries.

SECTION VII

ON

فصل في الخنثي.

Khunsa, Hermaphrodite

٦٢ - للخنثي المشكل
اقل النصيبين اعني اسوء

62. For that *Khunsa*, hermaphrodite, whose case is difficult,[1] its sex

---

I found that Maulana Nizam-uddin Kirawani in his work on the Law of Inheritance published by the Mujtabai Press, Delhi, (1904) has also pointed out the same mistake.

According to Imam Abu Yusuf, on the paternal side there are two sons S_1 and S_2, and two daughters D_3 and D_4 descendants of the Paternal Uncle's daughter and Aunt's son, and hence counted as four daughters. Hence the distribution will be into eight parts,

i.e., $S_1 = 2/8$ of $2/3 = 1/6 = 5/30$

$S_2 = 2/8$ of $2/3 = 1/6 = 5/30$

$D_3 = 2/8$ of $2/3$ (in double capacity) $= 1/6 = 5/30$

$D_4 = 2/8$ of $2/3$ (in double capacity) $= 1/6 = 5/30$

Similarly S_7 and S_8 will be counted as four sons being descendants of maternal uncle and aunt, and along with D_5 and D_6 the distribution will be into ten parts,

i.e., $S_7 = 4/10$ of $1/3$ (in double capacity) $= 4/30$

$S_8 = 4/10$ of $1/3$ (in double capacity) $= 4/30$

$D_5 = 1/10$ of $1/3$ . . . . $= 1/30$

$D_6 = 1/10$ of $1/3$ . . . . $= 1/30$

Thus in short according to Imam Abu Yusuf the division is into 30 parts and according to Imam Muhammad it is into 36 parts. The *Fatwa* accords with Imam Muhammad's opinion, hence his system of distribution relating to the distant kin ed class is to be followed.

[1] That is if the hermaphrodite closely resembles a male he would inherit as a male or if he resembles a female he would inherit as a

الحالين عند ابي حنيفة
رحمه الله تعالي و اصحابه
و هو قول عامة الصحابة
رضي الله تعالي عنهم و
عليه الفتوى كما اذا ترك
ابنا و بنتا و خنثي للخنثي
نصيب بنت لانه متيقن و
عند الشعبي رضي الله
تعالي عنه و هو قول ابن
عباس رضي الله تعالي

being doubtful, the rule is to assign to him the smaller of the two shares, [1] the worse of the two conditions in accordance with the opinion of Imam Abu Hanifa and his followers. This is also the common opinion of the Companions of the Prophet and the *fatwa* accords with it *e.g.*, a person dies leaving a son, a daughter and a hermaphrodite:

---

female. The Sirajiyyah here discusses the case of the hermaphrodite whose sex is doubtful and who cannot be described as a male or a female or closely resembles both sexes. The chief test to determine the sex is physical appearance of the male or female generative organs and such physical signs as the beard or a woman-like breast and menstruation.

[1] The small share that he would get as a male or a female.

It will be seen that the Sirajiyyah has not mentioned that a hermaphrodite would always take as a daughter, some people are likely to think that the share of the daughter is always less than that of the son; but this is not so, under certain circumstances the heir may take more if it were a daughter, *e.g.*, a person leaves a husband, father, mother, and a hemaphrodite :—

	Husband	Father	Mother	Hermaphrodite
If the hermaphrodite takes as a female	1/4 3/12	1/6 2/12	1/6 2/12	1/2 6/12
Reduced to unity by the doctrine of Increase	3/13	2/13	2/13	6/13
If the hermaphrodite takes as a male	1/4 3/12	1/6 2/12	1/6 2/12	5/12 (Residue)

Now 5/12 is smaller than 6/13, therefore the hermaphrodite inherits here as a son.

منهما للخنثي نصف نصيبين
بالمنازعة واختلفاني تخريج
قول الشعبي قال ابو
يوسف رحمه الله تعالي
للابن سهم و للبنت نصف
سهم و للخنثي ثلثة ارباع
سهم لان الخنثى يستحق
سهماً ان كان ذكراً او
نصف سهم ان كان انثى
، وهذا متيقن فياخذ نصف
النصيبين او النصف
المتيقن مع نصف النصف
المتنازع فيه فصارت له
ثلثة ارباع سهم و مجموع
الانصباء سهمان و ربع سهم
لانه يعتبر السهام والعول
، تصح من تسعة او نقول

in this case the hermaphrodite would get the share of a daughter, for that is so[1]; and according to Shabi, who adopts the view of Ibn Abbas, the hermaphrodite is to take half of the two collective shares by reason of controversy, but the ***sahibain*** (Imam Abu Yusuf and Imam Muhammad) have differed in interpreting the doctrine of Shabi, for Imam Abu Yusuf says that if the son takes one share, and the daughter one-half the hermaphrodite would take 3/4, because the hermaphrodite is entitled to one share in the capacity of male and to a share in the capacity of a female, and this is the certain share;[2] thus

---

[1] Because that is the smaller share :—

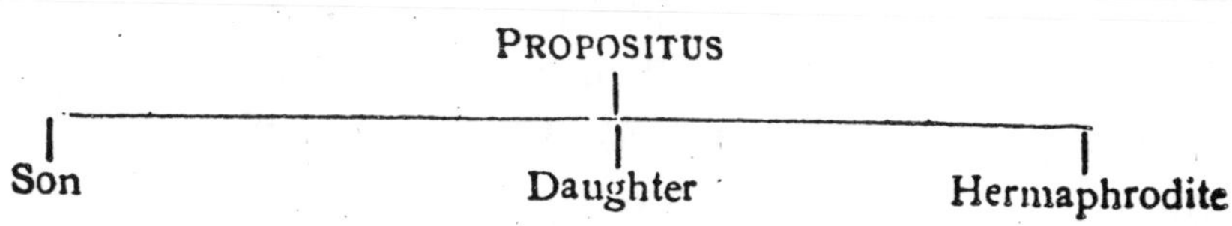

If the Hermaphrodite takes as a daughter :—

Son 2/4, Daughter 1/4, Hermaphrodite 1/4

If the Hermaphrodite take as a son :—

Son 2/5, Daughter 1/5, Hermaphrodite 2/5.

Now 1/4 is less than 2/5, therefore the Hermaphrodite takes 1/4 as a daughter.

[2] In the above example, Imam Abu Yusuf is simply fixing the *ratio* among the son, daughter and hermaphrodite and not assigning shares; 3/4 is equal to 1/2 of the share of the son plus half of the share of the daughter, that is $1/2+1/4=3/4$.

للابن سهمان و للبنت
سهم و للخنثي نصف
النصيبين و هو سهم ونصف
سهم و قال محمد رحمه
الله تعالي ياخذ الخنثي
خمسي المال ان كان
ذكرا و ربع المال ان كان
انثي. فياخذ نصف النصيبين
و ذالک خمس و ثمن
باعتبار الحالين و تصح
من اربعين و هو المجتمع
من ضرب احدي
المسئلتين و هي الاربعة في
الاخري و هي. الخمسة
ثم في الحالين فمن كان له
شيء من الخمسة فمضروب
في الاربعة و من كان له شي
من الاربعة فمضروب في الخمسة
فصارت للخنثي من الضربين
ثلثة عشر سهماً و للابن

the hermaphrodite would take half the sum of two shares, that is he would take half of the certain share[1] and half of the disputed share[2] so that he receives 3/4 and the total sum of shares is $2\frac{1}{4}$ because Abu Yusuf pays attention to the share and applies the doctrine of Increase and *masala* will be by 9;[3] or we may say that the son has two shares and the daughter has one share and the hermaphrodite has half of these two shares, which is $1\frac{1}{2}$. According to Imam Muhammad the hermaphrodite will take 2/5 of the property if it is a male and 1/4 if it is a female, and so he takes half of the two shares and he will get 1/5 and 1/8 in consideration of both sexes and the *tashih* will be by 40 *i.e.*, we multiply the two *masala*[4] that is 4 and 5 together and the product is multiplied in the two conditions, that is by 2, then the share of that heir who takes in fifths is to be multiplied

---

1 Possibly to which he belongs.

2 To which class he may not belong.

3

Son	1	4/4	Applying Increase reducing shares	4/9
Daughter	1/2	2/4		2/9
Hermaphrodite	3/4	3/4		3/9
Total ...		$2\frac{1}{4}$		

4 $4 \times 5 = 20 \times 2 = 40$. *Tashih masala.*

ثمانية عشر سهما و للبنت تسعة أسهم –

by 4 and the share of that heir who takes in fourth is to be multipled by 5. The distribution would be 13 shares to the hermaprodite, 18 shares to the son, and 9 shares to the daughter.[1]

---

1 PROPOSITUS

Son — Daughter — Hermaphrodite

Taking the Hermaphrodite as a son ;

Son 2/5, Daughter 1/5, Hermaphrodite 2/5.

Taking the Hermaphrodite as a daughter ;

Son 2/4, Daughter 1/4, Hermaphrodite 1/4.

According to the rule Hermaphrodite gets 1/2 (2/5+1/4)= 13/40.

Therefore the residue is 27/40. Hence the Son gets 2/3 of 27/40 =18/40. And Daughter gets 1/3 of 27/40=9/40.

The Sirajiyyah works out according to the following method.

Share of the son :

2 of the 5th multiplied by 4=2×4= 8
and 2 of the 4th multiplied by 5=2×5=10
—
18

Share of the daughter :

1 of the 5th multiplied by 4=1×4= 4
and 1 of the 4th multiplied by 5=1×5= 5
—
9

Share of the hermaphrodite :

2 of the 5th multipled by 4=2×4= 8
and 1 of the 4th multipled by 5=1×5= 5
—
13

N.B.—If the hermaphrodite is the only heir he would receive the whole property.

SECTION VIII
ON
Pregnancy

فصل في الحمل -

٦٣ - اكثر مدة الحمل
سنتان عند ابي حنيفة
رحمه الله تعالى و عند ليث
بن سعد ثلث سنين
و عند الشافعي رحمة الله تعالى
اربع سنين و عند الزهري سبع
سنين و اقلها ستة اشهر و

63. According to Imam Abu Yusuf the maximum period of pregnancy is 2 years,[1] and according to Lais bin Sad it is 3 years and according to Imam Shafi it is 4 years, and according to Alzuhri it is 7 years; and the minimum period[2] of

---

[1] A child may be an absolute excluder, that is, he may absolutely exclude the existing heirs or he may reduce their shares; if he could be an absolute excluder then the estate cannot be distributed *e.g.*, a person dies leaving a full-brother's pregnant widow and a full-brother's son's son and in this case if a male child is born then he would exclude brother's son's son; but if a female child is born she would take nothing, being a distant kindred as against the brother's son's son, since it is a possible case of absolute exclusion, the estate cannot be distributed until the birth of the child.

Two years is the maximum period of gestation ***provided the woman declares within the period of her iddat or divorce*** that she is pregnant; in the absence of such a declaration within this period, the rule of 2 years cannot be applicable; For further discussion see "A Dissertation on the Muslim Law of Legitimacy and Section 112 of the Indian Evidence Act" by the present author.

The normal period of gestation is from nine to ten months. Section 112 of the Indian Evidence Act limits the period to 280 days, the Code Napolean fixed 300 days, but according to some best authorities (*vide* Taylor's Medical Jurisprudence or Lyon's), the maximum period has been 308 days and in certain cases 315 to 322 days. The Muslim rule of 2 years is to cover these abnormal periods, provided a declaration has been made during the observance of *iddat* by the woman. In the case of pregnancy the *iddat* will continue till delivery, but this declaration must be made within 4 months and ten days after death of the husband and within three months after divorce. *Vide* "Dissertation on the Muslim Law of Legitimacy and Section 112 of the Indian Evidence Act," by the present author.

The Shafii jurists have mentioned several persons who were born during 4 years of pregnancy *e.g.*, Zuhak and Abdul Aziz Majshuni.

[2] The minimum period is 6 months, or six lunar months according to Muslim jurists, that is it will vary from 174 days

يوقف للحمل عند ابي حنيفة
رحمه الله تعالى نصيب
اربعة بنين او اربع بنات
ايهما اكثر و يعطي لبقية
الورثة اقل الانصباء و عند
محمد رحمه الله تعالى
يوقف نصيب ثلثة بنين او
ثلث بنات ايهما اكثر رواه
عنه ليث بن سعد و
في رواية اخري نصيب
ابنين و هو قول الحسن
واحدي الروايتين عن
ابي يوسف رحمه الله تعالي
رواه عنه هشام و روي
الخصاف رح عن ابي يوسف
رحمه الله تعالي انه يوقف
نصيب ابن واحد او بنت
واحدة و عليه الفتوى و
يوخذ الكفيل على قوله
فان كان الحمل من الميت
و جاءت بالولد لتمام اكثر
مدة الحمل او اقل منها

pregancy is 6 months, and according to Imam Abu Hanifa for the child in the womb there shall be reserved shares of the four sons or the shares of four daughters, whichever is greater and the smallest allotment will be made to the other heirs; and according to Imam Muhammad for the child in the womb shall be reserved a share of three sons or three daughters, whichever is greater, and this report of Imam Muhammad is from Lais bin Sad and according to another report the share of two sons shall be reserved and this is the report from Hasan, and of the two reports of Abu Yusuf one report is from Hisham and the other is from Alkhassaf, namely for a child in the womb shall be reserved share of one son or one daughter whichever is greater and the *fatwa* accords with this opinion; and according to Imam Abu Yusuf security will be taken.[1] And if a woman is pregnant from the deceased and she has a child at the

---

to 180 days and according to the best authorities reported in Medical Jurisprudence, (Lyon's or Taylor's) there is a case of a child born 174 days after the last menstruation, *i.e.*, the famous Jardine's case is the rearing of a 174 day child.

[1] Security will be taken by the Kazi from the heirs of the deceased. The security will be taken of the possibility, that is if more than one child is born then in consideration of his right the heirs will give part of his or their estate; that is each will return a part of the inheritance received by him according to the right of

و لم تكن اقرت بانقضاء العدة يرث و يورث عنه -

maximum time of pregnancy or within it and the woman had not admitted that her *iddat* has terminated then the child will be an heir and so would others inherit from him.

٦٤ - و ان جاءت بالولد لاكثر من اكثر مدة الحمل لا يرث و لا يورث و ان كان من غيره ، جاءت بالولد لستة اشهر او اقل منها يرث و ان جاءت به لاكثر من اقل مدة الحمل لا يرث -

64. But if a child is born after the maximum period of gestation then it shall not inherit nor would others inheirt from him and if the pregnancy was from a person other than the deceased and the child is born within less than six months then that child shall inherit; but if it were born after the minimum period of gestation he shall not inherit.[1]

٦٥ - فان خرج اقل الولد ثم مات لا يرث

65. And if a little part of the child comes out and it dies it shall not in-

---

inheritance of the child born, because according to Imam Abu Yusuf we have only reserved the share of one son or one daughter, whichever is great.

[1] *e.g.*, a person A dies and he leaves his father's wife pregnant (so the woman is pregnant from another) or his grandfather's wife pregnant, and a child is born within six months or less than six months after the death of father or grandfather then that child will inherit from A because it is conclusively established that the child in the womb was a child of the father or of the grandfather; but if the child were born after the minimum period of gestation then he shall not inherit from the deceased A. This case is different from the wife of the deceased being pregnant in which case the maximum period of gestation would be two years. However the child born to father's or grandfather's wife would inherit from the father or grandfather provided it were born within the maximum period of gestation. This is a case of a child of another's pregnant wife inheriting and not a child of his own wife.

و ان خرج اكثره ثم مات
يرث فان خرج الولد
مستقيما فالمعتبر صدره
يعني اذ اخرج الصدر
كله يرث و ان خرج
منكوساً فالمعتبر سرته -

herit;[1] but if a greater part comes out and then it dies, it shall inherit; and if the child comes out with the head first, then his chest will be considered; that is, if his chest has come out it shall be considered to be alive and shall inherit; but if it comes out with his feet first then his navel will be considered.[2]

٦٦ - الاصل في تصحيح
مسائل الحمل أن تصحح
المسألة على تقديرين اعني
على تقدير ان الحمل ذكر
و على تقدير انه انثي ثم
تنظر بين تصحيحي
المسئلتين فان تو افقا
بجزء فاضرب و فق احد
هما في جميع الاخرو ان
تباينا فاضرب كل واحد
منهما في جميع الاخر فالحاصل
تصحيح المسئلة ثم اضرب
نصيب من كان له شيء
من مسئلة ذكورته في
و من كان له شيء من

66. Ṭhe rule for *tashih-i-masala* in the case of pregnancy is that the case should be arranged on two assumptions *i.e.*, assuming that the child born is a male or a female, then compare the two distributions, and if the numbers are *mutawafiq*, multiply the *wafq* of any one of them with the other, and the resulting product would be the *tashih-i-masala*; if the numbers are *mutabayin* then multiply the whole of the one into the whole of the other, the product will be the *Tashih masala*. Thereafter multiply the share that each heir will

---

1 A dead-born child is not an heir.

2 That is, if the child upto his navel has come out, and was alive then it shall inherit; but if the navel has not come out though the child had come out apparently alive, it shall not inherit.

The following passage occurs in Sir William Jones' Translation: "now the way of knowing the life of the child at the time of its birth is that there be found in him that by which life is proved as a voice, or sneezing, or weeping, or smiling, or moving a limb." But this passage is not found in the text of the Sirajiyyah it is from its commentary Sharifa.

مسئلة انوثته او في وفقها
من مسئلة انوثته في
مسئلة ذكورة او في وفقها
كما في الخنثى ثم انظر في
الحاصلين من الضرب ايهما
اقل يعطى لذالك الوارث
والفضل الذي بينهما موقوف
من نصيب ذلك الوارث
فاذا اظهر الحمل فان كان
مستحقا لجميع الموقوف
فيها و ان كان مستحقا
للبعض فياخذ ذالك
والباقي مقسوم بين الورثة
فيعطى لكل واحد من الورثة
ما كان موقوفاً من نصيبه
كما اذا ترك بنتا و ابوين
و امراته حاملا فالمسئلة
من اربعة و عشرين علي
تقدير ان الحمل ذكر و من
سبعة و عشرين علي تقدير
انه انثي فاذا ضرب وفق
احدهما في جميع الاخر
صار الحاصل مائتين وستة
عشر اذا علي تقدير ذكورته
للمراة سبعة و عشرون و
للابوين لكل واحد ستة
و ثلاثون و علي تقدير انوثته
للمراة اربعة و عشرون و
لكل واحد من الابوين
اثنان و ثلاثون فتعطى
للمراة اربعة و عشرون و
توقف من نصيبها ثلثة اسهم
و من نصب كل واحد
من الابوين اربعة اسهم و
تعطى للبنت ثلثة عشر سهما

receive on the supposition of the child being male by the *masala* on the supposition of the same being female or by its *wafq* as stated in the case of the hermaphrodite, then consider the two products and that what is the minimum will be given to that particular heir and the difference between these two shares will be reserved (for later distribution) and when the child is born if he happens to be such a one who is entitled to the whole of that what has been reserved then it is all right; but if he is entitled to a part then he may take that portion and the residue will again be distributed among the heirs by giving to each one of them what we had reserved from the other distribution, *e.g.*, a person leaves a daughter, mother and father and a pregnant wife, here the *masala* is by 24 if we assume that a male child will be born, and the *masala* will be by 27 if we assume that a female child will be born. Then when we multiply the *wafq* of the one by the whole of the other we shall get 216, and on assumption the fact that a male child is born, the wife will receive 27 shares and mother and father each 36 shares and assuming that a daughter is born the wife will receive 24 shares and father and

لن الموقوف في حقها
نصيب اربعة بنين عند

mother each 32 shares.[1] Thus in these circumstances the wife will be given

---

[1] CASE I.

	Mother.	Father.	Wife.	Daughter and Child
If a son is born	1/6	1/6	1/8	(Both take the residue, the son taking double share.)
	4/24	4/24	3/24	Residue 13/24
In all cases reducing to Common Denominator.	36/216	36/216	27/216	117/216

CASE II.

				Two daughters
If a daughter is born ...	1/6	1/6	1/8	2/3
	4/24	4/24	3/24	16/24
Applying doctrine of Increase, reduce shares ...	4/27	4/27	3/27	16/27
In all cases reducing to Common Denominator	32/216	32/216	24/216	128/216

CASE III.

If a dead child is born ...	1/6	1/6	1/8	1/2
	4/24	4/24	3/24	12/24
		1/24 (Residue)		
In all cases reducing to Common Denominator	36/216	36/216	27/216	108/216
		9/216 (Residue)		

	Mother.	Father.	Wife.	Daughter.	Reserved shares.
The allotted shares are...	32/216	32/216	24/216	[13/216]	115/216

We have seen from the above figures that the smallest shares taken by Mother and Father are each 32/216 and by the wife 24/216. These shares will be given to them, and we shall

ابي حنيفة رحمه الله تعالي
واذا كان البنون اربعة فنصيبها
سهم و اربعة اتساع سهم من اربعة
و عشرين مضروب في
تسعة فصار ثلثة عشر سهما
و هي لها والباقي موقوف

24 shares and 3 shares will be reserved out of her allotment and 4 shares will be reserved out of the allotment of father and mother each and according to Imam Abu Hanifa the daughter will receive 13 shares,

---

reserve 4/216, and 4/216 in the case of Father and Mother and 3/216 in the case of wife. The shares assigned to the Daughter and male child or children are 117/216 as in case I and the maximum shares as in Case II are 128/216. If one or more daughters are born then they all shall share out of 128/216. If one son or more are born then the distribution will be as in Case I. Here the daughter receives 13 shares on the supposition that 4 sons are born. 1/9 of 13/24=13/216 residue.

If a dead child is born the distribution will be as in Case III, the residue 9/216 being given to the Father who is a residuary.

The Sirajiyyah works out the problem in this manner:

If a son is born the *masala* is ... 24
If a daughter is born the *masala* is ... 27.

24 and 27 are *mutawafiq* by 3 the *tashih masala* is obtained by multiplying *wafq* of one by the whole of the other namely,

$8 \times 27 = 216$ or $24 \times 9 = 216$.

	Mother.	Father.	Wife.	Daughter and child.
If a son is born	36	36	27	117
If a daughter is born ...	32	32	24	128
If a dead child is born ...	36	36	23	108
		Residue 9		

	Mother.	Father.	Wife.	Daughter.	Reserved shares.
The allotted shares are...	32	32	34	13	115

If 4 sons are born, the daughter would take 13 shares and the residue 115 would be reserved.

If one or more daughters are born the Sirajiyyah says all the shares reserved will be given to the Daughters namely, 4 from Father, 4 from Mother, 3 from Wife and 128 or, in other words, the distribution will be as in Case II.

If one or more sons are born the Sirajiyyah says that the reserved portions will be given to the Father and Mother and to Wife, and the residue together with 13, that is 117 will be given to the children. Father and Mother would receive 36/216 shares each that they will be given the reserved 4/216 shares in addition to 32/216 shares already given and similarly the wife will get 27/216 *i.e.*, 3/216 shares more, reserved. *Vide* Case I.

وهو مائة و خمسة عشر سهماً
فان ولدت بنتاً واحدة
او اكثر فجميع المرقوف للبنات
و ان ولدت ابناً واحداً
او اكثر فيعطي للمراة و
الابوين ماكان موقوفا من
نصيبهم فما بقي تضم اليه
ثلثة عشر ويقسم بين الاولاد
و ان ولدت ولداً ميتاً
فيعطى للمراة والابوين
ما كان موقو فامن نصيبهم و
للبنت الي تمام النصف و
هو خمسة و تسعون سهماً
والباقي للاب و هو تسعة
اسهم لانه عصبة -

reserving shares for the 4 sons, that is when there are four sons the share of the daughter will be $1\frac{4}{9}$ shares[1] and the *masala* being 24 the *tashih* will be by multiplying it by 9 and thus we get 13 shares for the daughter and the residue 115 shares is reserved [2] and if there is born one daughter or more then all the shares reserved will be given to the daughters and if one son or more are born then it shall be given to the mother and father and to the wife what has been reserved from their shares and the residue together with the 13 shares will be distributed among them; and if a dead child is born then it must be given to the widow and both parents what has been reserved from their shares and the daughter will be given one-half, that is, 95 shares more[1] and the residue which is 9 shares will be given to the father who belongs to the class of residuaries.

---

[1] After assigning shares the mother, father and wife the residue is 13/24 and distributing this amount between four sons and one daughter the share of the daughter is $1\frac{4}{9}$ only and by *tashih* it would be 13 shares *i.e.*, 1/9 of 13/24=13/216.

[2] 128 – 13=115 *vide* Case II.

[1] The daughter has received 13 shares+95=108 shares as in Case III.

SECTION IX

ON

A Missing Person

67. As regards his property, *Mafqud*, a missing person, is considered as alive so that nobody would inherit from him, and as regards the property of another he will be considered as dead to that extent that he will not inherit from anybody.[1]

68. The property of a missing person shall be reserved until his death is ascertained or a certain period has elapsed. Opinions differ regarding this period. The accepted view is this: when no one of his like age is alive then he will be presumed to be dead, and Hasan *ibn* Ziyad reports from Abu Hanifa that this period is 120 years from the date of his birth, and according to Imam Muhammad the period is 110 years and according to Abu Yusuf it is 105 years and some of our jurists have said that it is 90 years and the *fatwa* accords with this view. Some jurists have said that the property of a missing person shall be reserved until the decision of the Imam[2] and

فصل فى المفقود •

٦٧ - المفقود حي في ماله حتي لا يرث منه احد و ميت في مال غيره حتي لا يرث من احد-

٦٨ - و يوقف ماله حتي يصح موته او تمضي عليه مدة و اختلفت الروايات في تلك المدة ففي ظاهر الرواية انه اذا لم يبق احد من اقرانه حكم بموته و روي الحسن بن زياد عن ابي حنيفة رحمهما الله تعالي ان تلك المدة مائة و عشرون سنة من يوم ولد فيه المنقود و قال محمد رحمه الله تعالي مائة و خمس سنين وقال ابو يوسف رحمه الله تعالي مائة و خمس سنين وقال بعضهم تسعون سنة و عليه الفتوي و قال بعضهم مال المفقود موقوف الي اجتهاد الامام وموقوف الحكم في

---

[1] This passage is not found in Sir William Jones' Translation.

[2] That is until the Imam decides concerning the death of the missing person, which power is discretionary, and it is also the Shafii Law, some people take advantage of this provision, that is they obtain a judicial order on producing evidence confirming the death

حق غيره حتي يوقف نصيبه من مال مورثه كما في الحمل فاذا مضت المدة فماله لورثته الموجودين

as regards his right to succeed to another person, the veiw is that his share, which he would inherit from his ancestor shall be kept reserved as in the case of pregnancy[3] and when the period expires then his property will be given to his heirs who will be present when the decision

---

and according to some jurists the Kazi may pass an order after four years after the fact is brought to h's notice, and some say it is four years from the date of disappearance of the person. According to Imam Malik if a person is absent for four years the Kazi can cause separation between him and his wife and the woman will have to observe *iddat*.

In British India the period would be governed by Sections 107 and 108 of the Indian Evidence Act, which is 7 years.

[3] If the missing person is an absolute excluder then nothing from the property of his ancestor shall be given to other persons; but it he is a partial excluder then in that case the smaller share will be given to other heirs on the assumption that the missing person is alive.

If along with the missing person there is such an heir who is excluded if the missing person were present then that heir would get nothing, *e.g.*, a person dies leaving 2 daughters, a son's son and a missing son :—

	2 daughters.	Missing Son.	Son's son.
i. If the missing son is alive ...	1/2 3/6	1/2 3/6	0 0
ii. If the missing son is dead ...	2/3 4/6	0 0	1/3 2/6

The two daughters may take 3/6, but nothing can be given to son's son, and residue 3/6 will be reserved, if the son presents himself within the period, he takes 3/6 if not the daughters will again take 1/6 and the residue 2/6 will go to the son's son.

عند الحكم بموته و ما كان موقوفا لأجله يرد إلي وارث مورثه الذي وقف ماله-

concerning his death is made; and whatever share was reserved for him, will be given to the ancestor from whose share it was reserved.

٦٩ - و الاصل في تصحيح مسائل المفقود ان تصحح المسئلة علي تقدير حيوته ثم تصحح علي تقدير وفاته و باقي العمل ماذكرنا في الحمل-

69. The rule of ***tashih-i-masala*** concerning a missing person is that the ***masala*** must be corrected on the assumption that the missing person is alive and again it will be corrected on the assumption that the missing person is dead and thereafter we act as we do in the case of pregnancy.[1]

---

[1] The following interesting example is found in the Sharifa. A woman dies leaving her husband, two sisters and a missing brother :—

	Husband.	2 Sisters.	Brother.
CASE I.			
If the missing brother is alive ...	1/2	2/4 of 1/2	2/4 of 1/2
	4/8	2/8	2/8
Reducing in both cases to L. C. D. ...	28/56	14/56	14/56
CASE II.			
If the missing brother is dead ...	1/2	2/3	
	3/6	4/6	
Applying the doctrine of increase ...	3/7	4/7	
Reducing in both cases to L. C. D. ...	24/56	32/56	
			Reserved shares.
The shares assigned are	24/56	14/56	18/56

Thus, if the brother appears, the distribution will be as in Case I, and if his death is proved the distribution will be as in Case II. It may be seen that the husband benefits if the brother is found to be alive as he takes 28/56 *vide* Case I which is more than 24/56 *vide* Case II.

فصل في المرتد -

SECTION IX

ON

Apostate

٧٠ - اذا مات المرتد علي ارتداده او قتل او لحق بدارالحرب و حكم القاضي بلحاقه فما اكتسبه في حال اسلامه فهو لورثته المسلمين و ما اكتسبه فى حال ردته يوضع فى بيت المال عند ابى حنيفة رحمه‌الله تعالى و عند هما الكسبان جميعاً لورثته المسلمين و عند الشافعي رحمه‌الله تعالى الكسبان جميعاً يوضعان في بيت المال و ما اكتسبه بعد اللحوق بدار الحرب فهو فئ بالاجماع وكسب المرتدة جميعاً لورثتها المسلمين بلا خلاف بين اصحابنا -

70. If an apostate from Islam has died or has been killed or has migrated into *Dar-ul-harb* and the Kazi so decides that he has migrated into *Dar-ul-harb*, then whatever he earned while he was a Muslim will be given to his Muslim heirs and whatever he earned since his apostacy will be kept in *Bait-ul-mal*, State treasury, that is the view of Imam Abu Hanifa. And according to them (Imam Abu Yusuf and Imam Muhammad) both these acquisitions will be given to his Muslim heirs [1], and according to Shafii both these acquisitions will be kept in *Bait-ul-mal*; and whatever he has earned in *Dar-ul-harb*, if secured will be confiscated as agreed by all, and similarly the property of a woman apostate will go to her Muslim heirs and there is no disagreement among the jurists on this point.

---

1 In India The *Fatwa* accords with this view, because there is no *Bait-ul-mal* here.

In British India the Caste Disabilities Removal Act 21 of 1850 has removed the disability of an apostate heir to inherit from a Muslim or from a non-Muslim by birth or by apostacy. So this part of the Muslim Law has been superseded in British India.

٧١ - واما المرتد لا يرث من احد لا من مسلم ولا من مرتد مثله وكذالك المرتدة الا اذا ارتد اهل ناحية باجمعهم فحينئذ يتوارثون ۔

71. An apostate cannot inherit from anybody, neither from a Muslim nor from another apostate like himself; similarly a woman apostate, cannot inherit; but if the whole of the city has been apostatised, in that case they would inherit *inter se* among themselves.

SECTION XI

ON

Prisoner

فصل في الاسير -

٧٢ - حكم الاسير كحكم سائر المسلمين فى الميراث ما لم يفارق دينه فان فارق دينه فحكمه حكم المرتد فان لم تعلم ردته ولا حياته ولا موته فحكمه حكم المفقود ۔

72. The law concerning prisoners is the same law with regard to their inheritance which applies to Muslims provided they have not given up their faith. And if they have given up their faith then the law concerning them is the same as in the case of an apostate; but if it is not known whether a person has become an apostate or whether he is alive or dead, the law concerning them will be the same as in the case of a missing person.

SECTION XII

ON

Persons Drowned, Burned or Buried in Ruins

فصل فى الغرقى والحرقى والهدمى -

٧٣ - اذا ماتت جماعة ولا يدري ايهم مات اولاً

73. When a group of persons are dead and they are related to one

جعلو كانهم ماتوا معاً فمال
كل واحد منهم لورثة
الاحياء ولا يرث بعض
الاموات من بعض هذا هو
المختار و قال علي و
ابن مسعود رضى الله تعالى
عنهما يرث بعضهم عن بعض
الا في ما ورث كل واحد
منهم من صاحبه والله
اعلم بالصواب واليه المرجع
والماب -

another and it is not known which of them died first, then it shall be presumed that all of them died together and the property of each of them would be given to his heirs and it will not be distributed *inter se* among the dead ;[1] this is the better opinion ; but Ali and Ibn Masud (peace be on them) according to one of the two reports say that some of the deceased would inherit from others except in that what each of them inherits from his own colleague who met the same fate.[2]

---

1 The first Khalifa Abu Bakr followed this practice, and he did not permit dead men to inherit from the other dead; hence the heirs would inherit from the deceased. The same practice was followed by the second Khalifa Umar when a number of persons had died as a result of plague and a similar practice was followed in the battles of Jamal and Siffin. A *hadis* to this effect is reported in the *Muwatta* by Imam Malik.

2 The following example is given in the Sharifa : two brothers, one older than the other die in a shipwreck and each of them leaves 90 dinars and the survivors are their mother, daughter and an emancipator *i.e.*, a residuary. The distribution would be as follows :—

PROPOSITUS

Mother | Daughter | Emancipator

Under the Hanafi Law the mother will get 15 and the daughter 45, and the emancipator will get 30 and the same distribution will be in the second case.

According to the method of Ali and Ibn Masud they will get as follows.

Distributing the property of the elder brother :—

Mother	Daughter	Younger Brother
1/6 = 15	1/2 = 45	residue = 30

This 30 is again distributed : 5 to the mother, 15 to the daughter and the residue 10 goes to the emancipator. Similarly would be the division if we were to divide 90 dinars left by the younger brother.

THE END

The Koranic verses relating to the law of Inheritance

The Koranic verses relating to inheritance are not many and all of them are to be found in the Surah-an-Nisa, the Fourth Surah of the Holy Koran. The surah itself is called " The women " as it particularly deals with the rights of the women. The historic date of revelation is immediately after the battle of Uhad, for many Muslims were killed at Uhad. Noldeke assigns the date " between the end of the third and the end of fifth year " of the Holy Prophet's reign in Medina, [1] and Mr. Marmaduke Pickthall puts it between the end of the third year and the beginning of the fifth year.'[2] As stated by the Muslim writers the period of revelation of Surah-an-Nisa is the fourth year of the Hijra, it was revealed in Medina. The surah occurs in part fourth and sixth of the Holy Koran. The following passages occur in *'ayat* verses 7, 11, 12, 33, and 177.

[سورة نساء آيت ٧]

للرجال نصيب مما
ترک الوالدان والاقربون -
وللنساء نصيب مما ترک
الوالدان والاقربون مما
قل منه او كثر نصيباً
مفروضا •

VERSE VII

For men, (of a family) there is a share in what their parents and near relations leave and for women there is a share in what their parents and near relations leave, whether it be little or much, it is a legal share.

[سورة نساء آيت ١١]

يوصيكم الله في اولادكم
للذكر مثل حظ الانثيين •

VERSE XI

Allah commands you concerning (the provision for) your children: for the male there is a share equivalent to two females.

---

[1] Geschichte des Qorans. (2nd ed.) Part I, p. 195.

[2] The Glorious Koran, p. 91.

فان كن نسآء فوق
اثنتين فلهن ثلثا مما ترك
وان كانت واحدة فلها
النصف *

And if there are women more than two, then for them there is two-thirds of the inheritance, and if there is one then it is half.

ولابويه لكل واحد
منهما السدس مما ترك
أن كان له ولد - فان لم
يكن له ولد و ورثه ابواه
فلامه الثلث - فان كان له
اخوة فلامه السدس من
بعد وصية يوصي بها
اودين *

And for parents for each there is one-sixth of the inheritance if there is a child, but if there is no child and his parents are his heirs, then for the mother there is one-third, but if there are brothers or sisters then for the mother there is one-sixth after meeting legacies if any and his debts.

[سورة آيت ۱۲]

VERSE XII

ولكم نصف ما ترك
ازواجكم ان لم يكن لهن
ولد - فان كان لهن ولد
فلكم الربع مما تركن من
بعد وصية يوصين بها
اودين *

And for ye there is one-half or that which your wife (or wives) leaves if there is no child, and if there is a child then it is one-fourth of what she leaves, after meeting legacies if any and her debts.

ولهن الربع مما تركتم
ان لم يكن لكم ولد - فان
كان لكم ولد فلهن الثمن
مما تركتم من بعد وصية
توصون بها اودين *

And for them (wife or wives) there is one-fourth in what you leave if there is no child, but if there is a child then it is one-eighth after meeting legacies bequeathed and debts.

وان كان رجل يورث
كللة او امرأة وله اخ او
اخت فلكل واحد منهما
السدس فان كانوا اكثر
من ذلك فهم شركاء في
الثلث من بعد وصية يها
يوصى دين غير مضار *

And if a *Kalala* man or woman (*i.e.*, one who has no parents and no children) is dead leaving a brother or sister (on the mother's side) then for each of them there is one-sixth, and if they be more than two then there is one-third for them after paying legacies bequeathed and debts.

[سورة نساء آيت ٣٣]

ولكل جعلنا موالي
مما ترک الوالدان
والاقربون *

VERSE XXXIII

And for all we have assigned a share of that which parents and relations leave.

[سورة نساء آيت ١٧٧]

قل الله يفتيكم في
الكلالة ان امرء هلک
ليس له ولد وله اخت
فلها نصف ماترک وهو يرثها
ان لم يكن لها ولد فان
كانتا اثنتين فلهما الثلثان
مما ترک وان كانوا
اخوة رجالاً و نساء فالذكر
مثل حظ الانثيين *

VERSE CLXXVII

Say Allah has commanded ye concerning a *kalala* relation, if a person dies childless and he has a sister then for her there is a half in what he leaves, and similarly he would inherit from her if she dies childless. And if there are two sisters then to them is given two-thirds of inheritance and if there are brothers with sisters then for the males there is a share of two females.

Thus we see from the above Koranic verses that the portions fixed by the Koran are six, namely 1/2, 1/4, 1/8, 2/3, 1/3 and 1/6, and in opposition to the customary Law the Koran gave specific shares to the females who were excluded in ancient Arabia from participation in inheritance. It may also be noted that the Koran does not specifically mention the true grand-father or true grandmother, they are deemed to be included by our jurists under the general term parents and further the expression 'female children,' is understood to include son's daughters, and the term 'sister' includes full sisters and consanguine sisters. On the whole it may be admitted that the Koran attempts to provide for all near relations though the actual amount received by them may be little. The Sunni jurists in developing the law of inheritance have excluded daughter's children from the first class of heirs, and have put them in the distant kindred class, in fact it seems that the tendency was to prefer the agnates paticularly the uncle and his male issue, and in that sense the Muslim Law may be said to be patriarchal. However, the Shia jurists have put the son's children together with the daughter's children in the first class, thus showing their preference to near cognates. The reason assigned for this difference of treatment of daughter's children is partly due to the ancient customary law of Arabia, which like the Hindu law and the Roman Law, considered, a daughter after marriage and her children as members of her husband's family, and not of their own ancestral family, and it seems that the Muslim jurists could not break away from this custom, and they took advantage of the absence of any specific provision in the Koran.[1]

We have said that the Koran specifically allotted shares to the females in opposition to the customary law, accordingly we have under the Sunni system Twelve shares including two sharers by reason of marriage and out of these there are four male sharers and eight female

[1] On the other hand some writers assign a political reason for the exclusion of daughter's children from the first class, *viz.*, the Abbaside Khalifs who were the Prophet's uncle's descendants wanted to have their claims recognised in preference to the Fatimides who were the Prophet's daughter's descendants, and to trace it further some say the object was to exclude Imam Hasan and Husain, the sons of Fatima, daughter of the Prophet from any claim as rightful successors of the Prophet to the Khilafat. It may however be noted that Imam Hasan and Husain were just as much descendants of the Prophet's uncle as the Abbaside Khalifs, so if this political doctrine is to be supported, then Imam Hasan and Husain would be preferred to the fourth Khalif Ali, their own father. However it seems futile for our purpose to discuss the reasons for the exclusion of daughter's children from the first class as under the Sunni system or their inclusion in the first class as under the Shia Law.

sharers. The male sharers are, 1. Husband, 2. Father, 3. True grand-father, 4. Half brother by mother (uterine brother) and the female sharers are :—5. Wife, 6. Mother, 7. True grandmother, 8. Daughter, 9. Son's daughter, 10 Full sister *i.e.*, by the same father and mother. 11. Half sister by father (consanguine sister), 12. Half sister by mother (uterine sister).

After reading these few simple verses of the Koran one really wonders when he studies the elaborate principles and rules of the law of inheritance as developed by the Muslim jurists, a system rendered to perfection.

The Traditions of the Prophet relating to the Law of Inheritance.

There are six well-known works on the *Hadises*, traditions, of the Prophet. They are known as *al Kutub as sitah fi al Hadis*, namely the works of Imam Bukhari, Muslim, Tirmizi, Abu Daud, Nasai, and Ibn Majah. The Muwatta of Imam Malik is also a small well-known work on the *Hadis*. I have selected traditions from the above works and for the sake of brevity I have avoided repeating them again and again and have simply indicated that they are to be found in these works.

The following three *Hadises* are the great historical *hadises* They show the origin or the cause of revelation of the Koranic verses on the law of Inheritance. They show that the Prophet of God himself at first was unable to solve the problem of general distribution of property.

احاديث في ميراث الصلب

Hadis relating to children.

From Jabir bin Abdullah—

عن جا بربن عبدالله

قال جائي رسول الله صلى

"The Prophet of God came to see me. I was unwell while among the

الله عليه و وسلم يعودني
و انا مريض في بني
سلمة فقلت يا نبي الله
كيف اقسم مالي بين ولدي
فلم يرد علي شيئا فنزلت
يوصيكم الله في اولادكم
للذكر مثل حظ الانثيين الاية *
(ترمذي جلد ۲ - مسلم
جلد ۳ بخاري و انظر
في الموطا لامام مالك)

descendants of Salma. I said, 'O Prophet of God how shall I distribute my property among my descendants.' The Prophet did not reply. Subsequently the Koranic verse relating to inheritance *Usikumullah fi awlad ekum* was revealed." [Bukhari, Muslim, Trimizi and also in Muwatta of Imam Malik.]

احاديث في الكلالة

Hadis relating to sister and brother.

عن جابر بن عبدالله قال
مرضت فاتاني رسول
صلي الله عليه و سلم يعودني
فوجدني قد اغمي علي
فاتاني و معه ابو بكر و هما
ماشيان فتوضا رسول الله
صلي الله عليه و سلم فصب
علي وضوءه فافقت فقلت
يا رسول الله كيف اقضي
في مالي او كيف اصنع
في مالي فلم يجبني شيئا
و كان له تسع اخوات
حتي نزلت اية الميراث
يستفتونك قل الله يفتيكم
في الكلالة * (ترمذي
جلد ۲ بخاري ابو داؤد جلد
۲ - مسلم الموطا جلد۳)

From Jabir bin Abdullah—

"I was unwell when the Prophet of God visited me. Abu Bakr had come also with him. The prophet found me seriously ill. He after making *wazu* (ablution) sprinkled the water on me. I became better and I said 'O Prophet of God, how shall I distribute my property, what shall I do with it.' The Prophet gave no answer and he had nine sisters until revelation of the Koranic verse *Yastaf tuneka Qul ilahu Yuftikum fil kalala.*" [Trimizi, Bukhari, Muslim, Abu Daud, Ibn Majah and also in Muwatta.]

احاديث في ميراث البنات

Hadis relating to the right of daughter.

و عنه (جابر) رضي الله
تعالي عنه قال جاءت امراة

From Jabir bin Abdullah—

"A certain woman came with her two daughters before the Prophet of

بنبتين لہ افقالت يا رسول
الله هاتان بنتا ثابت بن
قيس قتل صعک يوم احد
و قد استفاء عمهما مالهما و
ميراثهما كله فلم لا يدع لهما
مالأ الا اخذه فما تري
يا رسول الله فوالله لا
تنكحان ابدا الا و لهما
مال نقال البتي صلي الله
عليه و آله و سلم يقضي
الله في ذلک فنزلت
سورة النساء يوصيكم الله
في اولاد كم الاية فقال
رسول الله صلي الله عليه
و سلم ادعو الي المراة
و صاحبها نقال لعمهما
اعطهما الثلثين و اعطا
مهماالثمن و ما بقي
فهولک * (مسلم بخاري
ابو داؤد ترمذي ابن
ماجد موطا)

God and said 'O Prophet of God these two daughters are of Sabit bin Qais[1] who was killed in the battle of Uhad, their uncle has taken away the entire property and has left nothing for them. It is not possible to get them married without property.' The prophet answered, "God alone could decide." Thereafter the Koranic verses as stated in Sura Nisa *Usikumullah fiawladikum* were revealed. The Prophet sent for the woman and the uncle and told him to give two-thirds to the two daughters and to take for himself the residue." [Abu Daud, Trimizi, Muslim, Bukhari, Ibn Majah and also in Muwatta.]

Besides these three great historical *hadises* there are number of them which may be called law-making *hadises*, the cases having been decided by the Prophet himself.

احاديث في ميراث الجد

Hadis relating to the right of the grandfather.

From *ibn* Abbas—

فانه انزله ابا او قال
قضاه ابا حديث ابن
عباس (بخاري)

"The grand-father is either treated or dealt with as the father." [Bukhari.]

---

[1] Trimisi speaks about Saad bin Rabbia.

عن معقل بن يسار
المزني قال صمعت البني
صلي الله عليه و سلم اتي
بفريضة فيها جد فا تاه ثلثا
او سد سا * (ابن ماجه)

From Maqal Bin Yasar—

"The Prophet of God gave to the grand-father amongst us one-sixth." [*Ibn* Majah].

عن عمران بن حصين
قال جاء رجل الي النبي
صلي الله عليه و سلم فقال
ان ابن ابني مات
فمالي من ميراثه فقال
لك السدس فلما ولي
دعاه فقال لك السدس
الاخر فلما ولي دعاه قال
ان السدس الاخر لك
طعمة *
(ترمذي - ابو داؤد)

From Imran bin Hasin—

"A person came to the Prophet of God and said, 'My grandson is dead what is my inheritance.?' The Prophet said 'one-sixth', and when the man was going away the Prophet called him and said 'for you there is another sixth.' When the man went away he was again called and the Prophet said 'there is another sixth for you by way of *toma*.'" [Trimizi and Abu Daud].

احاديث في ميراث الجدة

Hadis relating to the right of the true grandmother.

عن بن عباس ان
رسول الله صلي الله عليه
و سلم ورث جدة سدسا -
(ابن ماجه)

From *ibn* Abbas—

"The Prophet of God gave to the grandmother one-sixth" [*Ibn* Majah].

عن ابن بريدة عن
ابيه عن ابيه ان النبي
صلي عليه و سلم جعل
للجدة السدس اذ لم تكن
دونها ام *
(ابو داؤد جلد ٢)

From *Ibn* Baraida reporting from his father—

"The Prophet of God allotted one-sixth to the grandmother when there was no mother [Abu Daud]."

The following *Hadis* relating to the right of inheritance of the true grandmother shows how the Khalifa Abu Bakr and Umr in the ence of the Koranic injunction on the question attempted to find out if there was any *Hadis* not known to them on the point.

عن قبيصة ابن ذويب
قال جاءت الجدة ام
الام ام الاب الي ابي
بكر فقالت ان ابن ابنتي
مات و قد اخبرت ان
لي في الكتاب حقا فقال
ابو بكر ما اجد لک
في الكتاب من حق و ما
سمعت رسول الله صلي
الله عليه و سلم قضي لک
بشي و سا سأل
الناس قال سأل الناس
فشهد المغيرة بن شعبه ان
رسول الله صلي الله عليه
و سلم اعطاها السدس
قال و من سمع ذلک
معک قال محمد بن
مسلمة قال نا عطاها
السدس ثم جاءت التي
تخالفها الي عمر قال ان
اجتمعتما فهو لكما و ايكما
انفردت به فهو لها •
(ترمذي جلد ۲ ابو
داؤد جلد ۲ و ابن ماجه
مؤطا امام مالک)

From Qabisah bin Zueb.

"A grandmother (mother's mother or father's mother) came to Abu Bakr and said 'My grandson (son's son or daughter's son) is dead, I understand that I have a right under the Book' Abu Bakr replied, 'There is nothing as to this stated in the Book nor have I heard the Prophet giving anything to the grandmother, but I shall enquire from the people.' He asked the people. Mughirah bin Shubah answered that the Prophet of God gave one-sixth to the grandmother. Abu Bakr said, 'Who heard this along with you.?' Then Muhammad bin Muslima said 'The Prophet gave one-sixth.' Later a certain person came to Umr disputing the right of inheritance with the grandmother, Umr said 'Whether she inherits along with other heirs or alone her share is the same.' [Trimizi, Abu Daud, *Ibn* Majah, and in Muwatta].

The following is an important Hadis and is the solitary exception to the general rule of the Muslim Law of inheritance that no female is primarily a residuary but only becomes so when coexisting with a male residuary. Here in this tradition the full sister has been preferred to other remote heirs. The sister inherits as a residuary. The exception being based on a decision of the Prophet which has been accepted though it conflicts with the general rule of inheritance.

احاديث في ميراث ابنة و ابنة واخت لاب و ام

Hadis relating to inheritance concerning a daughter, a son's daughter and a sister of the same father and mother.

عن هزيل بن شرجيل قال جاء رجل الي ابي موسي و سليمان بن ربيعة فسالهما عن ابنة و ابنة ابن واخت لاب و ام فقالا للابنة النصف و للاخت من الاب و الام مابقي و قالا له انطلق الي عبدالله فاسأله فانه سيتابعنا فاتي عبدالله فذكر له ذلک و اخبره بما قالا قال عبدالله قد ضلت اذاً و ما انا من المهتدين و لكن اقضي فيها كما قضي رسول الله صلي الله عليه و سلم لابنة النصف و لابنة الابن السدس تكملة الثلثين و للاخت ما بقي ٭ (ترمذي جلد ٢ - ابن ماجه - ابوداؤد جلد ٢ و بخاري -

From Huzail bin Sharjil—

"A person came to Abi Musa and Sulaiman bin Rabia and asked them about the right of inheritance of a daughter, a son's daughter and a sister by the same father and mother. They replied that the daughter is to be given one-half and the residue to the sister, and advised him to consult Abdullah remarking that he would agree with them. The person went to Abdullah and told him what they had advised. Thereupon Abdullah said 'I shall be a sinner and not on the right path (if I agreed with them) I shall say what the Prophet of God had observed. That is one-half is the share of the daughter and one-sixth for the son's daughter thus completing two-thirds and the residue is for the sister." [Trimizi, Bukhari, *Ibn* Daud, and *Ibn* Majah.]

احاديث في ميراث الخال

Hadis relating to the right of the maternal uncle.

عن عائشة قالت قال رسول الله صلي الله عليه و سلم الخال وارث من لا وارث له ٭ (ترمذي جلد ٢)

From Aisha—

The Prophet of God, said "The maternal uncle is the heir of one who has no heir." [Trimizi].

عن ابي امامة بن سهل بن حنيف قال كتب معي عمر بن الخطاب الي ابي عبيدة ان رسول الله صلي الله عليه و سلم قال الله و رسوله مولي من لا مولي له و الخال وارث من لا وارث له * (ترمذي جلد ٢ ابن ماجه)

From Abi Imama Shuhail bin Hanif—"Umar bin Khatab wrote through me to Abi Ubaidat stating that the Prophet of God had said, that God and the Prophet are the guardians of those who have no guardians, and the maternal uncle is the heir of one who has no heirs." [Trimizi and Ibn Majah.][1]

احاديث في ميراث العصبة

Hadis relating to the right of the residuaries (Asbah) in general.

عن ابي هريرة قال قال رسول الله صلي الله عليه و سلم - انا اولي الناس بالمؤمنين من انفسهم فمن مات و ترك مالا فماله لموالي العصبة * (بخاري ومسلم)

From Abi Huraira—"The Prophet of God said, We are nearer to the believers than themselves. And who so ever dies and leaves property, it is for the residuaries [Bukhari and Muslim].

عن ابن عباس عن النبي صلي الله عليه و سلم قال الحقوا الفرائض با هلها فما بقي فهو لا ولي رجل ذكر * (ترمذي جلد ٢ ابن ماجه بخاري (ابو داؤد جلد ٣ و مسلم جلد ٣)

From Abn Abbas—The Prophet of God said "Distribute the inheritance to those who are entitled and the residue is for the residuaries *i.e.* the best male relations" [Trimizi Bukhari, Ibn Majha, Abu Daud and Muslim.]

احاديث في مولود يستهل ثم يموت

Hadis relating to children who are born alive (cry) and then die.

عن جابر عن النبي صلي الله عليه و سلم

From Jabir—"The Prophet of God said, No prayer shall be said

[1] The above two Hadises relate to the right of the uncle and also establish the law of guardianship under the control of the state.

قال الطفل لا يصلي عليه
و لايرث و لا يورث حتي
يستهل * (ترمذي
جلد اول ابن ماجه)

(funeral) for a child, nor can inherit from him unless he is born alive" (lit. cries) [Trimizi, and Ibn Majah.]

عن ابي هريرة رضي الله
عنه عن النبي صلي
الله عليه و سلم قال
اذا استهل المولود ورث *
(ابو داوٗد)

From Abi Huraira—"The Prophet said When a child is born alive (lit. cries) it inherits." [Abu Daud].

احاديث في ابطال
ميراث القاتل عن ابي
هريرة عن النبي صلي الله
عليه و سلم قال القاتل
لايرث * (ترمذي جلد ٢
و ابن ماجه)

Hadis relating to exclusion of Murderers.

From Abi Huraira,—"The Prophet of God said a murderer cannot inherit." [Trimizi and Ibn Majah]

The following *Hadis* however appears to make a distinction between intentional homicide.

عن عبدالله بن عمر ان
رسول الله صلي الله عليه
و سلم قام يوم فتح مكة
فقال المرأة ترث من دية
زوجها و ماله و هو يرث

From Abdullah bin Umr—"The Prophet of God thus spoke on the day of conquest of Mecca, 'A woman inherits her husband's property and *diat*,[1] the blood money, and *vice*

[1] By *diat* we mean compensation to be paid by the wrong doer to the aggrieved party and in case of murder blood money is to be paid to the heirs of the deceased. For example the compensation for the injury to one's one finger (cutting off the finger) is ten camels, thus for two fingers it would be twenty and so on and for murder it is either 12 Twelve thousand *dirhams* according to Imam Shafi and ten thousand *dirhams* according to Imam Abu Hanifa or it may be paid in kind *viz.*, 30 she-camels four years old, 30 she-camels five years old, 40 pregnant she-camels, and anything else which has been *mutually* agreed. The fine is to be realised from the tribe.

For minor injuries the *diat* is five camels. The relatives of the dead person also have the option to put the murderer to death. In Ancient Arabia crime was not considered as an offence exclusively against the state. This is the modern idea.

من ديتها و مالها مالم
يقتل احدهما صاحبه فاذا
قتل احدهما صاحبه
عمداً لم يرث من ديته
و ماله شيئا و ان قتل
احدهما صاحبه خطأً ورث
من ماله و لم يرث من
ديته * (ابن ماجه)

versa so long as one of them does not murder the other, and if one of them kills the other intentionally he or she cannot inherit the property or the blood money but if the killing was by accident he or she can inherit the property but not the blood money."[1] [Ibn Majah.]

احاديث في ابطال
الميراث بين المسلم والكافر

Hadis relating to exclusion between Muslims and non-Muslims.

عن عمرو بن شعيب
عن ابيه عن جده - ان
رسول الله صلي الله عليه
و سلم قال لا يتوارث
اهل ملتين * (ابن ماجه
و ترمذي ابو داؤد)

From Umr bin Shuaib—per his father. "The Prophet of God said, That persons of different religions cannot inherit from each other" [Ibn Majah, Abu Daud and Trimizi.]

عن اسامة بن زيد ان
رسول الله صلي الله
عليه و سلم - قال لا
يرث المسلم الكافر و لا
الكافر المسلم * (ترمذي
بخاري مسلم ابوداؤد
موطا و ابن ماجه)

From Asama bin Zaid—The Prophet of God said, "No Muslims can inherit from a non-Muslim, nor a non-Muslim from a Muslim." [Trimizi. Bukhari, Abu Daud, Muslim, Ibn Majah and also in the Muwatta].[2]

---

[1] This is rather ambiguous, it apparently means that a woman who kills her husband is liable to pay *diat* and at the same time she would become entitle to inheiit it as part of the inheritance in the capacity of wife, this she cannot be allowed under any circumstances.

[2] *e.g.*, According to a decision of the Prophet Ali the fourth Khalif and his brother Jafar who were Muslims were excluded from inheriting from their father Abu Talib whose property was given to Aqil and Talib who were at that time non-Muslims.

احاديث في ميراث ولد الزنا

Hadis relating to illegitimate children.

عن عمرو بن شعيب عن ابيه عن جده ان رسول الله صلي الله عليه و سلم قال ايما رجل عاهر بحرة او امة فالولد ولدزنا لا يرث و لا يورث (ترمذي جلد ٢ و موطا)

From Umr bin Shuaib—*per* his ancestor—"The Prophet of God said, 'When a man has a child born of illicit intercourse with a woman or a slave, the child is the result of fornication, and cannot inherit from the father nor he from him." [Tirmizi and Muwatta.]

Under the Hanafi Law, but not under the Shia Law, the mother is entitled to inherit from an illegitimate child and so can the child from the mother. The following *Hadis* supports this view.

عن واثله بن الاسقع قال قال رسول الله عليه و سلم المرءة تحوز ثلاثة مواريث عتيقها و لقيطها و ولدها الذي لا عنت عنه * (ترمذي جلد ٢ - ابو داؤد جلد ٢ و ابن ماجد)

From Wasila bin Alska—"The Prophet of God said, a woman possesses three capacities of inheritance namely by reason of emancipation, by birth of child and from a child repudiated by the father *i.e.,* illegitimate '[Tirmizi, Abu Daud and Ibn Majah].

احاديث فيما يبدأ بالدين قبل الوصيه

Hadis relating to payment of debts before legacies.

عن علي انه قال انكم تقرؤن هذه الاية من بعد وصية توصون بها او دين و ان رسول الله صلي الله عليه و سلم قضي بالدين قبل الوصية * (ترمذي جلد ٢)

From Ali—"You know the Koranic verse *Min badi wasiatain tusoon beha awdain.* The Prophet of God ordered payment of debts prior to legacies [Tirmizi]."

عن سعد بن ابي وقاص قال جاء النبي صلعم

From Sad bin Abi waqqas—"The Prophet visited me while I was ill in

يعودني و انا بمكة و
هويكره ان يموت بالرض
التي هاجر منها فقال
يرحم الله ابن عفراء قلت
يا رسول الله اوصي بمالي
كله قال لا قلت فالشطر
قال لا قلت فالثلث قال
الثلث و الثلث كثير
انك ان تدع ورثتك
اغنيا خيرمن ان تدعهم
عالة يتكففون الناس في
ايدهم ٭
(صحيح البخاري جلد
اول و صحيح المسلم
جلد رابع و صحيح
الترمذي جلد ثاني
صحيح ابو داؤد جلد
ثاني موطا لمالك و
صحيح ابن ماجه)

Mecca, and I did not like to die at the place, thence I migrated. The Prophet said, 'God be kind to the son of Afra.' I said, 'O, Prophet of God can I bequeath as legacy my whole property?' The Prophet said 'No.' I said 'then Half'? He said 'No' I said then, 'One-third'? He said, 'One-third and that is too much' for it is good that you should leave your heirs well provided rather than in need and begging (lit: holding their palms for assistance towards the hands of men)" [Bukari, Tirmizi, Muslim, Abu Daud, Ibn Majah also in the Muwatta].

عن شرجيل بن مسلم
قال سمعت رسول الله صلعم
يقول ان الله قد اعطى
كل ذي حق حقه فلا وصية
لوارث ابو داؤد جلد
ثاني و ترمزي جلد
ثاني و ابن ماجه و
انظر موطا امام مالك
و صحيح البخاري
جلد اول

From Sharjil bin Muslim per Abu Amama—"The Prophet of God said' The God has given the right to all deserving persons but there is no legacy for an heir" [Abu Daud, Tirmizi, Ibn Majah, Bukhari, and Muwatta.]

Under the Hanafi law a *bequest* to an heir is not valid unless the other heirs give their consent after the death of the testator, and under the Shia law the heirs may give their consent during the lifetime of the testator.

GENERAL INDEX

[The references throughout are to pages]